*Chicago History of
American Religion*

*A Series Edited by
Martin E. Marty*

American
Indians
and
Christian
Missions

*Studies in
Cultural Conflict*

Henry Warner Bowden

*The University of Chicago Press
Chicago and London*

The University of Chicago Press, Chicago 60637
The University of Chicago Press, Ltd., London

HENRY WARNER BOWDEN is professor
of religion at Douglass College of
Rutgers University. He is the editor of
the volume *Religion in America* and
author of *Church History in the Age of
Science, The Dictionary of American Religious Biography,* and numerous scholarly
articles.

Library of Congress Cataloging in Publication Data

Bowden, Henry Warner.
    American Indians and Christian missions.

    (Chicago history of American religion)
    Bibliography: p.
    Includes index.
    1. Indians of North America—Missions—History.
2. Culture conflict—United States—History. I. Title.
E98.M6B64   266'.273   80-27840
ISBN 0-226-06811-0

In Memoriam

James Albert Bowden
(1919–1980)

Christian   Soldier   Patriarch

Contents

Foreword

From about 13,000 years ago until nearly 500 years ago the descendants of Asian peoples who wandered across what is now a submerged land bridge from Siberia spread across the Americas undisturbed. They developed numberless languages, cultures, and religious outlooks. Remains of their ways of life give evidence that, like all other human beings, they experienced conflict within and between their groups. The evidence also suggests that they reinforced their conflicts with religious dances, symbols, and motifs.

After 1492, conflict among these native American peoples took a new turn. The European explorers and settlers arrived with books and bullets and changed all the terms of "Indian" life. A cultural evolutionist would say that they began to exploit the energy resources of the American environments more efficiently than the longer-term residents had and therefore inevitably prevailed, pushing back to reservations the natives they did not put to death or those whom the newly imported European diseases did not kill.

Today their repentant Euro-American heirs and virtually all contemporary Indians would stress the word "exploit" in that cultural-evolutionary language.

Since they underpopulated the two vast American continents, the natives did not have to overuse the resources of lake, hill, and mine. They could live with the rhythms of the seasons and respond to, not dominate, the world of nature. The white people, on the other hand, were in a hurry. Their Bible told them to claim dominion over the created world and to get other peoples, the "heathen," to convert and yield to the will of the already-saved. Given such impulses, they usually saw little incompatibility between the ideas of saving and enslaving the Indians. The result of their exploitation, according to almost universal scholarly opinion, is a devastated race of natives, on the one hand, and, on the other, a legacy of shame.

The conflict between Europeans and native Americans occurred on an epochal scale and belongs to the language of epic. Whenever latter-day Americans are thoughtful about their past, the Indian story becomes central to their self-understanding. Whenever the earlier Americans, misnamed Indians, reflect on their plight, they cannot help but see it as a legacy of the European intrusion.

Historians today busy themselves with many dimensions of the conflict, but the religious aspects often go neglected. Histories of Christian missions to Indians, particularly stories written in earlier times, when the mission had defenders, are plentiful. Accounts of native American religions, particularly on a tribe-by-tribe, people-by-people scale, are coming to be familiar, though works of synthesis that attempt to see Indian religion as a whole are still few. However excellent the books on these separate subjects may be, most fail to do justice to the urgent point of interaction between Indians and whites, especially when it comes to religion.

Students of religious history have learned that religion works two ways in relation to conflict. It tends to make bad wars worse and good peaces better. When one can call upon the spirits or the Spirit, the gods or God, in support of violent ventures, the killers claim more warrant than before to be cruel and vindictive. The conflict between encroaching Europeans and outnumbered, out-armed, and generally doomed natives could have proceeded to its almost inevitable end without benefit of clergy. The stakes were high enough for the hasty white people, but they regularly found support in their Bible and their churches for their exploitative activities. That plot is familiar. Sad to say, if this aspect shows that religion makes "bad wars worse," there have been too few days of concord to make possible a telling of how European religion in America helped make "good peaces better."

How can one tell the story of the conflict, which this book sets out to do? It makes no sense apart from some chronicling of the two antagonistic religious clusters, or, shall we say, cluster of clusters, for they both included many varieties. To do justice to all the brands of American religion of the sorts imported from Europe or later improvised on the basis of imports would itself fill long textbooks if not whole libraries. To do justice to the varieties of American Indian religious experience is an equally numbing task. While many of us historians are audacious enough to generalize about the thousands of religious groups that exist among two hundred million white and black North Americans, anthropologists generally shy away from synthetic or synoptic works dealing with Indian spirituality. Though the American white counterculture of the 1960s and '70s romanticized the Indian world as one of great simplicity, these anthropologists point to its complexity. They are willing to be asked about one rite of one tribe but not more rites of more tribes. For that reason it is almost impossible to come across good texts on Indian religion as such. Shall a historian of conflict, then, deal with a void?

Henry Warner Bowden has found a way to address the problem. Long at home in the study of European religion in America and a historiographer and encyclopedist of note, he applies the same technique to both sets of peoples. Picture him as having read widely, taking countless closeup pictures, as it were. Then follow him in his effort to get distance on the subject. We use one kind of snapshot to learn about neighbors or microbes. We use another kind of camera if we wish to produce topographic outlines, where the distance of satellites has proved to be of great use.

This book has the expansive topographic interest in mind. Bowden has to introduce us to the way the land lies as it looks from a distance, so that we can get a feeling of contour and outline. Then he zooms in, or, to change the metaphor a bit, he opens the album of closeups so that we can become more confident that we are understanding the ways of life of the people who occupied the vast landscape and who moved through such grand periods of time.

The effect of his endeavor is to give us three books in one: a short history of Christian missions among the natives; an overview of American Indian religion of a sort that has textbook values of its own; and, most of all, the story of intergroup conflicts in a religious context. I know of no similar work.

The state of conscience and the fashions of perception in the era in which they write color the inquiry and work of historians. Bowden writes in a time when most Americans have lost faith in the attempt to convert Indians, a time when they have come to respect the integrity of native American faith, to see missionary efforts as intrusive, and to regard "civilizing" efforts as condescending. He cannot escape something of the climate that produced that loss of faith and sees no moral reason to abandon the at least implied criticism of missionaries. Yet, for the sake of understanding, he also seems to be asking for momentary suspensions of impatience and criticism. One must endeavor to get inside the lost world of the converters and would-be civilizers. Few of them took native American religion on its own terms, as Bowden does and as his contemporaries often try to do. Only a few saw traces of valid "natural religion" in Indian practices and beliefs. But the missionaries often did go out in a humane spirit. They believed they were doing the natives a favor by offering them hope of a better afterlife even as they and their colleagues were trampling on Indian hopes in this one. Without the missionaries, the conquerors were coming anyhow. Industry, technology, urbanization—all these were, willy-nilly, destroying Indian culture. The missionaries at least set out to serve as critics of many of the advancers, to buffer the shocks of change, and to offer some sort of alternative world-view when the old one was so severely challenged. They did not do so consistently or elegantly, having had no precedent or practice for such civility. For that reason there are not many bright spots in Bowden's story.

On the other hand, he does not fall into the opposite, countercultural, trap, in which white writers serve as uncritical defenders of every aspect of Indian life. No way of life survives intact the scrutiny of historians, even of those who suspend a spirit of judgment as consistently as Bowden does. Not for him are there visions of an Edenic innocence in the older American landscape or of peoples whose religions simply reposed them in nature and left them at peace with each other. Native American religion in many cases helped its bearers and believers to intensify conflict in reaction and counterstrike. For those who seek "knee-jerk" expressions of white self-hate in the face of native American life, this will be a disappointing book.

Heirs of missionaries and heirs of the earlier native peoples who have read the manuscript without anti-missionary obsessions or romantic notions about Indian life have remarked on the confidence the Bowden approach breeds. On these pages he does what a historian should do. He has become familiar with the overabundant resources left by the literate aggressors and the often more meager sources that remain from the objects of their missions and their militancies. From this he has discriminatingly put together a narrative that sets out less to condemn than to lead to an understanding. Naught is here for the comfort of the majority peoples of North America. There is, on the other hand, much here that will lead to new awareness and may help produce a new spirit of responsiveness and empathy.

Martin E. Marty
The University of Chicago

Preface

In this book I have tried to show what was at stake when Christian missionaries and American Indians confronted each other. While using ethnographic and historical materials, I have followed no single anthropological theory and no predetermined view of historical development, and I have sought to avoid comment on ultimate truth in religions. In describing the conflicts that arose between Indian cultures and white missionaries, I have defended neither the Christian agents nor the natives opposed to conversion. Missionaries were not heroes who sacrificed themselves to save red savages; natives were not innocent victims who watched evangelists ruin aboriginal value systems. Those convenient stereotypes may satisfy current ideological needs, but they impede objective inquiry into the past. I have tried as much as possible to provide detached analysis of volatile issues and a chronological survey of their prolonged conflict.

Perhaps no topic discloses as much irony in human experience as the religious aspect of cultural conflicts. Nearly five hundred years of American history show that interaction between Indians and Christian spokesmen produced tragic results. White clergymen who tried to convert natives may have been prompted by altruistic ideals, but their daily activities helped destroy the cultures of people they wanted to aid. Contrasts between what may have been positive motivations and obviously disastrous results point to an irony not adequately explained by standard categories germane to red-white conflict. Missionary activity was not characterized by the pattern of greed and malice that was usual in most intercultural dealings. The fact that the missions were in any case a general failure makes it even more important to investigate the complicated nature of religious dialogue. I have thus tried not only to chronicle but to explain what lay behind those confrontations.

Another perspective underlying this study is that beliefs and activities in a culture tend to reinforce each other. Using "world-view" and "ethos" to describe these complementary components, I have presented religions as performing the central function of synthesizing ideas and actions within each cultural context. A third conviction of mine is that all cultures have led flexible but cohesive existences. Long before white men came to the New World, Indians developed various cultures, with religious ideologies and institutions to complement them. Through internal modification or external borrowing they adopted new features and adjusted to innovations. Such changes were marks of dynamic cultural creativity. After 1500, European cultures accelerated the rate of change and radically altered the options, but red-white interaction did not introduce a new social process. Studying religion in this context sheds light on the realities of cultural tension and on the persons faced with trying to resolve them.

When writing a brief survey, an author must condense topics and periods that deserve far more elaborate treatment. My method has been to treat of representative cultures, emphasizing Tanoan-, Iroquoian- and Algonkian-speaking groups from three major linguistic stocks found in North America. These groups, further narrowed to Tewa, Huron, and Massachuset tribes for precise reference, also corresponded to the areas of early Spanish, French, and English contact. After a review of pre-Columbian civilizations, chapters 2, 3, and 4 encompass those topics, for precedents in those areas may serve as

lenses for studying later white attitudes and behavior toward red men. Since ethnographic data on single tribes are
incomplete, studies of neighboring groups help flesh out a
synthetic viewpoint for fuller understanding. Thus a discussion of "Pueblo beliefs" or "Algonkian ceremonies"
draws on phenomena from contiguous tribes and blends
their emphases into an overview. Not all parts of the resulting generalized description derive from specific
thoughts and activities found in tribes or representative
villages mentioned in ethnographic studies, but it should
go without saying that such efforts at collective reporting
stay as close as possible to concrete evidence.

Later chapters do not allow as much space for analyzing
native cultures as do the first four, but they still contain
attenuated descriptions of important Indian groups, introducing new cultures when missionaries confronted
them and continuing the familiar pattern that followed
from earlier precedent. In chapter 5 the Delaware Indians
are a focal point for the eighteenth century, when English
culture began to dominate missionary activity. That epoch
started in 1701 with the Society for the Propagation of the
Gospel in Foreign Parts and reached a turning point in
1795 with the Treaty of Greenville. Chapter 6 covers
selected nineteenth-century developments, beginning
with the Louisiana Purchase in 1803 and ending with the
debacle at Wounded Knee in 1890. It focuses on the
highly acculturated Cherokees and the much less flexible
Dakotas as representative groups caught in the strident
white nationalism of that period. Chapter 7 treats of developments since then, including church and government
policies as well as Indian responses, such as the Native
American Church and revitalized indigenous rituals.

In writing this compact overview I have used terminology familiar to general readers, knowing that it does not
pass scientific scrutiny. References to "Indian" and "red
man" abound even though such words are not technically
correct. Similarly, "America" applies here to land that later
became the United States. This usage acknowledges that

other parts of the Western Hemisphere are fully American too. I have also designated sections of the country by their current names—for example, "the Southwest," "Oklahoma," "the Great Lakes"—even though Indians and white explorers used different names to identify them. Each chapter except the first and last contains a discussion of similarities and differences between native and Christian religions. These comparisons of ideas and behavior are my own reconstruction and serve as additional observations alongside the narrative of what actually occurred at the time. An analysis drawn logically from what might have been recognized does not conflict with what really happened. Instead of distorting history, it helps expand our awareness of alternatives in given situations and allows us to assess factual eventualities in light of wider possibilities. So while not technically historical, such comparisons do contribute a dimension on their own.

No chapter accounts for all tribes in a region at any single time nor fully conveys the rich diversity of native materials. The work is intended to describe precontact civilizations in a general way, to chart the role of religion in subsequent cultural conflicts, and to assess the priority Indians still give to their own religions. Readers should be able to acquire a basic understanding of native religions and Christian missions through this introductory volume. Specialists in anthropology, comparative religions, and cultural history can use these pages to supplement their own knowledge with information synthesized from other disciplines.

Portions of the following chapters were delivered at New Brunswick Theological Seminary as the William H. S. Demarest Lectures in March 1977. I am grateful to officers of that venerable institution for letting me share ideas about this material with their constituency. Several colleagues to whom I am deeply indebted read this manuscript and offered helpful suggestions. More than others, Edwin S. Gaustad (University of California, Riverside),

Bruce D. Forbes (Morningside College), Neal Salisbury (Smith College), Sam Gill (Arizona State University), and William S. Simmons (University of California, Berkeley) made particularly trenchant observations that saved me from errors and added qualities beyond my own capacity. I should also like to thank Martin E. Marty, series editor, whose encouragement and guidance were instrumental in bringing this work to completion.

1   *Pre-Columbian Cultures and Values*

At some remote point in time intelligent human beings first entered the Western Hemisphere. Millions of years had already passed since people had learned to use tools, so all their experience in the New World came after they had reached the status of *Homo sapiens.* Compared to our standard conceptions of early civilizations, drawn from Egypt and Mesopotamia, human life in North America covers a much more extensive period of time. Indian cultures in this country stem from a truly ancient sequence of events. Some evidence suggests habitation as early as 40,000 to 80,000 years ago, but there is no general confirmation of human presence that far back. Purists hold that no conclusive proof of human existence extends beyond 13,000 years ago, but more and more specialists are now accepting earlier datings. The best estimates of the dates of the last great Ice Age indicate that people have been living on this continent for 20,000 to 30,000 years.

Regardless of exactly when they arrived, humans came to this continent on foot, following game animals with as little intention of inhabiting a new world as did the creatures they hunted. When huge icecaps formed during the glacial periods, the sea level fell hundreds of feet. Shallow straits became dry land, and miles of new coastline were exposed. At such times a land bridge connected Siberia and Alaska, allowing free movement between the continents. Grass on the tundra provided grazing for countless

wild herds, and nomadic hunters kept pace with the desultory movements of big game. In time they made their
way southward and eastward through corridors left by re-
ceding glaciers, responding to vistas of new territory and
fresh opportunities that beckoned ahead.

The oldest datable evidence of integrated human cultures exists in the center of North America. Sites in Colorado (Lindenmeier), Montana (Anzik), and New Mexico
(Sandia Cave, Clovis, Folsom) show that people had
established a distinctive way of life by 15,000 B.C. Artifacts
tell us that they utilized bone awls, punches, and needles,
together with stone tools: choppers, scrapers, flaked
knives, and projectile points, such as the Clovis Fluted and
the more aesthetically pleasing Folsom. Because of such
intelligently fashioned stone points, this early culture stage
is generically termed Lithic. At other times the sites themselves justify calling it the Llano-Folsom-Plano tradition.
We know nothing about the clothing, shelters, or social
organization of the peoples who constituted this tradition
and very little about their appearance, values, and religious
orientation.

Folsom culture flourished generally on the grassy plains
of mid-America, dependent on the large warm-blooded
animals that abounded there. For at least ten thousand
years hunters stalked long-horned bison, camels, and
ground sloths, mastodons, mammoths, and horses. Human
debris—mostly stone tips for killing and charcoal for
cooking—is associated with remains of those herd animals
until they became extinct. Why such species of wild game
died out is a puzzle, but climatic change and wasteful
hunting methods probably contributed to their demise. As
they gradually disappeared, around 5000 B.C., Lithic culture also disappeared, surviving in isolated pockets for no
more than another thousand years.

There is little hard evidence to tell us about the inner
life of Folsom people, and we can only speculate on their
attitudes about nature, neighbors, or the spirit powers
connected with hunting dangerous game. We do know,

however, that these people developed ritualistic means of responding to death. Not many graves have been found, but the few that have been show us that humans were interred with large numbers of artifacts. Mourners sprinkled bodies with red ochre and deposited material goods, such as hunting gear, with them, apparently to give the departed something to use in the next world. They deliberately broke the bone foreshafts of tipped projectiles before placing them in graves. Some kind of belief in an afterlife, only vaguely conveyed to us by present findings, probably sustained people in Lithic times. Those convictions must have afforded enough of a sense of order and purpose to make life seem meaningful in that violent ecological context. Such beliefs also continued long after Folsom culture faded into obscurity.

Archaic Cultures

Another cultural system also emerged at the time of the big-game hunters, distinctive in both its origins and its adaptation to environmental conditions. Known as the Archaic tradition, whether found in the arid Southwest or in the eastern forests, this versatile way of life was richer and technologically more advanced than the Lithic style. Beginning between 15,000 and 13,000 B.C., various groups independently developed subsistence patterns that exploited a full range of animal and vegetable foods. The members of these Archaic-culture groups hunted small game and utilized fishing too, but they supplemented that fare with seeds, nuts, and roots. Because of their efficiency they survived the extinction of the large cold-adapted animals at the end of the last Ice Age. They became less nomadic and, content to live in smaller territories, developed an admirable stability and diversification. By adapting to local resources, which varied with climatic circumstances, Archaic peoples spread from the Great Basin and southwestern deserts to virtually every ecological system east of the Rockies. Archaic peoples adapted variously to plains, prairies, and woodlands and in time extended their lifeways through diffusion as far as the Atlantic.

Southern Arizona has yielded early Archaic sites, known there as the Cochise culture, that date back to Folsom times. We know nothing of their appearance, housing, or burial customs, but Cochise inhabitants definitely relied on a food-gathering economy. Crudely made milling stones predominate at the sites, whereas projectile points are rare. Hunting even small game was probably secondary to using wild plants to sustain human life. For well over ten thousand years this foraging pattern of existence continued with little contact or exchange with the richer cultures that flourished farther south.

Two later culture complexes emerged after the Cochise variant of Desert Archaic: the Hohokam, in southwestern Arizona, and the Mogollon, in southeastern Arizona and southwestern New Mexico. The more innovative, perhaps due to direct colonization from Mexico, was the Hohokam, which introduced new techniques sometime around 400 or 300 B.C. The people of this culture developed a distinctive pottery style and engineered impressive networks of irrigation canals to aid horticulture in arid terrain. Hohokam sites have also yielded clay figures, which probably played a part in religious activities. We know nothing else about Hohokam ideas regarding the spirit power of animals and plants or the proper respect due them. During a later epoch (A.D. 700–1100) the Hohokam people incorporated more influences from Mexico, such as ball courts, mosaic plaques, clay effigy vessels, loom weaving of cultivated cotton, copper bells, and shell ornaments. They also cremated their dead and buried them in urns. It is only speculation to think that this comprehensive practice of cremation and burial without grave offerings indicates pessimism about an afterlife. Such a conclusion does not necessarily follow, but the fact remains that Hohokam culture was one of the few that burned all its dead and deposited them without ostentation.

Building on local culture traits of considerably earlier lineage, the Mogollon peoples also emerged with their own particular emphases around 2,500 years ago. Gradually improving on the foraging pattern, they learned to produce crops of pod corn (maize), beans, and squash. A few sources indicate that domestic plants were used in Cochise times (as early as 2000 B.C.), but Mogollons were the first to use them in a way that we can call true farming. They also learned to make pottery, probably introduced by neighboring Hohokams after 300 B.C., and ceramics became one of their most distinctive traits. Mogollons usually lived in shallow trench houses and kept surplus food in storage pits. Quite early they also built large ceremonial buildings sunk deep in the ground, separate from the smaller family dwellings. Mogollon peoples almost always buried their dead in a flexed position, knees drawn close to the chest, with each individual receiving separate interment.

The Anasazi, last and perhaps most influential of southwestern pre-Columbian civilizations, also drew on Desert Archaic by blending Mogollon traits with items from the Caddo area farther east. By A.D. 300 they emerged with a notable culture system based on distinctive pottery and versatile basketry techniques. Their dwellings evolved from wattle-and-daub affairs to pit houses and then to mortared stone houses above ground. The Anasazi food supply expanded to include the staple crops of corn, beans, and squash that were destined to serve as standard fare in many native American communities. By A.D. 700 their weapons changed too, progressing from dart- and spear-thrower (atlatl) to the bow and arrow. The Anasazi flourished in northern New Mexico and southern Colorado for a millennium, especially during their great classical period, A.D. 1050–1300. Innovative ceramics and complicated basketry were outstanding characteristics of their material culture during the time that they occupied such magnificent settlements as Mesa Verde and Chaco Canyon.

Early remains of Anasazi culture show that they took particular care of their dead. They occasionally buried persons aboveground in slab-lined boxes called cists; more often they interred them in pits, tightly flexed and surrounded with many possessions. Graves of this period have yielded sandals, blankets, digging sticks, beads, and conical smoking pipes. We know little about their mortuary practices after A.D. 700. Another important indication of religious consciousness among the Anasazi was their use of special ceremonial buildings. As pit houses gave way to free-standing masonry dwellings, people retained the old architectural form for religious purposes. Underground chambers, perhaps derived from Mogollon ceremonial precedents, became the focal point of Anasazi rituals. These sacred rooms, later known as kivas, were the place where men assembled to ensure fertile crops. There they invoked cooperation from sunlight and rainfall, attempting also to propitiate the troublesome causes of storm and blight. Later, plazas or dance courts appeared, providing room for public participation in these vital ceremonies.[1] In historic times these underground sanctuaries and open plazas continued as important characteristics of pre-Columbian folkways.

By A.D. 1100 the distinctive southwestern cultures had been modified by a sharing of common features. Residential areas remained essentially the same, but housing, pottery styles, and ceremonial practices disclose increasingly similar patterns. Then, between A.D. 1276 and 1299 an extended drought caused widespread disaster and drastic changes. The drought, accompanied by famine and probably disease as well, significantly reduced the population in Anasazi, Mogollon, and Hohokam cultures. Fighting may have broken out as a result of disputes over remaining food supplies, and the situation was likely aggravated by predatory Navajos and Apaches, who entered the region at about that time.

Whatever the causes, by A.D. 300 the once-stable southwestern peoples had abandoned familiar landmarks

and moved to new localities in search of a better future.
The Hohokams trekked west, becoming ancestors to historic tribes known as the Pima and Papago. The Mogollons
ventured north, to central Arizona, and formed there a
base for historic descendants called Zuni. Anasazi migration went in two directions; forsaking their awesome cliff
dwellings, some moved southwest into Arizona and became ancestors of the Hopi, while others, occupying the
upper branches of the Rio Grande, became the prototypes
of a remarkably complex association of tribes known collectively as Pueblos. In spite of population loss, migration,
and resettlement, each Indian group held fast to its customs
and religious institutions. Their economy, architecture, social organization, and resilient ceremonialism were still
thriving when the Spaniards confronted them in 1540.

Data about Eastern Archaic life-styles are not as numerous, but some that date back to 9000 or 8000 B.C. confirm
what we know about their ability to use food sources
efficiently. A few more recent sites (5000 B.C.) also show
that proper burial techniques received strong attention,
with perhaps even greater significance attached to them
than in western territories. Sites in Tennessee (Eva) and
Kentucky (Indian Knoll) have revealed adult corpses,
bound in tightly flexed positions, in round pits. Young
children received the same treatment, except for the infants, who were buried in extended positions, strapped to
their cradleboards. Many graves also contained the bodies
of dogs. In addition to those traveling companions, the
dead were given many things, such as red ochre, weapons,
and tools. Mortuary gifts included bone awls, fishhooks,
whistles, bone and copper beads, bowls, axes, turtle-shell
rattles, freshwater pearls, and the canine teeth of bears,
drilled to be worn as pendants. These mortuary goods
indicate that Eastern Archaic peoples responded to death
in a manner eloquent of a belief in life's persistence in
another realm. People gave the dead material goods for a
pleasant afterlife because existence was thought to proceed there in much the same way it had been enjoyed

here, even to having one's favorite dog to share the experience. All types of Archaic cultures, desert and woodland, dealt with life on earth more adequately than the Folsom tradition did. It is also clear that they provided similarly thoughtful means of dealing with life beyond the grave.

Woodland Cultures

Between 1500 and 1000 B.C., in the eastern part of the continent, a slow transition from Archaic to Woodland culture occurred. Pottery appeared as an early manifestation of this gradual transformation. Its decorations and tempering procedures differed from southwestern styles, indicating a possible stimulus from somewhere in the Northwest. Early Woodland peoples still utilized a hunting-and-gathering economy in small settlements, but along with their acceptance of pottery they also adopted concepts and techniques associated with agriculture. Subsistence patterns were revolutionized along the Mississippi and Ohio rivers, especially after tropical flint corn was introduced—an element undoubtedly derived from Mesoamerica instead of the Northwest. Other Woodland features included extensive trading networks, burial mounds, large earthworks, social classes, and specialized ceremonial items. Burial practices had received notable attention in Archaic times, but the Woodland tradition augmented them. Integrating all these traits with impressive social organization, Woodland peoples achieved some of the most outstanding cultural expressions ever displayed in North America.[2]

A complex known as Adena, which emerged in the Ohio Valley around 1000 B.C., typifies the Woodland life-style. It represents a cultural tradition not simply distinct from other groups scattered between the western plains and Nova Scotia, for in its day Adena epitomized the height of civilized grandeur, in much the same way as Rome contrasted with barbarians from the steppes. The people lived in strong circular houses, formed by log posts, and they developed a thick type of pottery. They used grooved axes plus notched, leaf-shaped stone points and were satisfied with relatively simple burials in low mounds. Later sites disclose a richer use of materials for tools and more impressive earthworks. This elaboration of artifacts and general broadening of Adena cultural resources probably stemmed from a neighboring complex known as Hopewell,[3] but, despite these borrowings, Adena residents seem to have remained independent from Hopewellians. The fact that they could borrow selectively yet maintain a persistent cultural autonomy has not yet been adequately explained.

Well-developed ritual practices in Adena culture honored at least the important dead with burial in large earthen constructions. Most sites show clusters of conical mounds, all made with soil heaped basketful by basketful by possibly thousands of laborers. The mounds themselves vary in size, and clusters of them are often enclosed by long ridges, with ramparts and gateways, which form square or circular designs, sometimes five hundred feet in diameter. We know little about the Adena economy and settlement patterns, but the size of their engineering projects indicates a large population, capable of organizing its food resources and manpower to facilitate work on the mounds.

The Adena mounds infrequently contained a single body; most of them were the scene of numerous burials. The standard practice was to leave individuals in extended positions and place them in log-lined receptacles that held up to three persons. Mourners fashioned a tomb by using more logs for a roof and then covering the whole affair with earth. Occasionally bodies were simply deposited on the mound's surface and covered. As they laid each corpse on the common site, survivors spread a fresh mantle of soil over the entire edifice, increasing its overall dimensions with each new burial. Cremation was widespread too, with all or part of the body burned in a special pit, but inhumation was the dominant practice. Isolated skulls have also been found in many tombs or at random in the fill. They may represent trophies; relics of conquered enemies that honored the deceased; or possibly they were the heads of servants who accompanied their master into the next life.

Compared with the grave furniture of earlier epochs, Adena sites are rich indeed. They reveal that this culture responded to death with a massive affirmation of belief in an afterlife, at least for those prominent enough to warrant special burial in one of the mounds. Deposits have commonly yielded red ochre and other pigments, bone awls, arrow points, and a variety of polished stone tools. Bar- and reel-shaped gorgets abound, together with other ornaments, such as bracelets, rings, and beads, many made of copper obtained from the Great Lakes region. One gorget was created from part of a human skull. Graves also contained a number of stone-tube smoking pipes, some of them carved in animal shapes. Artisans produced not only small stone tablets, decorated with ornately engraved geometric patterns or stylized birds, to place with the dead, but thin sheets of mica, decorated with various designs and animal forms. Adena mounds contained two additional items that found more elaborate articulation in later complexes: the predator bird and the hand-eye motif, usually found on beaten copper plates or carved mica. These two themes, plus all the other mortuary furniture, indicate that effective religious institutions presided over a widely supported optimism about life beyond the grave.

The Adena complex remained geographically circumscribed, but other populations were strongly affected by it, particularly in Illinois. Sometime after 300 B.C. these more western people improved on the adopted models to develop their own distinctive cultural tradition, whose artifacts are recognized wherever they are found. This fusion of borrowed precedents and new creativity spread from the Illinois River Valley through southern Indiana to an apex in central Ohio. Named after a characteristic site each mound contains several individuals who belonged to a cult requiring their common burial within a relatively short period of time.

Hopewell craftsmen made an unequaled variety of objects for use in the ritual observances that culminated in burial. Some of the grave goods drew on earlier traditions and included bone tools, flaked knives, fishhooks, and stone axes. Following Adena prototypes, there were gorgets, pottery, bear teeth, and freshwater pearls woven into heavily encrusted robes or beadwork. Mortuary artisans also produced new ceremonial offerings of remarkable beauty and craftsmanship. A complete inventory would be too long to include here, but even a partial list shows how much time and energy went into burial customs. Hopewellians used obsidian from Wyoming for knives and other blades, copper from Minnesota for panpipes, earplugs, breastplates, and nonutilitarian axes. They cut mica from North Carolina into delicate ornaments and headdresses. Shark and alligator teeth from Florida decorated the important dead. Sculptors made human figurines of a quality surpassing previous attempts. They also used Gulfstream conch shells to fashion bowls, gorgets, and beads. But excelling all the rest was their unique creation: platform smoking pipes of stone carved into strikingly realistic shapes of birds and other animals. This rich profusion of mortuary furniture stands as a lasting tribute to the cultic observances that expressed Hopewellian values. Lofty artistic standards point to a complex of religious institutions, architectural accomplishments, and social management that found many converts in less-developed areas of the American woodlands.

Hopewell's integrated system of religion and culture affected many peoples in its enlarged sphere of influence. As ideas spread through personal advocacy or simple diffusion, new converts embraced a fresh perspective on this life and the next, one that not only gave reinvigorated meaning and purpose to such mundane pursuits as trade, farming, ceramics, and social organization but reoriented there, Hopewell culture existed alongside Adena for centuries, and not necessarily on amicable terms. When its more spectacular traits were reaching a peak in Ohio, the new practices reached out in all directions. Many simpler groups learned about farming and burial mounds for the first time under Hopewellian influence. Superseding the more isolated Adena tradition, Hopewell phenomena became the major agents of material and spiritual transformation throughout the eastern half of the continent.

The Hopewell builders raised even larger conical mounds and earthwork configurations than the Adena ones. In many places parallel earthen walls twelve feet high connected large opposing enclosures shaped as circles, squares, or octagons. To complete such impressive ceremonial centers—the biggest one covers four square miles—the Hopewellians must have been well disciplined and skilled enough in management to integrate large numbers of workers. There is little evidence that people resided in these structures. Apparently they lived in small riverine settlements and visited the sanctuaries only on special occasions. An adequate food supply, based on diversified farming, allowed artisans to concentrate on producing grave offerings while freeing laborers to prepare the arenas for mass participation in the burial cult. Far-flung trade networks brought rare items and exotic materials from the Rocky Mountains, Lake Superior, and the Gulf of Mexico for the same purpose.

Some of the mounds are enormous, but they did not follow the Adena example of acquiring layer upon layer for generations. Radiocarbon datings for some of the largest structures show that builders conceived them as single edifices from the start. Additional interments found in these unitary mounds probably represent related burials, supplements to the important individual for whom the mound was primarily intended.[4] We do not know whether these ancillary figures were kin to the central dignitary or accompanied him merely as servants, but it is clear that

tion was the dominant practice. Isolated skulls have also
been found in many tombs or at random in the fill. They
may represent trophies, relics of conquered enemies that
honored the deceased; or possibly they were the heads of
servants who accompanied their master into the next life.

Compared with the grave furniture of earlier epochs,
Adena sites are rich indeed. They reveal that this culture
responded to death with a massive affirmation of belief in
an afterlife, at least for those prominent enough to warrant
special burial in one of the mounds. Deposits have commonly yielded red ochre and other pigments, bone awls,
arrow points, and a variety of polished stone tools. Bar-
and reel-shaped gorgets abound, together with other ornaments, such as bracelets, rings, and beads, many made of
copper obtained from the Great Lakes region. One gorget
was created from part of a human skull. Graves also contained a number of stone-tube smoking pipes, some of
them carved in animal shapes. Artisans produced not only
small stone tablets, decorated with ornately engraved
geometric patterns or stylized birds, to place with the
dead, but thin sheets of mica, decorated with various designs and animal forms. Adena mounds contained two additional items that found more elaborate articulation in
later complexes: the predator bird and the hand-eye motif,
usually found on beaten copper plates or carved mica.
These two themes, plus all the other mortuary furniture,
indicate that effective religious institutions presided over a
widely supported optimism about life beyond the grave.

The Adena complex remained geographically circumscribed, but other populations were strongly affected
by it, particularly in Illinois. Sometime after 300 B.C. these
more western people improved on the adopted models to
develop their own distinctive cultural tradition, whose artifacts are recognized wherever they are found. This fusion
of borrowed precedents and new creativity spread from
the Illinois River Valley through southern Indiana to an
apex in central Ohio. Named after a characteristic site

in strong circular houses, formed by log posts, and they developed a thick type of pottery. They used grooved axes plus notched, leaf-shaped stone points and were satisfied with relatively simple burials in low mounds. Later sites disclose a richer use of materials for tools and more impressive earthworks. This elaboration of artifacts and general broadening of Adena cultural resources probably stemmed from a neighboring complex known as Hopewell,[3] but, despite these borrowings, Adena residents seem to have remained independent from Hopewellians. The fact that they could borrow selectively yet maintain a persistent cultural autonomy has not yet been adequately explained.

Well-developed ritual practices in Adena culture honored at least the important dead with burial in large earthen constructions. Most sites show clusters of conical mounds, all made with soil heaped basketful by basketful by possibly thousands of laborers. The mounds themselves vary in size, and clusters of them are often enclosed by long ridges, with ramparts and gateways, which form square or circular designs, sometimes five hundred feet in diameter. We know little about the Adena economy and settlement patterns, but the size of their engineering projects indicates a large population, capable of organizing its food resources and manpower to facilitate work on the mounds.

The Adena mounds infrequently contained a single body; most of them were the scene of numerous burials. The standard practice was to leave individuals in extended positions and place them in log-lined receptacles that held up to three persons. Mourners fashioned a tomb by using more logs for a roof and then covering the whole affair with earth. Occasionally bodies were simply deposited on the mound's surface and covered. As they laid each corpse on the common site, survivors spread a fresh mantle of soil over the entire edifice, increasing its overall dimensions with each new burial. Cremation was widespread too, with all or part of the body burned in a special pit, but inhuma-

human lives and gave them a sense of both improved out-
look and correct behavior. The groups adopting the new
patterns of course added them to local customs. Dynamic
Hopewellian themes blended with regional traditions and
facilitated beneficial cultural interaction in most cases.
Recognizable variations flourished in Minnesota, upstate
New York, Appalachia, tidewater Georgia, and the Mississippi delta.

One such variant, which flourished in a triangular area in
Iowa, Illinois, and Wisconsin, is known as the Effigy
Mound complex because of its distinctive earthworks.
Perhaps responding to additional stimuli beyond Hopewell, perhaps coexisting with other mound-builders in a
symbiotic relationship, these people constructed numerous mounds in animal shapes. Effigies of this sort appear in
other parts of the country too, notably the Serpent Mound
in Ohio, but they predominated in the northwestern
triangle. Low earthen outlines depict turtles, bison, pan-
thers, geese, and predator birds. One bird has a wingspan
of 624 feet, and there is a panther 575 feet long, but most
have dimensions averaging 100 feet. All of them suggest a
concern for ritual propriety consistent with Hopewell
characteristics. Scattered among the huge effigies are
familiar conical burial mounds containing from one to
three individuals but with almost no grave goods. This
shows how the overarching Hopewell tradition could
blend with local traditions, adding variety to the standard
themes that linked them together.

After spreading its material and spiritual influences to all
points of the compass, Hopewell culture gradually declined over a period of several centuries and ended sometime around A.D. 450. One indication of slow cultural
attrition is that the Hopewellian network of commercial
exchange atrophied, ending access to exotic materials for
grave goods. Few large, complicated mounds continued to
be built on valley floors; instead, smaller ones were
erected on hills and bluffs, with walls suggesting defense
against attacks. The graves now were stone-slabbed crypts

rather than the capacious log tombs of grander days. Cremation decreased, and there were more bundle burials, often with several people bunched together in single clusters. The amount of grave offerings became comparatively meager, and their quality was decidedly inferior. Most of the art found in late mounds exhibits drab and uninspired workmanship, posing a sad contrast with the excellent productions of preceding centuries. Whatever contributed to Hopewell's decline—changes in climate and food supply, disease, outside invasion, or internal dissension—most of its grandeur, together with the ideology that gave it life, had definitely collapsed by A.D. 600. Many woodland groups returned to localized ways of life, and their modest material accomplishments convey no hints about their religious orientation.

But cultures rarely vanish altogether. They often change shape and survive amid people who do not understand or acknowledge the roots of their heritage. Vestiges of Hopewell may have served as the basis for another vigorous culture, known as Mississippian. So named because its chief centers flourished along that mighty river, the core of this new civilization emerged between A.D. 700 and 900 on sites from Illinois to Mississippi. Although earlier cultures had depended on farming to maintain large populations, we have never accurately identified their domestic plants. But we know for certain that Mississippian groups relied on maize agriculture as their nutritional mainstay. One of the largest towns affording insights into this vital new complex is Cahokia, situated across from present-day Saint Louis. Cahokia covered an area of five and a half square miles on rich Illinois land, known as the American Bottoms. It held an estimated population of 38,000, making it one of the most densely settled aboriginal sites in North America. Its residents constructed large burial mounds, and later generations increased their size. By A.D. 1200 the biggest one towered 100 feet high and ran to 1,000 feet on its north-south base; its east-west base extended 710 feet. The entire structure remaining today contains over 22 million cubic feet of earth. With accomplishments like that, Cahokia set socioeconomic and religious trends for other civilization centers to follow.

Mississippian culture expanded southeast and southwest from the heartland. Apparently there were some attempts to spread northward too, but the culture did not thrive around the Great Lakes or the northeast Atlantic states above the Carolinas. The richest archeological sites indicate that it flourished best along an axis from Etowah, Georgia, through Moundville, Alabama, to Spiro, Oklahoma. People living at those centers reached a peak of cultural achievement between A.D. 1200 and 1400. During that time span, local traditions blended with Mississippian stimuli and imported Mexican themes to produce an advanced civilization of remarkable accomplishment, one knit together by shared material traits and religious practices.

The two classic features of Mississippian culture were shell-tempered pottery and mounds in the form of truncated pyramids. At its height the complex exhibited many inherited characteristics as well, but distinctive ceramics and architecture set it apart from all the others. Interestingly, these two new features both originated in Mesoamerica. At some early date, interaction began along the Arkansas River, a locale inhabited by Caddoan-speaking peoples. The Caddoans mixed patterns from Mexico with those of early Mississippian origin and produced a new synthesis greater than the sum of its parts. That dynamic complex in turn reverberated through the Southeast, spreading advantages to receptive inhabitants, who adopted them with energy and skill within a short period of time.[5]

The most tangible element pointing to Mexico's role as donor and to the Caddoans' role as intermediary is the "long-nosed god." By approximately A.D. 1000, small masks depicting a "long-nosed god" had been accepted in Oklahoma, Louisiana, upper Florida, and Illinois. Devotees most often fashioned their insignia from copper but sometimes used shell or stone that faithfully reproduced the copper prototypes. Standard artifacts are uniformly three inches high and display a shield-shaped face, slit mouth, and large circular eyes with round pupils. An excessive nose, measuring over six inches on some faces, protrudes from the center. Probably worn in pairs as ear ornaments, these small masks functioned as part of a ceremonial aggregate that quickly progressed through the Southeast. They were always associated with other ritual objects, such as stone axes, copper earspools, and oblong shafts termed "spuds." As Mississippian culture rose to its zenith, these ceremonial features combined with local elements and culminated in a socioreligious orientation sometimes known as the Southern Cult.

It is not clear how new themes moved from Mexico to the Caddo area and then into the fertile Southeast. The best theory is that Mayan-speaking traders from the Gulf Coast province of Huasteca carried their life-style northward. Such traders, called *pochtecas,* traveled extensively to obtain foreign materials for home markets. An important pochteca god was Yacatechutli, protector of travelers, and he was often portrayed with a long nose. These traders may have played a missionary role, spreading religious interest along with impressive new ceremonies while introducing new merchandise. Many oral traditions in the Mississippian region seem to confirm the Mesoamerican hypothesis. The Caddo revered two young culture heroes, who served as ceremonial intercessors. Muskhogean groups occupying central southeastern areas preserved the memory of those who first brought the new religion. Others, such as the Natchez, honored a tradition elevating one clan to aristocracy because of descent from the original cult-bringer. It is more than likely that individuals or groups of men really did pass through the region. As trader-missionaries, they succeeded in planting new ideas and themes that subsumed earlier patterns under a more sophisticated, comprehensive ideology.

One of the main points about this significant new complex is that preoccupation with the dead faded to secondary importance. Mounds built during this period were intended primarily for use by the living. Converts to the new ceremonial focus adopted distinctive ritual materials and helped spread them over a wide geographical area. Their rapid amalgamation suggests that religious convictions and behavior patterns probably flowed into a favorable matrix already prepared by Mississippian folkways.[6] The process also suggests no small measure of deliberate proselytizing, with natives actively extending the new cult through much of the southeastern woodlands.

Many prefer not to use the term Southern Cult when referring to Mississippian ceremonialism because for them the term "cults" implies devotion expressed by ineffective minorities on the fringe of society and so is inadequate. Whatever the term, the point here is that substantial aspects of Mississippian culture reached a high point between A.D. 1200 and 1400 because religious influences contributed to a widespread synthesis. This great pre-Columbian ritual movement crossed cultural boundaries and knit local variants together with tremendous integrative power. Considering its geographical coverage and persuasive force, a more appropriate term for this socio-religious phenomenon is the Southeastern Ceremonial Complex.[7]

The most impressive Mississippian buildings were truncated pyramids, not the cone-shaped mounds of Hopewell times. They featured ramps or log stairways leading up one side, reminiscent of Mexico's stone pyramids. Temples or chief's houses stood on the flat summits, and, when these significant halls were destroyed, a new superstructure was built over the original mound with countless basketfuls of soil. Some, enlarged as many as ten times through this process, occasionally reached a height of sixty feet. The temple mounds, with uniform rectilinear bases, frequently faced open plazas that served a number of purposes: as a ceremonial dance area, a playing field, a village commons. At some sites only temple mounds monopolized the scene, but often the old conoidal, accretional burial structures were there, too. A few graves have been discovered in the sides of temple mounds, but the two kinds of structure seem usually to have performed separate functions.

We are already familiar with burial practices at Mississippian sites, and they suggest ties with Adena-Hopewell precedents. They occurred in all forms: in flexed and extended positions, cremations, and bundle burials of previously exposed bodies; there were single and group interments in rectangular and rounded graves, in stone- and log-lined tombs. Much of the burial furniture offers no surprise either, except for its profusion. Graves have yielded tools and ornaments of wood, stone, shell, and copper; they also contained textiles, projectile points, mica, and red ochre. Many offerings were ceremonially "killed" or broken before burial, including large quantities of pottery with neat holes made in them even before glazing and firing. Sometimes additional people were placed in the graves, too; apparently they were ritually executed in order to accompany their kinsman, friend, or chief to the next life.

The Mississippian culture produced such strikingly beautiful mortuary artifacts as to place its accomplishments in a class by themselves. Distinctive items include conch-shell cups and beads, copper breastplates and fragile axes, stone animals, platform pipes, and several human statuettes.[8] The most important artistic theme represented is the hawk or falcon. Sometimes copper plates or engraved shells depict the bird itself, but they often portrayed men dressed to resemble the birds, epitomizing aggression and success in war. These impersonators wore feathers on their arms and displayed a forked-eye motif patterned after the fierce winged predators. One shell carving portrays a hawk-man brandishing a club in one hand and a human head (perhaps a head-shaped rattle) in the other. Several other motifs celebrated the martial spirit in addition to resplendent warriors: turkeys, because their long breast feathers resembled a human scalp, and woodpeckers, be-

cause their red heads suggested a clubbed victim. Mythological creatures, such as feathered rattlesnakes and
antlered beasts, also appear, as well as giant hawks locked
in battle with bird-claw-footed cougars. All these themes
glorified warfare, physical prowess in it, and the victories
that undoubtedly led to Mississippian domination of the
region.

People who spread the Southeastern Ceremonial Complex probably favored "red" themes of violence while con-
quering territories and forcing their ways on others. They
counterbalanced their aggressive tendencies with "white"
symbols of peace and forgiveness at their largest ceremonial centers. The most prevalent artistic motif in this second category is the circle with a cross in its center, occasionally stylized as a swastika. Another recurrent form is
the open eye, either depicted alone or in the palm of a
hand. The open eye seems to have been interchangeable
with the cross-and-circle, both representing the sun as the
deity who created fire and looked down on humanity from
above. Holy fire was identified with the sun in actual practice, manifested in temples by a perpetual fire fed with
four logs forming a cross oriented toward the principal
compass points. Such tangible symbols exist in great profusion, indicating widespread belief in a supreme sky god
who served his people as both judge and benefactor.[9]

Red symbolism must have predominated when warlike
activity demanded it. White ceremonies formed a regular
liturgical calendar highlighted by a festival now called
Busk, after the Creek word *poskita,* meaning "to fast."
Men prepared themselves by ritual fasting and by drinking
a powerful emetic from special conch-shell cups. After
vigorous purging, they were ready to proceed with solemn
activities inaugurating the new year, which began each August. Community efforts focused on purification and renewal, epitomized by extinguishing all village fires and
bringing down new fire from heaven. Old fires were
dangerous pollutants, just as new fire was considered
essential to village health and general well-being. Officials

prepared new fuel in the temple plaza and laid out four logs along the cardinal compass points. Ceremonial leaders kindled sacred fire in the temple, brought it down to the plaza, and distributed it among commoners for general use. This sacred act of renewal also stressed forgiveness and reconciliation throughout the community. Busk functioned as a type of universal atonement ceremony that wiped away all offenses (except murder) and celebrated new pledges of mutual friendship in a feast of newly harvested corn.

The Southeastern Ceremonial Complex featured belief in a heavenly deity and showed marked respect for fire as his earthly symbol. But the Busk ritual went beyond renewal, thanksgiving, and communal harmony. It also propitiated animal life, clan heroes, crops, such as corn, beans, and squash, and wild food plants as well. Busk was the occasion of prayers for adequate rainfall and fertility, for successful hunting and warfare, and indeed for all elements conducive to general prosperity in Mississippian civilization. Taken as a whole, temple-mound culture integrated a wide range of emphases into a balanced world-view that gave meaning and order to life. Its rituals and beautiful symbolism enhanced both social integration and defense against enemies. Political authorities often legitimated their position by associating themselves with the fire-sun-deity themes that vitalized daily life. Massive construction projects and the well-disciplined social organization necessary to carry them out also corresponded to the overall fitness of things when Busk climaxed each year with another gift of sacred fire from the sky god.[10]

But by the time whites arrived, Mississippian culture had been declining for a century. Temple mounds existed only in a small area controlled by the Natchez, and they built no new ones. The Natchez also continued to execute retainers for burial with an important chief, but no other southeastern group did. By A.D. 1400 the magnificent artistry of earlier times had all but vanished. Creeks, Chickasaws, Cherokees, and Yuchis still observed the Busk ceremony, but their mounds and temples were mere shadows of their former grandeur. Their ceremonial cycle, focusing on agricultural prosperity and tribal solidarity, proved to be an important factor in resisting white encroachment in the Southeast. However, in view of the deterioration already experienced, it appears that downward culture change following white contact was but an extension of the general decline in Mississippian culture from its classic fourteenth-century epoch.

Summary

Such are the Indian cultures known from archeological data. Other life-styles probably existed alongside them, but the evidence has disappeared or remains undiscovered. While we cannot describe pre-Columbian life in exhaustive detail, it is possible to generalize about a few characteristics before turning to the European explorers, colonists, and missionaries and their discordant and troubling perspectives.

Human beings have inhabited the Western Hemisphere for possibly 27,000 years, a relatively short time geologically speaking but quite long compared with standard references to "ancient" civilizations. At first dependent on hunting alone and then on more balanced subsistence techniques, the Indians developed distinctive life-styles over very long periods of time. People north of Mexico acquired new skills, such as farming and ceramics, through intermittent contact with southerly cultures. In time, material changes revolutionized everything, from economy to theology, north of the Rio Grande. As concepts and behavior patterns spread across plains and woodlands, they blended with earlier cultural orientations, producing many notable varieties and local emphases.

Long before contact with Europeans, several New World cultures had already experienced periods of vital expansion and subsequent decline. Their corresponding religious phenomena exhibited similar patterns of ebb and

flow. Still, when whites first arrived, there existed a remarkable profusion of native cultures with differing spiritual orientations. People spoke at least 200 mutually un-
intelligible languages north of Mexico, and there were
perhaps 350 in Mesoamerica and another 1,450 in South
America, making some 2,000 separate tongues for the
Hemisphere. New World population centered mostly in
the Mexican and Andean regions (up to 75 percent of the
total lived in those places), but probably no fewer than 10
million people lived in present-day Canada and the United
States.

Whatever their density and distribution, the Indians
followed cultural patterns noticeably different from those
of the intruding whites. Materially speaking, the natives
had domesticated no animals larger than the dog; they did
not use wheeled vehicles, plows, or iron implements. With
the exception of a few Mesoamerican groups, none employed written languages. Indian value systems did not
sanction acquiring wealth at the expense of one's fellow
tribesmen. Their attitude about group identity and its
corollary, communal ownership of the land, was one of the
most ubiquitous expressions of Indian priorities. It also
proved to be the one most often misunderstood by whites.
Ideas of perpetual kingship and warfare for territorial conquest or for imposing universal rule were also alien to
aboriginal values. Europeans commonly viewed the ab-
sence of such characteristics as evidence of low cultural
attainment. But while native Americans noticed differences between local and foreign cultures, they did not
immediately conclude that their own ways suffered by
comparison. We shall see how these divergent viewpoints
collided when white missionaries sought to affect Indian
cultures with their own syntheses of religion and folkways.

One principle to remember in these case studies is that
all human cultures are dynamic. People created them
through deliberate choice and under varying circumstances kept them alive by exercising intelligent options.
Before A.D. 1492 many native cultures had thus changed

to accommodate new tools, foods, social systems, and values; less flexible ones disappeared when their supporting environment collapsed. Some endured for centuries in comfortable isolation, introducing barely perceptible modifications. Others rose and fell dramatically, spreading their material and intellectual syntheses to new hosts, who embodied them in turn. But all cultures changed to a degree, because interaction and acculturation are natural to human collectives sustained by thoughtful behavior. When aboriginal cultures conflicted with those imported by Europeans, the result was often disastrous for native American life, but it would be wrong to assume that Indians confronted cultural change for the first time in the sixteenth century. Native cultures had been affecting each for better or worse through millennia, and similar interaction continued after whites began contributing to the process. After A.D. 1500 the only additional elements were quantitative: the differences were more radical and the rates of change were greatly accelerated. Pre-Columbian civilizations were not static, and local cultures did not disintegrate because Europeans introduced entirely new processes of social interaction.

The same principle holds in religious history. Ideological orientations, which give meaning and purpose to life, must constantly adjust in response to new perspectives. Whether modifications stem from internal reformations or external influences, religions exhibit the same pattern of metamorphosis as do material changes in a dynamic culture. At times native agents spread new ideas, symbols, and ceremonies because they thought their life-style could benefit others. When these advocates were successful, liturgical and behavioral alterations produced compelling new religions. People in many regions acclaimed potent new divinities, occasionally blending them with their own traditional figures and at other times expropriating a fresh cultus altogether. Religious interchange occurred among native cultures long before whites began their missionary work in the sixteenth century. Contrasts were sharper after A.D. 1500, but nothing qualitatively different confronted native Americans at that point. No living culture remains unaffected by proponents of physical or spiritual alternatives to current norms. Cultures survive through continual readjustment, and archeology shows that readjustment had been part of human experience in North America for thousands of years.

2

Southwestern Indians, Spanish Missions

The Pueblos

Long before Spaniards came to the American Southwest, the Indians there had gained sufficient knowledge of their universe to live well. Those with retentive memories preserved information about the gods and about early human attempts to enhance existence. They were adequately informed about proper conduct: how to live harmoniously within ordained patterns and ways of fulfilling divine injunctions. Their entire cultural complex—housing, cultivated plants, standard of living, social organization, priestly societies, dances, and prayers—had been bestowed on them by the gods in mythic times. Each village's officials worked to maintain harmonious relations between the human and spiritual worlds. Townspeople worked together to perform their common duty: assuring continuity with nature's basic rhythms so that people could survive and prosper within their appointed sphere.

All this was established before historic times. By the early 1500s, descendants of the Anasazis and Mogollons had settled in the upper Rio Grande Valley and other locations, farther west. From an earlier period a complicated distribution of languages and cultural affinities had developed. Close material similarities led outsiders to think of them collectively as "Pueblos," a Spanish word referring to permanent Indian towns, but linguistic differences prevented much cooperation among the tribes, who seldom communicated with each other. The Hopis, peaceful farmers who spoke a Shoshonean dialect, occupied at least eight villages in eastern Arizona. The Zunis, inhabiting three towns on the western border of New Mexico, spoke a language unrelated to all the others.

Most Pueblos lived on productive lands to the east and spoke variants of two other languages. The smaller of these groups spoke Keresan and resided in about fifteen villages between isolated Acoma mesa and such large towns as Santo Domingo and Cochiti. Other Pueblos spoke Tanoan, but three separate versions of that tongue produced more diversity than uniformity. Tiwa-speaking villagers lived in at least twenty places, including Taos and Isleta; Towa-speaking inhabitants occupied some twelve sites, including Jemez and Pecos. Tewa-speaking natives were not as widely scattered; their six pueblos, clustered around San Ildefonso and Nambe, formed a nucleus of aboriginal solidarity. Counting all these different people as parts of one material culture, they totaled approximately 40,000 persons living in an estimated seventy villages.[1]

Each town was an independent political unit that preferred its autonomous village councils to any overarching tribal association. Though each was free to cooperate with neighboring city-states or distant linguistic relatives, they rarely formed larger administrative units, a fact the Spanish failed to understand while trying to force centralization on them. There was no tradition of hereditary rulers, military leaders, or religious officials. The Spanish intruders sought to manage the Pueblos through a class structure based on political power and concentrated wealth, but none existed in precontact times.

They lived independently, pursuing rather tranquil lives, sustained by an agricultural economy. As a rule the men tilled fields of corn, beans, and squash to obtain the staples of their diet and raised cotton for weaving and small amounts of tobacco. Male labor also maintained irrigation ditches, and the Pueblos achieved impressive results

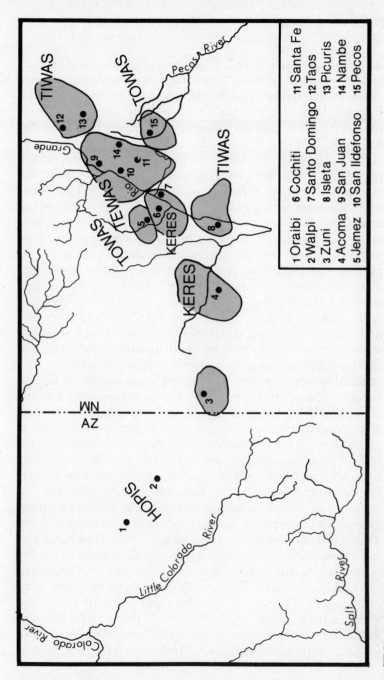

THE PUEBLOS

in watering arable land. Dietary supplements were acquired through hunting (especially deer and rabbits) and
through gathering wild items, such as piñon nuts. The
Pueblos kept domesticated turkeys but rarely ate them;
they prized the feathers for ceremonial decorations and for
fashioning warm, lightweight capes. Well-fed and well-
clothed, they lived securely in permanent dwellings made
of stone, wood, and mud plaster. Most towns were arranged to form a hollow square bounded by apartment
buildings two or three stories high. None of the living
units had doors or windows, and residents entered their
rooms by a ladder through a hole in the ceiling. Women
usually owned the houses, together with all they contained, including the food brought by male providers.
They also predominated in artistic crafts, producing textiles and pottery that embellished a comfortable life-style
with creative beauty. Compared with the impoverished
nomads around them, the Pueblos enjoyed a high standard
of living, as is evidenced by their durable residences and
by the subdued luxury of their everyday apparel.

Kinship systems and community organization followed
two basic patterns. Hopi, Zuni, and Keresan tribes utilized
clan identity as the primary unit of smoothly functioning
government, land use, and religious performance. Their
kinship groups were both matrilineal and matrilocal; that
is, one's mother determined one's clan membership. Marriage within the clan was forbidden, no matter how distant
the relationship might be. Exogamous clans defined the
station and duties of its members; they were essentially
independent corporate associations loosely united to form
a village. Tanoan-speaking Pueblos, on the other hand, did
not stress clans quite as much, nor did they accord females
such high status within the clan. Tanoans classified kin
bilaterally, tended to feature patrilineal descent, and were
nonexogamous. Instead of expecting clans to fulfill the
village's basic needs, they performed those tasks through
voluntary societies that drew members from the whole
village, without regard to kinship relations.[2] Special

societies often followed a winter-summer division of responsibility that made for strong political and ceremonial
organization. Most Pueblos along the Rio Grande did not
rely on clans alone to produce smoothly integrated participation in governmental and religious functions.

Regardless of how they defined kinship ties, all Pueblos
emphasized the values of conformity and a cooperative
spirit that promoted harmonious village life. Their existence revolved around five basic concerns: weather, illness, warfare, village harmony, and successful integration
with the world of plants and animals. Meeting these needs
required cooperative rather than competitive action.
Everyone was expected to take part willingly in such simple tasks as sweeping the plaza, grinding corn, and gathering firewood. There were even higher expectations for
joint effort in such essential duties as planting, harvesting,
and communal hunts. This emphasis on group consciousness was more than a rationale for efficient distribution of
labor; it set standards for personal worth. Among Pueblos
the self was subordinate to the group. Unique personal
qualities were of course recognized, but always in relation
to some larger whole. Individuals mattered only to the
degree to which they contributed to collective activities.[3]
Pueblo social values characterized ideal citizens as dis-
creet, prudent, and conformist—qualities that suppressed
egotism for the sake of other-directed serenity.

People shunned rather than sought individual distinction in Pueblo communities, and those who violated this
canon were open to serious reprisals. Individuals who
thirsted for power or nursed private ambitions received
nothing but censure and were often accused of sorcery.
Witchcraft and self-assertive nonconformity were almost
synonymous crimes. Braggarts and malcontents alienated
by pride or jealousy were as potentially dangerous to the
village as if they had plotted to cause epidemics or an
earthquake. Townspeople equated such uncooperative in-
dividualists with witches because their actions ended similarly: in harm to fellow villagers. The Pueblos believed that

witches could disrupt communal harmony or infect specific persons by shooting thorns, stones, or rags into the victim's body. Witches had the power to change shape, becoming at times a coyote, owl, or another human being for malevolent purposes.[4] If a community ever became convinced that a nonconformist was actually a witch, it ordered the death penalty and provided summary execution. So the golden mean of Pueblo ethics stressed village harmony at the expense of private ambition and placed severe sanctions on individuals unwilling to conform. In fact, this homogenizing norm was so widely accepted that those who defied it appeared to be fundamentally inhuman.

Voluntary societies existed to some extent in all Pueblo tribes, but they were particularly important in Tanoan villages. The emphasis on joining a society was so strong that persons were not considered fully mature until they had done so. Those who perpetuated life-sustaining activities through societies were the ones who really accepted full human responsibility. They were considered "cooked," while adults who did not join a society were still "raw," delinquent in the activities expected of them. The crucial element to notice about these societies and the psychological norm of community consciousness is that they provided tangible outlets for personal fulfillment through cooperative participation. While performing ego-satisfying labors, people accomplished tasks essential to corporate well-being too.

Recruiting practices differed, but the Tewas kept their small voluntary societies effective through vigorous solicitation among young adults. Some societies held vivid initiations, featuring ritual washing and symbolic whipping. Others relied simply on patient indoctrination of the lore and practices germane to their specific responsibilities. A few Pueblo tribes allowed women to participate in the male societies as auxiliaries; in others, women formed their own sodalities. In the western parts of the region, where women played a greater role in clan identity and property ownership, they also had greater access to

religious organizations than did women along the Rio
Grande. Leadership usually followed a single principle:
paramount offices were held for life and were transferred
to the next-senior member; this guaranteed that each society would remain cohesive and stable.

Virtually every pueblo contained societies that presided
over essential activities. The hunting society coordinated
communal hunts, because individuals were seldom free to
kill animals indifferently or at random. Warfare was
another component of tribal life, and the war society regulated joint efforts to protect the village. Pueblo war
societies differed from those of most other native American groups by seldom becoming aggressive. Many other
tribes exulted in armed conflict, but the Rio Grande conformists organized only for defensive war, not for asser-
tiveness and possible conquest. The members of a third
society, known variously as *kossa, kwirena,* or *koshare,* were
often characterized as "clowns," but they had a serious
purpose. The clown society used buffoonery as a means of
public ridicule to shame potentially troublesome citizens
into accepting community standards. Koshare served as
the local police force, dealing with social deviance to in-
sure the smooth operation of village life.

A fourth group responding to community needs was the
medicine or curing society. The Pueblos treated those
stricken by recognizable diseases or physical injuries with
normal skills and broad pharmacological knowledge, but
unaccountable illness was thought to derive from witchcraft, and curing societies accomplished their main purpose by dealing with victims of sorcery. Ceremonial curers
tried to identify the source of mischief, to combat alien
influences, and then to relieve the invalid's suffering. They
sought to remove the spell that had struck down their
fellow townsman by extracting, if possible, the foreign
objects (usually feathers or bones) that occasioned strange
maladies. Since curers had to defeat the prowess of sorcer-
ers and restore their patient's heart to proper equilibrium,
they emphasized ritual preparation and spiritual power in

their office. Such attempts at curing were not always successful, but the belief persisted that some sickness was a byproduct of witchcraft, and villagers regularly solicited the services of the curing society.

An important group of societies in each village concentrated on the agricultural cycle and on the different tasks requiring seasonal attention. Some integrated village activities with the rhythm of natural events and the spiritual power manifested in them. They prepared villagers for crucial episodes in the annual cycle, presiding over ceremonies at the winter solstice to lessen the cold or at the vernal equinox to bring buds, leaves, and blossoms to life again. Others prepared ritually for planting and for various harvests. In the arid zones to the west there were societies to secure rainfall, but along the Rio Grande they supervised the all-important mechanics of irrigation.

The primary responsibility of the various voluntary societies was to recognize the spiritual meaning behind natural changes and then plan the suitable human response in their village. They used elaborate dances to enact symbolically each cosmic event as it occurred in the ritual calendar. After performing that essential task, the pertinent society led villagers in such practical activities as planting, harvesting, hunting, and all the rest; for their duties extended to matters of physical subsistence, and their members were solemnly dutiful about these responsibilities. But the profound significance of their contribution lay in their careful maintenance of ceremonials as the key to proper orientation toward spiritual forces, the ultimate source of meaningful existence.[5] The Pueblo voluntary societies may appear simply to be dividing necessary labor into manageable tasks for different parts of the workforce, but it is a mistake to overlook their essentially ceremonial concerns. They were religious institutions whose ritual actions dealt with the fundamental components of life. Membership in them constituted priestly ordination, and their careful attention to liturgical continuity

made them the most cohesive religious structures found
among natives of North America.

They were priestly institutions because no new member
increased the dimensions of ritual, nor did ceremonial
patterns adjust to each neophyte's capacity. Members were
effective because the society made them so; the lore held
within each group caused its work to be efficacious. Leaders subordinated individual spontaneity to precise ritual
and perpetuated the canon faithfully. We shall see that
other cultures esteemed unregulated religious capacities
and unique personal qualities, but corporate action among
the Pueblos ruled out individualistic performance, and, in
the process, novices were transformed into priests. The
work they subsequently accomplished came not from in-
nate ability but from initiation and long training in a society's sacred teachings. We shall also see that their
successful resistance to white culture derived largely from
the fact that such societies were theologically and in-
stitutionally more cohesive than the religious leadership
found among other natives.

Priests in voluntary societies performed work considered holy by the entire community. They did so with great
reverence, conforming to precedent because they believed
their organizations preserved divine instruction within
established procedures. At the time of creation, or
"emergence," many deities, known as *kachinas*, lived
among human beings and taught them how to deal effectively with the newly inhabited world. These divine
teachings gave ceremonial form and practical substance to
every important facet of human survival, including
agriculture, hunting, warfare, the curing of disease, and
village cooperation. Priests who correctly performed traditional rites could expect other forces to cooperate by providing the necessities of life. If societies failed, by wrong
attitude or faulty observance, to maintain their rightful
place in the rhythm of natural events, they disrupted the
divinely instituted balance of things and exposed their

village to danger. Rather than bring illness, blight, or invasion on their people, priests continued to work in reciprocal harmony with gods and nature, expecting prosperity to follow from painstaking observance of ritual duty.

The central aspects of each society's work began secretly in a kiva, usually an underground ceremonial chamber prominently situated in the plaza of every pueblo. Some towns had two kivas, others more; most of them were circular or oval, but a few were rectangular. Regardless of number or shape, they were the place where activity originated in response to sacred teachings. At designated holy times only members of the priesthood of the society in charge could enter a kiva; at other times any male citizen could use them as a temporary home. These underground cells usually had smooth floors of packed earth with a small hole or depression in the center. Benches ran around the perimeter. At one end there were often an altar, stone effigies, dance paraphernalia, and masks. The Pueblos believed that their ancestors originated from under the earth, and most of their important ceremonial activities began there too. The underground sanctum gave ontological focus to every subsequent act performed by the appropriate priesthood and the community as a whole.

Information about how the members of a society prepared for ritual activities has always been restricted. Priests have kept most of their kiva responsibilities secret not only from curious outsiders, collecting fieldwork data, but from fellow tribesmen as well. But in general we know that the first steps of holy work involved days (usually four) of ritual preparation, including sexual abstinence, fasting, and mental discipline. These measures probably helped officiants achieve a frame of mind in which they could pursue their tasks with undistracted dedication. They might also have involved notions of personal sacrifice, to make each priest worthy of approaching the sacred realm. If masks or costumes needed repair, members refurbished them or made new ones during this time. The principal figures then

put on the masks and, in so doing, made the kachinas a
living reality again for all the people to see.

Dancing was the fundamental medium of public ritual.
Clothed in symbolic regalia and masked to represent sacred beings, performers filed out of the kiva to share their
work with the general populace. They embodied the
kachinas in appearance and act, recapitulating divine
essence in order to make spirit power live for public
benefit. Citizens caught up in the pageantry of the dance
did not see familiar townsmen in costume. They accepted
the performers rather as transfigured beings, representing
divinity in undeniable reality before them. Dances varied
in gorgeous profusion throughout the year; each society
had its distinctive colors and costume designs, copied since
earliest times. Regardless of variations in its duration or in
the number of participants, whether the mood was somber
or playful, dancing brought all the people together. It
served as a tangible reminder that holy purpose undergirded every significant human act. Mundane tasks necessary for community survival remained to be done, but
dances in the plaza linked secret kiva ceremonies with
these tasks, engendering public enthusiasm along the way.

The Pueblos had ways of demonstrating individual religious concerns in addition to the priestly societies and
their ceremonial cycle. One common device was the
prayer stick, often a short willow or cottonwood wand with
a tuft of feathers dangling from its tip. After making personal patterns from various feathers and symbolic colors,
suppliants placed the decorated sticks at localities holding
special importance for them. Prayer sticks could convey
simple feelings of homage and thanksgiving; they could
transmit specific requests for favor and protection. They
stood as silent votive offerings from individual hearts until
natural elements consumed them. Corn was another aid to
worship because it was a particularly sacred plant. People
sprinkled corn meal in short lines to "make a road for the
gods" and thus facilitate prayerful communication. Ubiquitous cornstalks, cornmeal, and multicolored ears show

that corn was a popular vehicle for private devotions. Roads for the gods were also made in the kivas, and animal fetishes and beautifully painted altars served as additional aids to meditation. The Pueblo religion knit ideas and actions together mostly with institutions supervised by priests for the community's good. At the same time, it was flexible enough to permit individual expressions alongside the dominant network of integrated rituals.

Pueblo life flourished within an ethos that had settled major questions about proper behavior. The native view of reality stood behind accepted ways of dealing with practical situations, and the life-style confirmed their perception of the cosmos. Religion united world-view and ethos into a mutually supportive system, rationalizing the nature of existence and directing human participation in it.[6]

Native views of the world stemmed ultimately from creation or emergence stories that spoke of origins and progressed to familiar realities. The Pueblo narratives told of an early time when insects, plants, animals, people, witches, and gods lived in a world beneath the present one. When it was time to leave the underworld, important animals helped them ascend through four lower spheres and finally emerge onto this world's surface. All beings passed through a roof of the last subterranean region, marked in some traditions by a lake but by dry ground in most. Linguistic differences allowed for various spellings of this sacred place, but it was known usually as *shipapu*.

Humans came out of the underworld somewhere to the north of their present location. At first the earth was too soft for them to walk on, but the gods dried it out, while providing light with the sun and moon. The gods taught the people to hunt, grow crops, and dance, how to cope physically with all tasks essential to effective living in their new homeland. They also instituted structures for proper social existence: the kinship systems, political organization, and voluntary societies with priestly officers and sacred duties. The Pueblos preserved these patterns of civilized life because the gods had ordained them. Even

the small hole in the floor of the kivas, the holiest locality
in each village, perpetuated the memory of shipapu and
the dawn of time, when the kachinas had given order and
purpose to all things.[7] Emergence symbolism thus provided orientation and proper definition for all facets of life.
In such a world-view, human experiences were in balance
with other parts of the cosmos, and the cosmic whole was
made intelligible by divine ordering.

Because the people found it too sacred to live indefinitely at shipapu, they moved south in search of more
acceptable places. Wherever they settled, each group had
the sense of living at the center of the world, midway
between the upper and lower planes. From that center
they oriented themselves toward the rest of the cosmos,
identifying six cardinal directions with colors, weather
spirits, and other supernatural beings. They rarely
mentioned life in the world above theirs. The middle
plane, or present location of human life, and the lower
realm, the place of origin and ultimate destination, were
more important spheres to them. From the beginning it
was understood that people would return to shipapu when
they died. Regardless of later migrations, they confidently
believed that, after death, a short journey would take each
person back to shipapu, to the place of emergence, where
they could reenter the underworld, the original source of
life.

Of all the divine beings who blessed the Pueblos, none
was more significant than Iatiku, a female deity revered as
Grandmother. Although portrayed sometimes as a spider,
her most important symbol was corn. When the people
moved away from shipapu, Iatiku remained there against
the day when she could welcome them back after their
earthly life. She gave them corn to sustain them in the
interim and to serve as a reminder of her constant presence. Corn was her heart, and it supplied strength for
human survival as if it were milk from her breasts.[8] Iatiku
also commanded reverence because of her omniscience;
she knew beforehand and without effort what others

strove to learn or decided to do. As early designer of the present world and companion of the dead, she contributed substantially to a view of the cosmos as stable and benign. Two other ranking gods were Masewi and Oyoyewi, twin war deities, whose importance fluctuated with military circumstances. These were the chief deities, but the Pueblos reverenced many guardian spirits associated with clouds, mountains, and other holy places. They interacted with the kachinas through the customs, rituals, and organized social patterns the gods had fashioned when they shaped the whole cosmos at the time of emergence.

The kachinas provided comfortable daily routines for Pueblo existence, and the pillars of each community sustained these orderly ways from one generation to the next. The Tewas called such individuals *Patowa* or Made People—those who, having become fully mature, were installed in responsible offices. They were recognized as complete persons because they observed duties initiated by primordial fiat. They thus performed the highest role anyone could achieve. As guardians of the ancient rituals, they directed all group activities and exercised much more power than mere political officials, for the Pueblos regarded the societies of Made People as holy institutions in both origin and purpose. After death, Made Persons returned to shipapu. Their service in priestly roles climaxed in posthumous reunion with the highest deities after a twelve-day journey back along the path of emergence.

When a common layman, or Dry Food Person, died, his soul joined its ancestors at one of the four directional shrines that bracketed the village. Senior relatives dressed the body and placed food with it. If persons were thought to have led a good life, their survivors provided only a small amount of food, because they would need but little sustenance in traveling straight to the afterworld. If departed souls had not been particularly virtuous, they received more food for the difficult journey that lay ahead. The Tewas supplied extra moccasins too, believing that such persons would encounter rocky roads and confusing byways before reaching their destination. But all the dead were thought eventually to reach their goal; the Pueblo cosmology did not recognize a place of eternal punishment.[9] However, even though Dry Food People could reach the place of origin, everyone was expected to become a Made Person and so be certain of returning to the earth's navel.

Still, no one violated the corporate texture of Pueblo existence by positing two completely different fates for villagers of unequal moral character. Other than that general assurance, ideas about souls in the afterlife specified no single task or locality. Departed spirits were free to move about in the underworld and also to inhabit lakes, mountains, or other places dear to people on the surface world. Death may have had a temporarily disquieting effect, but in the Pueblo scheme of things it held no lasting terror. The Pueblos had developed means of dealing with such anomalies as death as well as rebellion against community standards and sickness induced by witchcraft. In the last analysis, dying was not a fearful experience because it did not really involve termination; one simply changed residences and lived among the ancient powers where life had begun long ago.

The Pueblos thus viewed their universe as an orderly phenomenon, expressive of a reasonably good fit between perceived reality and practical experience. They defined "good" ideas and actions as those perpetuating human balance in the cosmos, "evil" as those disturbing harmony and equilibrium. If war captains, koshare, or other officials seemed authoritarian in demanding conformity, they did it to achieve the higher cooperative good required by traditional sanctions. Such procedures worked effectively for centuries, and as long as their world-view and ethos fitted together, Pueblo life remained unperturbed. But when the Spaniards arrived in force, they injected disruptive elements into the people's lives. When Pueblo behavior and conceptions of reality no longer supported each other, there were drastic results. Responses to foreign intrusion,

ranging from millennial visions to violent revolt, all sought
to integrate the new experiences into a stable order of
existence.

The Franciscan Missions

By mid-1521 Hernando Cortez had captured the Mexican
capital of Tenochtitlán, murdered its ruler, Montezuma II,
and stamped out the last pocket of resistance at Otumba.
Cortez thus added new territory to the Spanish realm;
what is more important, he fired imperialistic ambitions:
exploiting new land for riches and exploiting new peoples
for religion. After 1521 the Spanish conquistadores fanned
out in all directions, usually followed by Franciscan
missionaries, as dedicated to their own type of conquest as
their secular counterparts were to theirs.

Mineral wealth and heavy population led the Spaniards
to concentrate in the southern regions for fifteen years,
but then, suddenly, in 1536, certain officials heard of
fabulous cities in the uncharted north when two survivors
of an ill-fated expedition to Florida arrived in Mexico after
eight years of adventures. A young notary public named
Cabeza de Vaca and a black Moor known as Estevanico
told of shipwreck, enslavement, and wandering in the
Sierra Madres, but no part of their narrative fired the
imagination as much as their hints about the Seven Cities
of Cibola. This chimerical image had already persisted for
years in Spanish legend despite a lack of substantiating
evidence. When the bedraggled travelers spoke of Indian
stories of advanced cultures to the north, visions of rich
prizes danced again in aristocratic minds. Cortez and
Pizarro had acquired immense fortunes through daring
acts, and every young hidalgo felt that other plums were
waiting to be plucked. Many of them clamored for permission to enter the unexplored territory, but Cabeza de
Vaca's tales needed verification. In 1539 the authorities
sent Estevanico and Marcos de Niza, a Franciscan, adept in
native languages, to map the area and determine whether

the fabled riches actually existed. A small company made
its way to the Zuni pueblo of Hawikuh, where the Moor
was killed and Brother Marcos beat a hasty retreat. Back in
Mexico City, his fanciful reports confirmed preconceived
beliefs in wealthy civilizations ripe for the taking. The
stage was set for northern exploration, with most Europeans bent on personal aggrandizement and a few on the
salvation of souls.

In early 1540 Francisco Vásquez de Coronado launched
the first expedition in search of fabled Quivira. Five
months later he pushed into western New Mexico and
commandeered the town of Hawikuh, using it as a base for
further explorations. He searched for a year and a half,
reconnoitering territory from central Kansas and the Texas
panhandle to the Grand Canyon, but found no gold or
native culture advanced enough to satisfy Spanish expectations. A Franciscan, Juan de Padilla, who was part of the
company, remained in Kansas to establish a mission when
the soldiers retraced their steps, to winter again in New
Mexico. Later reports disclose that he was killed only a
short time thereafter. Coronado returned to Mexico in
1542 in disgrace, his health shattered and his fortune
wasted. But despite his failure, new expeditions set out to
prove that the northland would reward diligent seekers. In
1581 Agustín Rodríguez led a small band of missionaries
north of the Rio Grande; two years later Antonio de
Espejo mounted a relief party to locate and rescue them.
Neither contingent accomplished much except to reaffirm
the Franciscan policy of not allowing evangelists to precede Spanish troops. In 1521 Gaspar de Sosa received
swift punishment for organizing an illegal entrada, while
one led by Francisco Bonilla and Juan de Humana (1594)
fell victim to murder and leaderless collapse.

The failure of these desultory excursions led to more
systematic efforts. Juan de Oñate was appointed to head a
substantial colonizing force, and early in 1598 he led a
party of four hundred, including ten Franciscans, eight friars, and two lay brothers, up the Rio Grande Valley. By

May the entire procession of men, cattle, horses, and wagonloads of furniture, seeds, iron tools, and leather goods rumbled through El Paso, the last Spanish outpost. Two months later they arrived in the heart of Pueblo country and appropriated a native village as temporary headquarters. The intruders had no misgivings about their right to dominate local affairs or to enforce a new life-style on the natives. As conquerors, they justified themselves by claiming the right of discovery and by offering the benefits that accrued to Christian belief and political vassalage. They also threatened severe retaliation against anyone refusing to cooperate with the new scheme of things.

Oñate summoned the chiefs of neighboring villages to a council, where he explained his twofold mission. He promised that if they submitted to Philip II, the most powerful monarch in the world, Spanish arms would protect them from all enemies. More important than political reorganization, Oñate also raised the crucial issue of native souls. He warned the Pueblo leaders that, unless they accepted baptism and instruction in Christian doctrine, they would suffer not only immediate physical punishment but eternal torment later on. After listening to these new ideas, and undoubtedly recognizing the technological superiority enjoyed by the intruders, the Pueblo leaders expressed a willingness to adopt both the Spanish king and a new deity. Whether or not they understood every implication of Oñate's message, it seemed prudent to acquiesce in the new situation and await further developments. It may be that the Indians accepted the Spanish ultimatum because they perceived that refusal seemed to entail both earthly disadvantages and future damnation.[10]

Thus the Pueblos, who had been conditioned to conformity since childhood, accepted the new social forces that had entered their culture like the point of a wedge. In the ensuing years they faced all the institutions of Spanish occupation: those redefining land-ownership and distribution, those establishing missionary assignments and ecclesiastical tribunals, and those demanding native tribute

paid in labor and material goods. Modest adjustments to
early change went peacefully enough, but the Pueblos did
not know that the Spaniards planned to use these initial
accommodations as the means of transforming native life
into their own model of civilization, including its religion.

Oñate proved to be a bad governor. For a decade he
chased rainbows of imagined wealth, searching for pre-
cious metals, dabbling in textiles and hides, even hunting
Apaches and Navajos to sell as slaves in Mexico. Ranches
and farms languished under his indifferent supervision,
and the colonists began to talk of abandoning the entire
venture. Priests and people agreed that New Mexico was
an unprofitable land that did not deserve to be part of the
Spanish Empire. But, just as they had needed royal permission to enter the territory, so they could not leave
without specific authorization. In 1608, influential colonists therefore petitioned the Council of the Indies for
permission to withdraw from their distant and altogether
barren outpost of civilization. Supporting reasons included
the prohibitive cost of bringing fresh supplies from
Mexico. Few civil servants or soldiers volunteered for duty
there when the hope of easy riches died. The missionaries
had not mastered native languages, and so the harvest of
souls fell short of expectations. The situation discouraged
both religious and secular leaders, and almost everyone
trapped there wished to write off New Mexico as a bad
investment.

Officials in the royal chain of command took such argu-
ments seriously and were inclined to terminate the colony.
But in a curious reversal, never fully explained, the missionary fathers suddenly opposed the departure. They in-
flated the number of converts and maintained that it would
be unconscionable to abandon so many at a critical stage of
religious progress. Rather than allow the Indians to lapse
again into barbarism, the Franciscans urged that their spiritual condition and the salvation of future generations
were compelling reasons for staying. Royal opinion tacked
to sail with the clerical wind. The king decided not to give

up the region but rather to support it himself in order to sustain missions in his empire. In late 1609 he replaced Oñate and provided annual funding for sixty-six friars. Missionary rolls over the next seven decades never approached that maximum, but royal expenditures for evangelization amounted to a considerable sum, possibly a million pesos. Although a drain on the royal treasury, the colony survived, largely because of the missions, and it stood as a rare example of religious motivations overruling the quest for riches and power.

The Franciscans interpreted the king's decision as an affirmation of their central role in provincial affairs. Governors usually held office for no more than three years, but each found time to resent the friars' presumption that secular government existed primarily to serve religious interests. Thus, instead of cooperating to transform the Pueblo way of life, the Franciscans and the magistrates squabbled over who was entitled to guide the Indians' destiny. Unseemly disputes over ecclesiastical immunity and clerical interference in secular matters vitiated missionary efforts. This bickering caused many Pueblos to lose what little respect they had initially had for Spanish authority.

Such were the conditions under which the missionaries tried to work against the Pueblos' religious proclivities and convert them to Christianity. Their difficulties with the Spanish civil officials hampered their work in many ways, but their own internal policies also kept progress to a minimum. For one thing, there never seemed to be enough missionaries for the job. When the king rescued their work in 1609, their numbers had dwindled to three. The new governor brought nine new ones with him, together with military reinforcements and fresh supplies. Others came three years later, so that in 1616 there were eleven flourishing missions staffed by twenty friars. By 1622 the number of Franciscans had risen to twenty-four, centered around a monastery built at Santa Fe. Three years later Alonso de Benavides brought twenty-seven friars in his new capacity as *custodio* to plan mission strategy. The

crown ordered another thirty north in 1629, but, with
deaths and transfers, that raised the net total to approximately forty-six. During the next five decades there were
no more than forty Franciscans, and often fewer than
thirty, scattered among the pueblos. The official quota of
sixty-six was never filled, and, when disaster struck the
mission stations in 1680, only half of the allotted number
were preaching Christianity along the Rio Grande.

In 1610 the friars established a permanent base at Santo
Domingo, near the Rio Grande, and divided the territory
into seven administrative districts that covered 87,000
square miles. In their initial contacts with native peoples
they enjoyed the advantage of offering a package of new
materials and ideas. They brought domestic animals, an
array of food plants, metal tools, and weaponry, all of
which seemed connected with the religious concepts they
advocated. Early missionary work was thus clothed in an
aura of promising innovation, and perhaps because of this
many Pueblos accepted such new rituals as baptism and the
Mass. But instead of improving on these good beginnings,
most of the later friars settled for an unpretentious round
of daily Mass, vespers, and an occasional baptism, marriage, or burial. Rarely did they bother to learn the native
languages or to translate the liturgy into local tongues. A
few Indians memorized Spanish prayers phonetically, but
instruction in reading or writing Spanish was not a regular
part of the missionary program. Furthermore, the missionaries did not stay in one pueblo for long. They followed a policy of constant resettlement that moved them
from one language group to another and then, after an
average of ten years' service, back to Mexico. Im-
permanence and superficiality thus characterized the manner in which the Spanish friars confronted the native
Americans.

Still, the records indicate a surprising number of positive native responses. Enthusiastic missionaries listed a
total of 7,000 converts in 1608, and they claimed 10,000
more baptized followers by 1620. Five years later, reports

of Indian Christians in twenty-eight different pueblos went as high as 34,000; some irresponsible estimates numbered them at half a million.[11] But instead of increasing further, the number of converts decreased in the aggregate when overall population declined along with the number of inhabited villages. The estimated seventy pueblos of Coronado's day fell to about thirty-five by 1650 because conflicts with Spanish soldiers were added to the familiar problems of drought, disease, and raids by marauding Apaches. Spanish domination started dangerous trends in Pueblo life, and routine missionary practices did nothing to counteract the downward tendency.

Compatible elements between Spanish and Pueblo ceremonial styles could have encouraged missionaries to appreciate fundamental aspects of native life. Both traditions emphasized the importance of priestly leadership, and, whether buildings were called churches or kivas, each religion stressed a special place for ritual activity. Additional parallels can be seen in the use of altars, special ornamentation, ritual chants, sacred utensils, and a religious calendar that regulated community life. Crucifixes and rosaries bore some resemblance to prayer sticks as aids to private devotion. The use of holy water could be likened to the "clouds" of yucca suds and consecrated water that native priests used for bringing rain. Incense in churches resembled ceremonial tobacco smoke. Catholic saints who had once been human beings blended easily with departed Indian heroes elevated to the status of powerful spirits. The sacrament of baptism found a parallel in the Indians' ritual bathing, especially in connection with initiations into the voluntary societies, which involved head-washing and name-giving ceremonies. Even on the darker side of life, the Catholic clergy were as likely to envision demons as were their native charges, for Spaniards accepted witchcraft with a certainty that matched that of the Pueblos, who looked for sorcery behind illnesses and social deviance.

The world-views were similar too, for both stressed divinely ordered reality. Both groups believed that the world had been made by power beyond human control, and they agreed that nature and human life conformed to laws determined by godly fiat. Each religion in its own way emphasized divine power as that which gave meaning and purpose to human identity and conduct. Definitions of good and evil followed logically from that supernatural norm. The full range of injunctions about personal morality and social ethics in both religions derived from perceptions of life made dependable and reasonable through divine decree.

Both Spaniards and Pueblos thought that compliance with holy power brought practical benefits. One group might revere a solitary god in three persons while the other obeyed innumerable kachinas, but each side was convinced that blessings flowed from a proper relationship with supernatural authority. The missionaries assured native listeners that venerating the Cross would protect them from traditional enemies, drought, and toothaches.[12] The Pueblo priests reminded their fellow townsmen that correct performance of kiva rituals and plaza dances ensured favorable climatic conditions and produced bountiful harvests. Both religions saw a direct connection between divine will and personal fate coupled with national destiny. Conversely, each interpreted disease, drought, famine, and other catastrophes as punishment from demons or angry gods unwilling to overlook human failings. Between these positive and negative poles it would be difficult to say whether love of duty or fear of retribution predominated in the daily actions of either people.

Despite these compatibilities, the Pueblos' world-view and their conceptions of personal identity and moral obligation differed at important points from those preached by the friars. They referred to no exalted god who created matter ex nihilo, and the underworld, rather than a heaven beyond the sky, was the focus of their life. They thought

all things came from the earth's navel instead of a transcendent source; gods, people, animals, and plants had
emerged through the underworld's roof to dwell on this
world's surface. Christian references to Hell or Purgatory
in nether regions thus fell on uncomprehending ears, for
the Pueblos could not accept the upper cosmos as humanity's ultimate destination.

Differing ideas about the nature of divine power added
to the problems. The Spaniards were monotheistic in spite
of the fact that they spoke of God as three separate persons. This view contravened the Pueblos' belief that a
great number of divine beings were required to make the
world's components work smoothly. The friars emphasized belief in one God, depicted with primarily male
characteristics. The Pueblos viewed such male figures as
Jesus and Santiago (patron saint of Spain) as similar to the
twin war gods, Masewi and Oyoyewi, and they likened the
Virgin Mary to the venerable female deity Iatiku. But the
friars, glossing over these superficial resemblances,
stressed the unitary character of Christianity's solitary
deity, who ruled a cosmos that turned the Pueblo orientation upside down.

The Pueblo Indians gave the earth a respected status of
its own; they therefore could not share the Europeans'
belief that the natural world was simply an economic re-
source. Instead of using natural objects for secular purposes, the Pueblos had a more profound regard for their
sacred constitution. What really mattered to them was
locating human life at the center of reality, with sacred
space radiating in concentric circles throughout nature.
Everything, from the points on the compass to the changing seasons, was bounded and controllable by reference to
that center. Because of this orientation, the world was an
orderly environment that circumscribed the harmony of all
good things. The Pueblos affirmed mundane existence and
husbanded their lives, along with nature, as cooperative
parts of a sanctified ecosystem. For them it was a complete,

satisfying world, and people could live in it safely and well, knowing that they fulfilled holy purposes by respecting its established ways.

Another point at which the two cultures contrasted sharply had to do with personal identity. Just as their worlds were different, the Europeans and Pueblos regarded the people in them differently too. Spanish assumptions granted individuals freedom of choice and opportunities to distinguish themselves from others. Personal merit was a virtue to be prized and cultivated, whether accomplished through valor or charity, by prowess or austerity. The Pueblos, however, always defined personal identity in reference to the community, not at its expense. They submerged the self as any Spaniard would have defined it and emphasized collective values instead of individual repute. They shunned personal distinctions and discouraged competitive innovation because they found the true self in group action. Anyone setting himself apart from others was more likely to be ridiculed than honored, and, if his separatism continued, he might be executed as a witch.

Christian doctrines of salvation, and church practice as well, pointed up the contrast with Pueblo ideas about personal identity. From its beginnings Christianity had generally thought of its adherents as a distinct people, a faithful remnant saved from destruction by a merciful God. But the church's salvation of separate individuals usually included some degree of voluntary belief and personal morality, a combination of faith and works in which individual responsibility helped secure the final result. There were no such thoughts in Pueblo life. Everyone there belonged to the group, and each person was sanguine of returning to life in the underworld through shipapu regardless of his personal merits or demerits. The only qualification placed on this cultural universalism was the idea that less-virtuous tribesmen would have a more difficult time in reaching the place of original emergence.

There was no ultimate life of pleasure for the good and punishment for the wicked. The Pueblos had no conceptions of atonement, vicarious suffering, or redemption because none of these conceptions was necessary to their beliefs.

Christians came to Indians preaching a doctrine that required a psychological sense of separation from the aboriginal group. They saw the church as an institution composed of believers gathered in anticipation of rescue from earthly existence. This doctrine divided the Pueblo community because not all Pueblos would be saved, only the baptized. Only Indians or Spaniards gathered into the communion of saints were received at Mass. Church membership thus cut through families, clans, and voluntary societies, and Christianity's major threat to Pueblo life stemmed from its disruptive capacity to offer salvation only to individuals.

Differing ideas of moral obligation constituted a third area of conflict. The friars thought that their ethical guidelines derived from biblical and theological tradition, sources that transcended historical conditioning. The Pueblos derived their sense of duty from the local community and its pragmatic needs. The friars defined good and bad actions from an ecclesiastical perspective, basing standards on what they viewed ideally as a divine institution that did not coincide with any particular cultural unit. The Pueblos based ethical judgments on standards that complemented their social fabric, and, because the kachinas had established them, they did not see any reason to look elsewhere. The friars thought that sanctions against improper conduct would occur in the afterlife in addition to temporal punishment. The Pueblos considered it proper that sanctions, such as ridicule from the koshare or death for witches, belonged to this life alone, with no reward or punishment reserved for the future.

As the friars tried to convert the Pueblos, and the latter continued to follow their own view of right conduct, these fundamental differences became readily apparent. The

Pueblos had aligned ethics with a divinely appointed natural order and had organized morality in terms of ritual obligations. Their central duty was to participate in ceremonies that perpetuated a well-ordered life for the pueblo and met its physical needs. For them, sin was failure to sustain elements that gave meaning and orientation to life in the pueblo. But the friars stressed attendance at Mass, monogamy, with no divorce, and obedience to royal magistrates. The Pueblos did not understand why such activities might be significant. Furthermore, they saw no need for the Crucifixion story and the accompanying appeals for repentance and reconciliation with a God propitiated by Christ's sacrifice. They could not comprehend why the death of one individual, long ago, could affect their own sacred obligations, designed to provide adequate food, continuing health, village harmony, and military defense. The Spanish message of sin, divine redemption, and sacramental aids to salvation fell on stony ground in the Southwest.[13]

In trying to secure converts, the friars highlighted the elements that separated the two religious systems. By the late 1400s Christian wars against the Moslems had forged a strong alliance between the Catholic religion and Castilian customs. As Spanish arms advanced the cause of king and orthodoxy in the New World, it became increasingly easy to disdain all who differed from Spanish norms, and the missionaries pursued their evangelical program with iconoclastic zeal, convinced that all native beliefs were superstitions and that native behavior was depraved. As spiritual conquistadores, they regarded all Indians as barbarians, lacking any civilized notion of law, morality, or proper worship. Instead of beginning with compatible parallels and drawing the Pueblos through shared ideas to a specifically Christian perspective, they rejected Pueblo religion as utterly misguided. From the outset they sought to eradicate every vestige of Indian conduct and to fill the vacuum with Catholic doctrine and practice. After 1609 royal support added repressive power to the arrogance

born of religious certitude. At times they promised rewards to Pueblos who accepted the true faith, but condemnation was their dominant message. When Pueblo
loyalties persisted in the face of repeated denunciations,
the friars used force to destroy the base of local resistance.

Convinced that Pueblo rituals were totally wrong, the
friars seized kivas and confiscated as much ritual paraphernalia as they could find. They burned the sacred masks,
dance costumes, altar effigies, and prayer sticks. They tried
to seal off the sacred chambers and to prevent the voluntary societies from meeting in them. They forbade dances,
whether conducted secretly or in the public plaza. In sum,
the central features of local institutions, plus essential
duties required in priestly observance, were the targets of
all the destructive wrath the missionaries could bring to
bear on them.

The fact that it was necessary to raid the kivas over and
over again shows that the Pueblos persisted in their traditional ceremonies. Their institutionalized religion provided both a coherent rationale and a tenacious structure
for resisting the friars' onslaught. Interestingly enough,
the Spanish civil servants did not always cooperate with
the Franciscan leadership. Many governors resented
clerical tyranny and showed their displeasure by allowing
pre-Columbian habits to flourish under their administrations. But the friars remained adamant in their doc-
trinaire perspective. If pagans adhered to traditional
ways, the gentle sons of Saint Francis directed that they
be whipped as an obstacle to pacification in this life
and to their own bliss in the next.

In keeping with such forceful procedures, the friars also
dictated a specific regimen to natives who accepted Christianity. They gave neophytes European names and insisted
that they speak Spanish. But, curiously, they seem never
to have made language instruction or even catechizing an
integral part of missionary routine. The Pueblos had long
been accustomed to monogamous marriages, yet they frequently allowed divorce. The friars denounced these easy-

going ways as promiscuous and permitted divorce only in
extreme circumstances. They required daily attendance at
Mass for all baptized Indians and punished those who
failed to comply. Pueblos accepting baptism may have
done so for many reasons that did not exclude loyalty to
traditional patterns. The Spaniards viewed religion as an
exclusive loyalty, however, and berated their charges
for retaining old folkways after conversion. Delinquent
Pueblo Christians often felt the lash of disapproval from
their spiritual supervisors, either because they could not assimilate to Spanish standards or they clung to aboriginal
habits while adopting secondary customs to appease their
masters.

Repressive tactics were bound to create ill feelings
eventually, but the habitually self-effacing Pueblos rarely
expressed their discontent. In most cases they rebelled as
residents of isolated towns against local conditions; there
was no general rebellion against Spanish oppression at
first. Indians at Taos, for instance, killed two soldiers and
the resident priest in 1639 and destroyed the church and
friary before fleeing to escape reprisal. During the early
1640s several pueblos, including Jemez, demonstrated
against the imprisonment and flogging of natives who had
in secret carried on the ancient traditions; the Spanish
governor hanged twenty-nine leaders and jailed many
more. In 1650 various Tewas and Keresans from Cochiti
plotted to rid themselves of Franciscan domination, but
Spanish troops stopped the insurrection before it started;
nine conspirators were hanged on that occasion, and
others were sentenced to a decade of hard labor. For a
time it seemed that openly violent acts of rebellion had
ended, so church and state officials resumed the more
familiar pattern of squabbling with each other instead of
sharing administrative responsibilities. Then a unique
combination of events brought the pressure of intercultural conflict to a breaking point.

For five years, 1667–72, there was an extended drought
in New Mexico. When their crops failed, native farmers

began to question Spanish assurances that their trinitarian
God would bless agricultural work. In 1671 a great pesti-
lence carried off many inhabitants, whose resistance was
weakened by the inadequate diet. It began to appear that
the Christian deity was no better at preventing epidemics
than providing good weather. By 1672 the Navajos and
Apaches, whose hunting-gathering life-styles left them
more desperate for food than the Rio Grande farmers,
began raiding the pueblos. The king's promise to protect
his vassals proved as ineffectual as the other advantages
supposedly accruing to Spanish rule. Famine, disease, and
attacks from marauders convinced most Pueblos that they
had seriously erred in accepting elements of the intruders'
religion alongside their own.

Many had been willing to accept Christianity insofar as it
harmonized with their customary understanding of how
religion served material and social ends. Others had
adopted the externals of the new viewpoint as long as it did
not displace their traditional world-view and the activities
integral to it. But when the new ethos and its bewildering
world-view proved incapable of guaranteeing good harvests and peaceful villages, where was the advantage in
accepting Spanish ways? Despite Franciscan determination
to abolish ancient ceremonials, the Pueblos rejected the
foreign life-style because they thought it had caused their
present difficulties; they returned to the voluntary-society
rituals with increased dedication because a revitalized
tradition seemed the only practicable recourse in times of
stress.

Just at the time the Pueblos were reaffirming their traditional practices, the Spanish clerics and magistrates ended
their habitual antagonism against each other. Juan Francisco de Treviño became governor in the early 1670s and
placed his office at the disposal of missionary policy. As
more and more Pueblos rallied to their old faith, Treviño
swore to destroy it once and for all. In 1675 he arrested
forty-seven prominent Indians on the vague charge that
they had bewitched a clergyman. One Pueblo committed

suicide while in prison; the authorities hanged three others
and freed the rest, after severe beatings, when the townspeople demonstrated forcibly for their release. Among the
forty-three survivors was a Tewa religious leader named
Popé, from the pueblo of San Juan. Using distant Taos as a
secret headquarters, he persuaded leaders in other towns
to form an unprecedented intertribal alliance to resist
foreign oppression.

The united Pueblos struck in early August 1680. Using
a pincer movement that divided the Spanish forces, they
sent the enemy's southern contingent reeling downriver at
once. Then they concentrated on Santa Fe, where survivors had rallied to make a stand. In a few days they
crippled the garrison, and all the Spaniards fled south to El
Paso for refuge. The Pueblo warriors were content to let
them go, wishing them good riddance instead of death.
Out of 2,500 Spanish inhabitants in the province, the Indians killed only 380; they simply expelled the rest from a
land where they had never been welcome. But of thirty-
three missionaries in the area, twenty-one fell victim to
native retaliation. Angry warriors burned most churches
and obliterated tangible symbols of clerical influence,
such as records of baptisms, marriages, and burials, together with all the statuary and altars they could find. The
basically antiecclesiastical character of this revolt indicates
how much the Indians considered the priests to be the real
cause of their suffering. Missions had been essential to the
province's continuing existence, and so the missionaries
bore the brunt of the Indians' attempts to eradicate all
things Spanish. The revolt was the concerted act of a
people determined to reject Christian civilization because
it posed a direct threat to their integrated religion and
culture. The worsening conditions in the 1670s had
proved Christianity to be an unacceptable alternative to
the traditional safeguards of Pueblo survival. By late 1680
it seemed as if the kachinas had smiled on native efforts to
realign themselves completely with baseline culture.

For the next fifteen years, sporadic expeditions moved

north from El Paso to pacify the old colonial district. Popé
was unable to maintain the pragmatic union and disappeared from historical view because the Pueblos preferred local autonomy to his grand alliance. As a result, the
Rio Grande Pueblos once again fell piecemeal to Spanish
troops, now bent on revenge. By 1696, when the latter
had extinguished the last sparks of revolt, they had caused
many more native casualties than they themselves had
suffered fifteen years earlier. The native population had
been declining throughout the seventeenth century, dwindling to less than 20,000 after seventy years of Spanish
influence. The fighting that took place during the rebellion
and the reconquest lowered their numbers even further,
and by 1700 no more than 14,000 survived in the ancient
pueblos.

The Spaniards hoped that revised administrative procedures would cause fewer problems in future red-white
interaction. Since many investigators blamed missionary
tactics for earlier difficulties, one change they insisted on
was never to allow the Franciscans the power they had
once had. By 1700 it appeared that pacification was complete and that prewar economic and political habits could
be resumed. But thoughts on that score failed to note a
significant cultural change, especially on the basic level
where religion motivated human life. Many Pueblos had
emigrated west to find refuge among the Hopis. Those
who stayed in their traditional homeland found another
way to resist Spanish domination. They adjusted to the
foreigners' control over secular matters wherever necessary but rarely allowed Christianity to penetrate the private sphere of their religious sensibilities. By a com-
promising technique, known as compartmentalization, the
Pueblos cooperated outwardly with dominant social patterns while maintaining their ancient integrity. Precontact
kinship systems, especially the clans, which gave them
their primary sense of identity, remained intact and in
force. Imposed political offices, such as alcalde, did not
replace the traditional voluntary societies, which still em-

bodied each pueblo's real government. The native languages remained vibrant too. The Pueblos mastered
enough Spanish to function in the workaday world, but
they used the ancient tongues at home, and especially in
the kivas, to remind each other of the true ground of
reality.

Partly because of previous mistakes, partly due to
demographic changes, the Franciscans did not return in
large numbers. They never achieved effective contact with
the Indian leadership and in fact aided the compartmentalization process by evangelizing less aggressively. If the
Pueblos adopted elements of Hispanic Christianity, it was
only the externals of the European faith, to appease the
missionaries and keep them at arm's length. This double
standard of external acquiescence and internal resistance
assured Christianity only a peripheral status. The Pueblo
religion survived because its tenacious network of voluntary societies withstood every attempt to exterminate
them. These durable, highly sophisticated institutions
offer an important suggestion about what factors help native culture systems endure in the face of white domination.

Later generations of Pueblos grew up in an environment
in which one could be nominally Catholic and still be loyal
to another tradition. Church attendance and Hispanic holi-
days had some place in village routine, but Catholic elements that contrasted with baseline religious values were
politely ignored. Since 1700, the Pueblos have added an
unobtrusive Christianity to traditional patterns without
fundamentally altering their solid precontact core.[14] Such
compromises and the enabling compartmentalization
process have relegated Hispanic influences to secondary
importance. Christian agencies exist in the general sum of
things, but they have not really changed the world-view
and ethos that sustain Pueblo life.

Old ways persist today despite the missionary efforts of
various Christian denominations that compete for native
loyalty. Ancient beliefs and rituals have endured side by

side with ideas yet to be resolved into a new synthesis. The Indians learn English, but it is a second language. Many now live in single-unit houses instead of the old village structure, but they stay close to the land. Automobiles, electricity, and other technological changes affect native habits, but the ceremonial substratum of traditional existence survives. The organizational strength of Pueblo culture, embodied in its priestly and sociopolitical institutions, has been the key to native endurance over the past four centuries. It will probably withstand threats to its integrity in future times as well.

3   *Northeastern Indians, French Missions*

The Hurons

An estimated 10 percent of all Indians north of Mexico lived in the Great Lakes region. Among them were Iroquoian-speaking peoples who controlled the territory between Lake Huron and the Hudson River and from central Pennsylvania to the Saint Lawrence River. Some groups, such as the Tobacco, Erie, Neutral, and Susquehannock tribes, were independent, but most Iroquoians were clustered in two confederacies. The eastern one, in the Finger Lakes district of New York, consisted of Senecas, Cayugas, Onondagas, Oneidas, and Mohawks, who formed the Hodenosaunee, or People of the Longhouse. Algonkian-speaking Indians considered these people extremely dangerous and referred to them as "Iroquois," or vipers. They are known to history as the Iroquois League, a powerful force to be reckoned with in warfare, peacetime diplomacy, and trading alliances. The western confederacy, located between Ontario's Lake Simcoe and Georgian Bay, included four major tribes, known as the Bear, Rock, Barking Dogs, and White Thorns or Canoes. This second league used the collective name Wendat, usually translated People of the Peninsula, to indicate their geographic location.

When French explorers first encountered the Wendats, they called them "Hurons." Some think the bristly Wendat headdresses reminded the French of their native wild boar; others suggest that the name derived from a French slang term denoting peasant ruffians or any boor. But regardless of origin, the outsiders' term became generally accepted over indigenous usage—a common occurrence. The Hurons occupied an area no larger than thirty-five miles east to west and twenty miles north to south. Their Bear and Rock tribes, comprising well over half the population, had lived in the same locality since at least 1400. Tiny Huronia, which was one of the more densely settled parts of the region, sustained perhaps as many as 21,000 individuals by means of a diversified agricultural economy.[1]

Huron settlements contained a maximum of one thousand people, who protected their semipermanent villages with palisades of upright logs. Within the walls, the people lived in longhouses, some of them fifty to sixty yards long. Each longhouse was approximately thirty-six feet wide, and the roof arched twenty-four feet high to cover a spacious interior. Overlapping sheets of elm or cedar bark formed an outer covering, while support posts and ridgepoles strengthened the solid frame. There were no openings except for doors at each end and a few holes in the roof to let smoke escape. Cooking fires for perhaps a dozen families lined the central hallway, and around the interior wall a narrow shelf provided space for sleeping and storage. Since there were no partitions or apartments, privacy was minimal; everyone freely observed the domestic life of everyone else in each dwelling.

For food the Hurons depended heavily on domesticated plants, although they occasionally supplemented their diet with game animals. Climate and geology made their area one of the northernmost territories where maize horticulture was a viable enterprise. Situated on the edge of the Canadian Shelf, the Hurons had been growing corn since 1000, sunflowers since 1300, and beans and squash since 1400. Tobacco was another valued plant. After the men had cleared land in the classic slash-and-burn procedure, the women tilled the fields and owned all the pro-

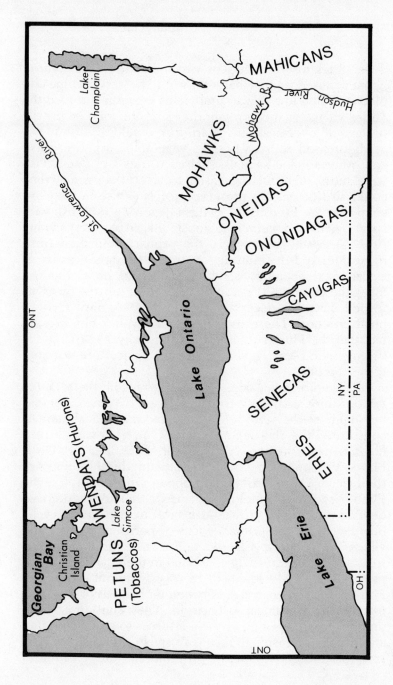

THE HURONS

duce. Lacking fertilizer or crop rotation, the Huron women raised annual harvests until the soil became depleted. When low agricultural yields eventually forced the entire village to move to another site, the men began the process all over again by clearing new fields.

Major food sources besides vegetable crops were fish and other aquatic animals, such as turtles and clams. Fish were more plentiful and easier to catch than game; they could also be readily preserved for later use in the corn soup that the Hurons ate twice a day. Men took fish with spears, nets, and weirs ingeniously placed across spawning runs. Deer and bears were the primary source of fresh meat. Men did the hunting, because it brought prestige as a warrior's secondary activity. Successful hunts did not meet the community's nutritional needs, but the skins afforded materials necessary for clothing. A third favorite meat was dog. These food items should not obscure the fact that the Huron economy was basically an agriculture-fishing complex rather than an agriculture-hunting-gathering one.

All Iroquoian-speaking Indians arranged their family relationships according to clans. In each village, persons belonging to the same set of extended matrilineal families constituted the clan segment. The Hurons acknowledged eight female totems—Turtle, Wolf, Bear, Beaver, Deer, Hawk, Porcupine, and Snake—as the mythical founders of their clans. These kinship units apparently did not, like the Pueblo societies, employ any managerial technique that divided physical and ritual duties through an annual cycle, but they were the primary focus of personal identity and village cooperation. Clanswomen owned the longhouses, together with everything contained in them, and residence patterns were determined by clan identification. The Hurons forbade marriage between individuals of the same matrilineal, matrilocal association. They considered such unions incestuous and, as such, a threat to social cohesion and ritually offensive to the clan's spiritual ancestress. The Iroquois observed incest prohibitions only within a

mother's clan; the Hurons observed a bilateral taboo by
not marrying close relatives on either the maternal or the
paternal side.[2]

Clan lineages were fundamental to political organization, even though they did not fit neatly within tribal
alignments. Each local family segment chose two headmen:
a civil leader responsible for social order and a war chief
concerned with military affairs. These headmen presided
over the village councils, where all clansmen deliberated
over questions of community welfare. When intertribal
councils debated issues touching the whole confederacy,
each village appointed additional orators and statesmen to
accompany the clan representatives and voice their collective opinion. Huron politics operated at three levels:
village, tribe, and confederacy. Village government
functioned best because it involved fewer people. Clan
chiefs organized village councils in which older men, and
women too, expressed their opinions on matters of mutual
concern.

No headman held an office inherently superior to his
counterpart in other clans in the village. A leader's value
lay in his personal performance, with prestige depending
on administrative ability, diplomatic skill, and solicitude
for the entire community. Official spokesmen lacked coercive power to force individuals or any group of them to
obey majority decisions. The council was not so much a
governing body as a sounding board for canvassing attitudes and pointing out the popular choice on specific
matters. Decisions made in the councils tried to reflect a
consensus, but they were not binding on anyone. Clans
could dissent from the village consensus, and villages
could refuse to cooperate with a tribal decision, as could
tribes with confederation policy.

The Hurons thus respected majority opinion, but they
also made room for individualistic behavior. Their social
values affirmed individual dignity and self-reliance alongside clan membership and its corporate identity. Characteristics such as permissive childrearing and a penchant for

impressive rhetoric indicate how much the Hurons valued
individualistic expressions. But harmonious community
relations dictated that personal initiatives be carefully balanced with general consensus. The Hurons thus tried to
accommodate private preferences to collective expectations in every area except murder, treason, and other serious crimes. Those who persistently violated these fundamental restrictions laid themselves open to the charge of
witchcraft. Community leaders usually viewed such non-
conformists as alien to the common interest and ordered
their execution because they threatened social stability.
The imperfect fit between government-by-consensus and
personal initiative gave Huron corporate structure both its
flexibility and its serious limitations. It allowed for private
distinction yet could not command obedience to the uni-
vocal decisions needed in a crisis. This flaw proved disastrous when the confederacy later came under all-out attack.

The Hurons pursued individual distinction in two principal occupations, warfare and trade. War was the most important way in which young men could exhibit their prowess and so gain respect. The opportunity for gaining
personal prestige was thus a major incentive for making war,
but the Iroquoians also fought to avenge earlier injuries inflicted on their tribe or confederation. Fighting between
Hurons and Iroquois constituted an endless round of aggression, reprisals, bitter memories, and vengeful feuding.
Once the cycle began, it never ended, and it found support
in religion. Every springtime, when food was plentiful
again, the warriors raided their traditional enemies to obtain captives, whom the townspeople usually slaughtered in
religious rituals that were thought to please the sun, their
god of war. Older headmen sometimes succeeded in ar-
ranging fragile peace agreements with enemy tribes, but
the young men clamored for war as the best means of
enhancing their reputations. The experienced councilors
found that restraining them from rash action required
great tact and wisdom. Quite often they had to invoke the

confederacy's higher interests before cooler thinking controlled youthful militancy.

Intertribal trade was one of the higher interests
threatened by unregulated warfare. The Iroquois used
their League primarily for aggressive purposes, to dominate tribes around them and exact annual tribute, but the
Hurons added mercantile considerations to their military
federation and became the most influential tradesmen in
their region. Since they valued trade and did not wish to
see feuding disrupt it, they made strong alliances with
many tribes. Peace meant prosperity, and council headmen
constantly sought to promote friendly relations with other
tribes as a means of securing greater economic advantages
for their confederacy. The chronic hostility between the
Hurons and the Iroquois, however, made lasting peace and
trade impossible between their mutually exclusive
alliances, but in their own territory the Hurons extended a
wide sphere of influence, acting as middlemen who traded
foodstuffs northward to nomadic Algonkians and carried
furs (and, later, French hardware) southward to agricultural tribes. They had acted that way since prehistoric
times. The coming of the white men may have accentuated
but did not appreciably alter any part of their precontact
habits or values.[3]

Since trading produced material prosperity, the Hurons
emphasized mercantile activities as the second important
means of acquiring personal prestige. Just as they admired
brave warriors and successful hunters, they also saw merit
in clever traders who could barter goods in exchanges
yielding a profitable surplus. Trading had an air of personal
adventure about it because individual initiative and shrewd
judgment came into play. It took courage and diplomacy
to open new trade routes or to organize a wide network of
business alliances. The Hurons respected those who were
adept at such activities and consulted them on the full
range of village issues.

Trading was valued for a more important reason than its

capacity to increase wealth. The Hurons wished above all to be honored by other members of their tribe, and generosity in material goods was the surest way to win affection. Individuals worked hard to accumulate extra food and furs for social use, not for personal profit. The principal aim of acquiring wealth was thus to give it away, to share with others—from clan to confederaton—and so to improve social status. Dormant wealth commanded no respect because natives did not regard property as an end in itself; beaver robes, wampum, and surplus tobacco were truly useful only when a tribesman could share them unstintingly with others. He then gained renown as an open-handed individual whose contributions to community needs showed a concern for his neighbors' welfare.[4] Since feasts and gifts depleted one's stock of goods, more trading was necessary next year. In this way individual enterprise fed, and reciprocally benefited from, Huron social values.

Attitudes about property show that the Hurons retained a sense of corporate identity in spite of giving wide latitude to individualism on the behavioral level. Individuals could express themselves through dissenting opinions in debate, by leading private war parties, and by engaging in personal business ventures, but they pursued their activities with due regard for blood relatives and village associates, without whose confirming support they could achieve nothing. Possessions acquired at the expense of family and townspeople or withheld from their enjoyment were no riches at all. They impeded the process of sharing that sustained the native group. Any type of individualism that emphasized accumulating things instead of augmenting corporate existence was a form of cultural suicide. It represented selfishness gone awry, redefining the ego outside the clan and tribal relationships, which provided the only satisfactory ground of identity.

One way to see how property facilitated community processes is to observe its role in settling grievances. Whenever someone committed a serious offense, community leaders tried to prevent retaliation by determining

who was really at fault; the guilty party then customarily
paid reparations to those he had offended. Even when the
crime was murder, material gifts were the acceptable way
of assuaging guilt and preventing a vicious cycle of further
reprisals. Thirty presents was the usual indemnity for killing a man, but the murder of a tribeswoman called for
forty gifts.[5] Whenever officials named a guilty party, his
clan and often the entire village acknowledged collective
responsibility for his actions. His kinsmen then vied with
each other to amass enough goods for the imposed pay-
ment. Similarly, the victim's kinsmen received part of the
goods distributed and thus overlooked their grievance. (Of
course, if the violence involved an outsider, the only answer was war; this explains why Indian warfare can usually
be described as an extended blood feud.)

The way property flowed in a never-ending circuit
through Huron social structures indicates how these Indians reaffirmed communal responsibility. Visitors from
outside were never refused hospitality, and no villager
went hungry or without shelter as long as anyone in the
community had something to share. Whenever accidental
fires destroyed goods in a longhouse, ready replacements
were supplied through the generosity of others in the village. Huron families competed with each other to give
away the most property at feasts, curing ceremonies, and
funerals. A personal donation to the community's reparations fund was another way of expressing solidarity with
the group. In a classless society these activities helped
prevent disproportionate accumulation of wealth in a few
hands. But, more important, they show how the Hurons
affirmed the corporate identity that ultimately defined
their existence and gave meaning to their daily activities.

Huron values found expression in religious rituals more
clearly than in social patterns, though their ceremonies
seldom had much formal structure. Like most other
American Indian groups, the Iroquoian-speaking Indians
did not confine their religious attitudes to a limited sphere,
with specific institutions to embody them. They had no

distinct priesthood to conduct regular ceremonies for tribal or village benefit; there were no special chambers for traditional rituals, no churches, no public shrines or altars where specialists conducted sacrifices according to a standard formula. Huron religiosity permeated every aspect of native life. The men believed they had special guardian spirits to help them in fighting, hunting, trading, and other private conquests. They invoked spiritual aid by fasting, prayers, and gifts of tobacco before embarking on journeys or a military raid. Charms, curiously shaped stones, or any object signifying a person's unique communication with the divine world afforded protection and presaged good luck. In these and countless other ways the Hurons tried to live harmoniously with the spirit powers who shared the natural world with human beings.

While they encountered the divine presence intermittently, they recognized that some persons communicated regularly with the supernatural. Such people were *aretsan,* or shamans, individuals singled out for excelling in activities everyone had the capacity to perform. Shamans received no special power through ordination or by virtue of belonging to an exclusive religious brotherhood. They demonstrated special capabilities through personal association with divine spirits, and their acceptance as religious leaders in Huron society depended on their ability to exhibit that power in concrete ways. Their fellow tribesmen believed that the shamans could control the weather, predict the outcome of military ventures, bring luck to hunters and fishermen, and recover lost objects. They respected such feats and rewarded the shamans well for serving communal needs in practical ways.[6] If a shaman failed repeatedly, people simply turned to others, never questioning shamanistic power or the benefits resulting from it.

Though shamans provided many services in Huron society, curing was crucial, because here they opposed the power of witchcraft. Witches were antisocial beings who were believed to cause many illnesses by magic spells.

They had the power to afflict innocent victims by shooting
hair balls, stones, shells, or nail parings into their bodies.
The villagers themselves felt helpless in the face of such
malevolence, but they believed that the shamans could
diagnose the cause and prescribe treatment. On the tangible level, shamans cured people by removing foreign
objects. Sometimes they administered emetics or prescribed a curing dance; more often they sucked or cut the
patient's body without harming it and displayed what had
been causing the trouble. On the intangible level, shamans
wrestled with wicked spirits and overcame their power. In
this manner they vindicated good over evil and maintained
their place as intermediaries between the spirit world and
common villagers.

Dreams were an extremely significant element in Huron
life, and shamans functioned importantly as interpreters.
Everyone was believed to have two souls, one to animate
the body and a rational one extending beyond physical
activities. In sleep the rational soul went on its own adventures, communicating with spirits and encountering
pleasure or pain with other human souls. Dreams occurred
when one's rational soul came back to the body and re-
counted its nocturnal experiences. Every Huron agreed
that it was essential to reenact these dream adventures in
order to unify the two souls and make each person whole
again. Failure to gratify the rational soul's wishes, literally
or figuratively, could result in what we would term schizo-
phrenia, a palpable illness that endangered the whole
community as well as the individual directly involved.[7] So
Hurons consulted shamans to interpret dreams, to determine the soul's wishes, and to prescribe palliative behavior. By unpeeling the layers of manifest and hidden
content in dreams, shamans relieved cumulative anxieties
that could emerge as psychosomatic disorders if left un-
attended.

One of the most significant Huron festivals centered on
dream fulfillment. Once a year, usually during the winter
solstice, in a three-day ceremony called Ononharoia, the

Hurons gave themselves entirely to fulfilling everyone's dream wishes. At such times they withheld nothing from a person if he or she claimed to have dreamed of receiving it. Villagers gave feasts, exchanged possessions, and relived fantasies in order to reconcile every dreamer's two souls. Not all dreams could be fulfilled literally: if someone dreamed that enemies had captured and tortured him to death, he of course had to find a substitute in lieu of actually killing himself. In one such case the Hurons made a straw man and then ritually killed it as they would a prisoner; the dreamer pronounced himself satisfied with this symbolic death because his souls felt back in place again. The shamans were particularly skilled in finding such metaphorical alternatives. But whether heeded symbolically or realistically, dreams directed personal affairs with great power, not only at the frenetic time of Ononharoia but on a daily basis.

The Hurons also treated captives with ritualistic attention to detail. Prisoners of war who survived long enough to reach a Huron town met one of two fates: adoption or execution. The triumphant village readily absorbed conquered women and children but accepted men less frequently. Huron families assimilated individuals to replace kinsmen lost in previous raids, and these adoptees apparently found little difficulty in accepting their new identity. But townspeople reserved most of the men for torture, a lingering death, which they supervised with the solemnity of a religious ceremony.[8] Torturing a prisoner was an important act dedicated to the sun, symbol and embodiment of their war god. Leaders urged the entire village to participate in a ritual devised to make the victim cry out in pain. If they failed to make the captive show fear, the villagers thought their god would be displeased and cause misfortune to befall them.

Torturing a prisoner began in the evening and could last as long as six days. It was necessary to keep the victim alive for at least one night because executions had to culminate at dawn, when the sun could view the offering made to

him. As the ritual began in a war chief's longhouse, women
and children beat the captive freely. They pulled out his
fingernails and made deep gashes in the fleshy parts of his
body, where they inserted live coals. Then others stripped
off his scalp and burned every inch of his body, sometimes
using hot resins that stuck to his torso and made him
writhe in pain. Whenever the prisoner seemed about to
expire from such treatment, he was revived with water and
rest. Throughout the process the captive would try to
endure his agonies stoically, singing a death song and actually encouraging his tormentors to acts of greater violence.
As dawn approached, the war chiefs led him to a platform,
built especially for the final act, where they quickly dis-
patched him and, if he had proved an admirable warrior,
ate his heart in order to absorb his courage. Then they cut
up the body and cooked it, inviting everyone in the village
to feast in symbolic triumph over a worthy opponent. These
practices of ritual human sacrifice and cannibalism may
have originated in far-off Mesoamerica, but they were fully
indigenized by the time white men arrived to see them
performed with jubilant ferocity.

The Hurons also treated their own dead with ceremonial propriety. When a local resident died, the relatives
decorated the body with ornamental paints and wrapped it
in a fine robe. Three days later they laid the corpse in a
bark coffin and placed it on a ten-foot platform in the
cemetery. When the funeral ceremonies were over, the
mourners took condolence gifts and distributed them
among the members of other clans who had attended to
the burial details. The Hurons did not honor slain captives
or tribesmen executed as witches. Instead of mourning
their passing, they contemptuously threw such offal on the
village garbage dump. Persons dying a violent death belonged to another special category; victims of warfare and
murder were buried in the ground as soon as possible,
their graves marked with simple bark huts. Infants were
also treated differently; they were buried secretly, along
pathways or at longhouse thresholds, so that they could

enter some woman's womb and be reborn for a second chance at life.

The platform burials were only temporary. The Hurons conducted the final and most impressive ceremony at intervals of approximately fifteen years, corresponding to the time of relocating the village at a new site. The Feast of the Dead provided eloquent and lasting testimony to the basic Huron value of corporate identity that nurtured personal well-being through all stages of life. When the designated time arrived, relatives removed bodies from the platforms, cleaned the bones, and wrapped them in new finery. They then invited members of the whole confederacy to attend this most significant of all festivals. Tribesmen brought gifts to honor the dead and to comfort those who mourned their departed loved ones. In an open field outside the village, the men dug a pit ten feet deep and at least fifteen feet wide. They built a large scaffold around the pit and arranged parcels of bones on it, together with gifts signifying the attachment people still felt for their dead kinsmen.

After several days of solemn feasting, it was finally time for the last interment. Mourners placed rich presents in the ossuary as final tokens of esteem and gave others to those attending the ceremony, to thank them for their expressions of solicitude and solidarity. Relatives lowered individual skeletons into the pit; the leaders then used poles to mix all the bones together in final community. This powerful symbolic gesture emphasized that Hurons belonged to one another in death as in life.[9] The Feast of the Dead reminded Hurons perhaps more graphically than any other ceremony that they were a people defined by the group and from it drew their abiding sense of being.

The Hurons did not, however, develop religious institutions as strong as those of the Pueblos. Shamans embodied the only localized religious leadership, and their stability did not match that of the Pueblos' voluntary-society priests. When white missionaries introduced an alternative faith and life-style, the Hurons, bewildered by

conflicting claims, had few institutional supports to fall
back on. Compared with priestly authority and tradition,
the idiosyncratic performance of shamans proved less capable of resisting white cultural influences.

The Hurons relied on a cosmology as well as shamans
and ceremonial customs to correlate proper actions in a
rational world. They saw no need for an elaborate account
of how life originated or for a precise pantheon of deities,
but within a rich mythological nexus they usually
mentioned the female deity Aataentsic as central to human
experience. Aataentsic originally lived in a transcendent
spirit world, but she fell through a hole in the sky, either
slipping accidentally or pushed through by her angry hus-
band. As she was falling, the Great Tortoise saw that
Aataentsic was going to plunge into the primordial sea and
possibly drown. Tortoise asked animals such as beaver and
muskrat to dive to the bottom of the ocean and bring up
mud. (Local variations differ on details of this story, but
the number four recurs in mentioning the animals involved and the number of times they tried to reach the
bottom.) At length they succeeded in piling enough earth
on Tortoise's back to provide a soft landing spot and a
congenial dwelling place for the mother of mankind.

Aataentsic was pregnant when she fell from the upper
realm, and in time she gave birth to twin sons, Iouskeha
and Tawiscaron. Variant narratives say that she was their
grandmother; if so, the intermediate parents played no
role in subsequent events. Iouskeha became the familiar
culture hero, creating lakes and rivers, causing corn to
grow, releasing game animals to roam the earth, and providing good weather. He also learned to make fire and
taught the people that valuable skill. When the brothers
grew up, Iouskeha fought with Tawiscaron and made him
run away bleeding. Drops of his blood turned into flint,
the most important material for Huron tools. Iouskeha
grew old but never died because he was able periodically
to rejuvenate himself. He lived with Aataentsic in an uneasy relationship, the male deity seeking to help mankind

and the female largely responsible for disease and death. Aataentsic reigned over departed souls and manifested little good will toward human beings, who ultimately derived from her. Iouskeha, on the other hand, was often identified with the sun and smiled on all Hurons, particularly warriors.[10]

The Hurons also referred to a wide range of localized spirit beings to explain how their world operated. They believed that everything, including lakes, rocks, plants, and even manmade objects, had souls. As living beings in a homogeneous universe, all things had power to communicate their will and to influence human experience to some degree. Sometimes the Hurons spoke of supernatural power in generalized terms, such as Orenda. More often they referred to a particular being as an *oki,* a spirit who figured importantly in immediate experience. Every oki had to be taken seriously, and most ritual behavior was an attempt to relate harmoniously with spirits who constituted the unseen portion of daily existence. Such powers were everywhere. People had to propitiate dangerous ones with prayers and offerings of tobacco and petition the benevolent ones for aid in war, hunting, and travel. Oki spoke to Hurons in dreams, granted successful fishing, aided political ambitions, and blessed business ventures. Even human beings with extraordinary personal qualities such as shamans, great warriors, and epileptics or lunatics were thought to be oki.[11]

Although it is difficult to establish a definite hierarchy among these spirits, the most potent element seems to have been the sky. An oath involving the sky was the most sacred one a Huron could make. In general, however, other than associating power indefinitely with transcendence, the sun, and mythopoeic figures, such as Iouskeha, Huron spiritualism concentrated on local spirits. People conducted their lives according to what they thought each oki expected of them. In that way they hoped to cooperate with the spiritual dimension and receive practical benefits from properly ceremonious relations with it.

They thought that life after death would continue in

much the same way as earthly existence. They believed
that each tribe had its counterpart in the land of the dead,
where kinsmen feasted, danced, and pursued the same occupations as before. One soul remained in the ossuary
after the Feast of the Dead, reaffirming common origins
and a shared destiny. The other soul traveled westward to
be reunited with townspeople who had died earlier. Such
happy prospects made no distinction between good and
bad tribesmen and did not mention separate places of reward and punishment. However, though souls were im-
mortal, not all reached the afterlife villages. Those of children and the very old lacked the strength to travel west;
they therefore stayed behind and inhabited the abandoned
sites of former villages. The Hurons also denied access to
the souls of those who had died violently, because they
considered them dangerous. Villagers taken captive and
possibly tortured to death in foreign territories were irre-
trievably lost, too. For all others, however, death involved
only a temporary separation from loved ones.[12]

All in all, Huron life was sensible and confident, with
few sources of traumatic anxiety in this world or the next.
Subsistence techniques supported the confederacy's population bountifully. Individuals acquired prestige through
warfare and trade but grounded this eminence in social
service and corporate existence. Their shamans provided guidance; dreams regulated personal affairs; community festivals such as Ononharoia and the Feast of the
Dead rounded out a full and gratifying life-style. The
Huron world-view and ethos blended in mutual confirmation, providing a context in which human acts had both
pragmatic utility and meaningful direction. Beyond that,
the Hurons anticipated continuing the same enjoyable
range of activities in the afterlife.

Jesuit Missions

French exploration of the Saint Lawrence Valley began in
1534 with three voyages by Jacques Cartier. Efforts languished after that for almost a century, but in 1608 Samuel

de Champlain planted French enterprise firmly in the valley and encouraged missionary activity among the native groups he met with for trading purposes. The first missionaries were a reform branch of Franciscans known as Récollets. Led by Joseph Le Caron, four of them traveled to New France in 1615 to work among tribes operating trade networks between Huron territory and important Laurentian villages. Champlain had secured strong alliances with the Hurons by then, and that inadvertently angered the Iroquois League which rarely forgave its enemies. Le Caron visited Huronia during the winter of 1615–16, but most Récollets stayed around Quebec and ministered to Algonkian groups called Montagnais. This went on for seven years until some Franciscans visited the Hurons again in 1623–24. As before, they rejected native hospitality by not living inside the Indian villages; consequently, they achieved minimal results. Since Franciscan missionary policy depended on European colonization, and the trading companies did not encourage permanent settlers, the missions to the Indians needed different personnel and another approach to be successful.

By 1625, volunteers from the Society of Jesus replaced the ineffective Récollets, who depended too heavily on outside help. One of the most influential Jesuits was Jean de Brébeuf, who first entered Huron territory in 1626. During the next three years he baptized only one dying child, but he learned to speak Huron. That accomplishment, together with his remarkable physical endurance, won grudging respect from the natives. Brébeuf returned to Quebec in early 1629 for consultations with his religious superiors, but British warships captured the town in July, and, for a time, all French operations in the region ceased. When a treaty restored New France in 1632, Jesuit missionary efforts began in real earnest and dominated spiritual activity for most of the seventeenth century. Brébeuf and several others were back among the Hurons by 1634, allowed to remain there as part of a renewed trade agreement between the Hurons and Champlain, who seemed

genuinely concerned about spiritual conditions among the
natives. This treaty had far-reaching consequences for
Hurons and Jesuits alike.

American Indians were not immune to diseases brought
by Europeans to the Western Hemisphere. Smallpox,
typhoid, and influenza affected everyone, but even less
virulent ailments, such as measles, chicken pox, and
streptococcus infections, took a disastrous toll in native
villages. Unfortunately for the Jesuits, their return coin-
cided with a serious epidemic among the Hurons. Traders
probably carried the contagion with them from Quebec,
but the natives blamed the resident missionaries, who insisted on sharing an intimate life-style with them. The disease, whatever it may have been, proved especially
destructive to children and old people. Loss of the young
necessarily involved a decline in tribal vitality, particularly
in military strength, while deaths among the aged decimated the craftsmen and cultural leaders who normally
kept traditions alive and perpetuated native lore. By 1640
an estimated half of the population had been swept away.
The Hurons numbered less than 12,000 by then and were
finding it difficult to maintain their precontact cohesiveness.

People in every culture use the known and familiar to
interpret what is new and unknown. Most Hurons viewed
the Jesuits as powerful shamans, never understanding the
concept of priesthood as embodying power through ordination in a special society. When disease broke out at the
first mission stations, Ihonatiria and Ossossane, death
spread in all directions. The natives naturally concluded
that the strange men in black robes were responsible for so
much human suffering. The Jesuits refused to baptize
healthy Hurons unless they were convinced that they were
genuinely converted and would reform their lives. Their
usual practice of baptizing only those who were about to
die confirmed the impression that Christian sacraments
threatened Indian survival. They seemed to be causing
death with their incomprehensible rituals, and many local

leaders called for their execution as villainous shamans. Most Hurons feared the Jesuits well into 1637, despite the fact that many of the Jesuits themselves were sick from the same maladies that infected their charges. That the Jesuits were not placed outside Huron law and killed as witches was largely due to the trading alliance with the French, coupled with the dominance of commercialism in the confederacy's value system.

In short, the native leaders tolerated the Jesuits because they wanted to preserve good relations with Montreal and Quebec.[13] The Jesuits, for their part, knew that the trade alliances were crucial to their protection while working among the Hurons, but they did not often try to further the commercial or political objectives of their fellow countrymen. There is no evidence that they considered themselves representatives either of fur traders or of the French government. They sought rather to serve Indian interests, though they defined these in Christian terms. Eventually their altruism contributed significantly to their being accepted as adjunct tribesmen.

In 1639 the Jesuits built Sainte-Marie, a special compound and headquarters for mission work. By 1643 resident priests had established themselves as permanent fixtures in several villages, and they visited others regularly on assigned circuits. Their determination to live among the people and share their style of living inspired confidence and gave continuity to the whole evangelical program. Only five men left the region because of poor health or incompetence during the sixteen years of Jesuit missionary work in Huron territory. Nineteen of the twenty-four sent there remained until the end or died at their posts. Such discipline and dedication were additional factors that persuaded the Hurons to make room for Jesuits within their sophisticated confederation.

Another reason why the Jesuits were accepted had to do with their favorable attitude toward the native religion. They recognized compatibilities between Huron spirituality and Christianity and used them. Europeans and Indians alike acknowledged that supernatural power directly influenced their lives. They thought such power was localized somewhere above—the sun or sky for the Hurons, in heaven for the Jesuits. Both also respected divine forces immanent in everyday affairs, but the "god above" motif provided an important basis for dialogue. Members of both groups believed in good and bad spirits who influenced daily experience. The Huron concept of oki easily corresponded to Catholic convictions about angels, and both believed that evil spirits preyed upon unsuspecting individuals. They agreed further that it was important to relate harmoniously with these supernatural beings, pleasing the forces sympathetic to human aspirations and combating powers inimical to them. Both understood ritual ceremonialism, social cooperation, and personal morality as the accepted means of living correctly with the directive spirits, and both saw that sanctions regarding proper conduct applied in all three spheres. Failure to behave satisfactorily could spell immediate retribution not only for an individual but for the group.

The Hurons placed a great deal of emphasis on personal contact with the supernatural realm. Everyone—especially a young man at puberty—was expected to find his own particular guardian spirit. Visions and dreams directed individual lives, while collective association with divine beings gave a characteristic Huron perspective to group activity. They communicated with the supernatural world through the natural one because they drew no sharp distinction between the two. Supernatural entities permeated natural existence with their own willful presence. In that homogeneous setting the Hurons understood their place and recognized the importance of living cooperatively with all other participants. The Jesuits similarly encouraged individual quests for spiritual guidance, and like the Hurons they valued fasts and vigils as preparations for meaningful religious experience. Christian prayers to Jesus found a ready counterpart in native ones to Iouskeha, who also blessed supplicants. The Jesuits relied on the church more than natural phenomena as a medium, but personal encounters with divine power served as a common bond between the two forms of religious consciousness.

That their attitudes were compatible found additional confirmation in their shared conviction that proper worship produced tangible effects. Jesuits may have had a longer perspective on the practical results, but both cultures agreed that religious behavior produced short-term benefits. One group sprinkled tobacco on a lake and talked to fish spirits before setting their traps, the other venerated saints and performed novenas, but at bottom they conducted themselves from day to day in ways easily understandable to each other. The native emphasis on sacrificial ritual and the Jesuit reliance on sacraments evinced a shared conviction that divine power controlled warfare, caused rain or drought, and allowed disease or provided health and good harvests. The common element of prayer further attested to shared beliefs that human contact with the spirit world yielded direct consequences. On occasion the Jesuits even used this underlying conviction to pray for rain. Like Elijah before them, they tried to prove that the true God would answer such prayers while frustrated shamans stood by in impotent rage.[14] Finally, both Indians and blackrobes accepted the idea of life after death. Though they differed on how people would participate in that afterlife, both relied on existence beyond the grave as an absolute certainty.

An analysis of Jesuit and Huron religious ideas also discloses elements in each that had no ready counterpart in the other. Chief among the differences was the Christian insistence that only one deity ruled the universe. This devotion to rigorous monotheism contrasted with the Hurons' belief in many deities whose power was manifest in different spheres. The Jesuits constantly fretted over the fact that the Hurons considered animals, stones, and sky to be living persons. Huron sacrifices to natural objects elicited even great dismay and sharper rebukes, because the missionaries saw nothing there but material

fashioned by a single Creator. In addition to finding polytheism objectionable, many Jesuits complained that Indian
languages were incapable of expressing Christian truths.
They argued that verb structure and the lack of abstract
nouns made it impossible to discuss all the nuances of
Christian doctrine in native idioms. Some observers have
since suggested that European cultural exclusivism made
this a foregone conclusion.[15] Right or wrong, seventeenth-century missionaries thought that the native languages were an obstacle to communicating such ideas as
the Trinity, the Incarnation, and substitutionary atonement.

Another set of contrasts centered on sexual behavior.
Huron marriages were monogamous, and the Jesuits approved this sanction of single-pair bonds as core family
units. But divorce was easy and frequent, and missionary
belief in the indissolubility of marriage was hardly compatible with that. For the Hurons, female lineage defined identity in clans and extended families, and, since children
belonged to the mother by definition, divorce did not en-
danger family stability. The Hurons could not see that one
lifetime marriage had much to recommend it. They also
failed to appreciate the Jesuits' own practice of celibacy.
They thought that heterosexual relations were normal,
that homosexual practices were acceptable though deviant,
but that it was abnormal to have no sexual contact at all;
they could never understand how the monastics derived
any benefit from sexual self-denial.

They also found it difficult to comprehend ideas about
grace conferred through the sacraments. Many reasons
precluded ready understanding. As noted above, the
Jesuits' baptismal practices in the early period, during the
epidemic, made the Hurons regard them as wicked shamans, practicing sorcery, and, when the plague had passed,
they still regarded the Jesuits as shamans and occasionally
sought baptism as a talisman to ward off disease. Inter-
preting new practices within familiar thought patterns made
it difficult for them to appreciate baptism, confirmation,

and the Mass for otherworldly reasons. Their perspectives stressed the way religion benefited earthly existence, and to many it seemed that baptism had no pragmatic significance. The Jesuits insisted that baptism was a means of preparing for death and the afterlife. It was incomprehensible to Indians that missionaries could rejoice when a dying person was baptized. The Jesuits were gratified that a soul had been saved, but the Indians saw only the loss of a villager and mourned accordingly. It was difficult to explain the essentially otherworldly orientation of this and other sacraments to native Americans, who expected beliefs and customs to yield practical benefits.

Human sinfulness and the need for salvation were probably the most important areas where missionaries found no common ground with native thought. Of course Indians distinguished between good and bad conduct in their villages and tried to ensure proper behavior with community rules. But it was difficult for them to fathom the concept of universal guilt, of a fundamental inadequacy in human nature. The Hurons spoke of misdeeds in specific contexts, not as an endemic human condition that only divine grace could rectify. They viewed sin as a limited circumstantial act, a social mistake, for which material gifts could atone. In contrast with European standards of justice, they could not understand how misdemeanors required punishment rather than compensation. They rarely agreed that anyone should die for a serious crime. Consequently, it made no sense for anyone to die for his sinfulness even if he acknowledged it. People accustomed to property compensation did not value blood sacrifice, even one involving the Son of God, because such sacrifices were exacted only from enemies. Christ's atoning death seemed to them as inappropriate as it was unnecessary. Their precontact frame of values and sense of personal esteem did not recognize sin as a pervasive category; salvation could not remedy a condition that they saw as needing no remedy.

A final difference between the two culturally conditioned religious expressions involved the question of life

after death. Like most native Americans, the Hurons believed that almost everyone would experience the same
pleasant afterlife regardless of how he had lived on earth.
The Jesuits insisted on the contrary view of ultimate reward for the justified and punishment for the wicked. This
notion of heaven and hell contradicted deeply held native
convictions about personal worth, family solidarity, and
social means of compensating for human failings. The
Jesuits warned the incredulous Hurons that death would
terminate their familiar habits and relationships. The pros-
pect of heaven or hell and the divisive necessity of
choosing one alternative over the other clashed with native
ideas about present reality and future destiny. Despite
such incongruities, the Jesuits maintained that the only
hope of escaping eternal torment was to accept the means
of grace offered through Catholic Christianity.

The Jesuits noted major incompatibilities between the
Indians and themselves, but that did not prevent fruitful
interchange because they chose not to stress religious differences. They observed Indian culture closely to determine how they could use indigenous ideas and customs
in fostering new Christian expressions. They analyzed Indian politics and religion fairly and recorded a wealth of
pertinent data in their annual reports *(Relations)*. They also
noted approvingly the way that group dynamics encouraged social harmony and mutual toleration and made it
possible to restrain violent crime without the death penalty. They were also glad to see that the Hurons had
already developed such traits as stoicism, generosity, sexual modesty, and monogamy. They did not approve of
divorce, blood feuds, torture, reliance on dreams, or habits
that to Europeans smacked of laziness and thievery. But
their negative judgments applied only to specific actions,
not to the total Huron life-style. Instead of rejecting the
entire social fabric, they hoped to improve on local customs and to approximate a Christian ideal of sanctified
conduct.

The international-minded Jesuits had developed a philosophical basis for their missionary methods long before the order came to America. Their monastic community made education and rigorous discipline the cornerstones of its training program. It had learned valuable lessons in Reformation-torn Europe, where frontal assaults on religious dissenters achieved little good. Practical experience had thus led to the conclusion that an accommodating posture would win more converts than reactionary combat with religious opponents. The Jesuits also espoused the philosophical rationale known as probabilism, holding that no universal moral code could apply to people in different cultures at all times. Rather than impose inflexible beliefs and conduct, the probabilists first considered the particularities of local circumstances before determining on possible improvements. They defined moral expectations in terms of individual conscience, a perspective relative to historically conditioned human discernment. Instead of insisting on a single moral standard without regard to local contexts, they used cultural realities to set realistic goals for behavioral change.[16]

The Jesuits thus refined missionary techniques at stations around the world by adapting to the limitations of specific circumstances. Instead of condemning existing cultures outright, they tried to build on common denominators and gradually reshape native ways toward closer approximations of a Christian norm. They hoped eventually to persuade indigenous peoples, through tact and forebearance, that biblical standards were worth accepting. This approach precluded the arrogance and impatience that characterized forced acculturation. As early as 1583 the Jesuit Matteo Ricci had chosen this manner of converting the Chinese literati. He wore the robes of a Mandarin scholar and spoke only of those Christian ideas that did not offend his hosts. Ricci postponed mentioning abhorrent facts, such as Christ's crucifixion, and did not oppose traditional Chinese ancestor worship. Similarly, in early seventeenth-century India, Robert de Nobili trained himself to be a Brahmin. He wore the clothes of that caste

and observed Hindu laws to facilitate communication between his own religious message and indigenous patterns.
Many Catholics criticized Ricci and Nobili for making such
compromises, but they pioneered innovative missionary
procedures within their religious order.

Jesuit missionaries to the New World were confident
that their discriminating approach would work as well
among native Americans as it had in Asia. In fact they had
already established a successful mission among the
Guarani Indians of Paraguay that did little violence to the
precontact economy, kinship relations, and social values.
Thus the French-speaking Jesuits in Ontario were simply
following a precedent familiar to all members of their
order. In keeping with the probabilist view that cultural
differences called for discerning patience rather than in-
discriminate uniformity, they hoped to create a reservoir
of good will among the Hurons by respecting the integrity
of local culture traits. Once gradual change had begun with
friendly encounters, they planned to transform native
communities through gradually increased influence. Such a
process let converts absorb Christianity at their own pace.

The Jesuit missionaries expected to accomplish all this
in an isolated geographical setting, independent of European settlements embodying their own versions of Christian practice. They did not want to force the Hurons into a
satellite community, allowing the French to control their
economy or politics. They did not intend to undermine
precontact institutions or manipulate local policy on the
assumption that Indians existed to serve European interests. As they had done in Paraguay, the Jesuits sought to
engender a hybrid native state, protected from all outside
influences except Christianity, which could help native
customs function better. They tried to retain aboriginal
values and practices that did not openly contravene
essential Christian teachings, and they jealously guarded
their native charges against too much contact with other
Frenchmen. In this way they hoped to blend the best of
both world-views and behavioral systems, creating an im-

proved culture that preserved Indian identity and developed an indigenized Christianity belonging exclusively to the local residents.[17]

They expected a modicum of change, though, and urged reforms as practical steps to conversion. Of course they identified Christian values with European norms to some degree, but, compared with other missionaries in North America, the Jesuits read fewer culturally determined preconceptions into the gospel. They insisted on curtailing easy divorce and preached that marriage should be binding for life. While not advocating austerity, they objected to frequent feasts because consuming huge amounts of food at one time encouraged gluttony. They found eating human flesh at such festive occasions abhorrent and often asked that the practice be stopped. They argued that undue reliance on dreams and participation in curing ceremonies were detrimental to Christian conduct. They also condemned blood feuds, failing to notice how deeply these were ingrained in the Huron value system as a practice that combined group solidarity with personal initiative. Many native headmen said that to abandon such habits would destroy the carefully integrated Huron way of life, but the Jesuits continued to oppose what they considered atavistic ungodliness.

Recognizing the difficulties inherent in cultural interaction, the Jesuits tried to reduce tensions by tailoring their religious advocacy. They knew that Christian ideas had originally included Near Eastern assumptions about social relationships, political authority, and punitive justice. So it was necessary to screen out these culturally conditioned expressions, which violated local priorities, and deliberately to base a revised gospel on the Huron view of reality. They were careful not to transgress on the host culture even when discussing Christian worship. For instance, they did not mention eating the body of Christ and drinking his blood because it could have been equated with the ritual cannibalism they disparaged. Brébeuf explained the concept of the Eucharist by using a Huron word for thanksgiving festivals, a purely memorial ceremony. He must have considered it worthwhile to obviate Tridentine statements about transubstantiation and simultaneously avoid aboriginal connotations of absorbing an enemy's courage by eating him.

In addition to presenting Indians with a gospel fashioned to their understanding, the Jesuits used local customs to enhance acceptance; for example, when Brébeuf learned that the Hurons attached special significance to red colors, he immediately painted every cross red. Then, though they were often frustrated by the powerful influence that dreams exerted over everyday Huron decisions, they quickly sanctioned dreams as valid grounds for accepting Christianity when some Huron dreamed of experiencing the joy of heaven or the pain of eternal torment. Family ties were another trait they exploited. Of course they started by offering salvation to individuals, and the impact of conversion disrupted traditional identity patterns. But, once individual changes began, they used the Huron sense of group loyalty to develop momentum and enlist more converts. After someone became a Christian, the Jesuits warned his relatives that death would separate them unless they too adopted the new faith. Strong attachment to family solidarity created a siphon effect, producing further conversions through the strength of ancestral bonds.

The Hurons were preeminently a people who esteemed property, so the Jesuits used gifts to advance their evangelical program. In the early days they reinforced acquisitive habits by rewarding converts, but in 1641 giftgiving reached a new plateau: in that year the French governor presented Charles Tsondatsaa with a gun to celebrate his baptism. He was the first Indian in the entire confederacy to own such a weapon, and the lesson must have been clear to others who yearned for a similar possession. Many reasoned that Christianity might be worth the trouble if it facilitated acquiring such tangible magnificence. The new faith was also particularly beneficial to

those who traded at Quebec and Trois Rivières. Hardly
more than 15 percent of the Huron population had been
converted by 1648, but more than half of the men who
traded downriver had accepted baptism or preparatory instruction. Apparently the special perquisites given to
Christian traders persuaded many Hurons to adopt Christianity for mercantile advantage. A third property-related
incentive appeared at times of crisis. In difficult times the
French opened their private stores and donated charitable
relief to Christian Indians first. Sometimes they were the
only natives to receive aid. Thus, immediate material gain
apparently induced many to adopt the new religion.[18]

Once the Hurons showed a minimal interest in Christianity, the Jesuits incorporated native exhorters in their
evangelical program. They did not accept them as ordained
priests but employed them instead as catechists, because
they had better command of local idioms. Native spokesmen called *dogiques* performed many duties when the missionaries were away and mediated significantly between
the European and Indian cultures. What is perhaps even
more remarkable in the light of Catholic practice today,
there were women dogiques, too, who brought Christian
witness into accord with the Hurons' deeply entrenched
matrilineal patterns. The Jesuits also played on aboriginal
fears to produce more believers and prevent converts from
backsliding. They emphasized the torments in store for
those who refused God's salvation, drawing explicit parallels between eternal punishment and the tortures the
Hurons inflicted on captives. With such vivid examples
already before their listeners, evangelists used familiar imagery to depict the agonies of souls lost in hellfire.

Their acquaintance with local customs thus led the
Jesuits to pursue a variety of missionary tactics. They
avoided direct conflicts with precontact culture whenever
possible, they induced conversions by exploiting native
proclivities, and they threatened recalcitrants with consequences everyone could easily understand.

At times they must have found it difficult to fathom the

varying reasons that prompted the Hurons to request baptism. Personal friendship and family loyalty often motivated an initial interest. After one had been baptized (perhaps on his deathbed), his clansmen might ask for baptism to make sure that they would be with him wherever Christians met in the afterlife. Others considered baptism necessary after dreaming of the rite; physical reenactment was simply the second phase of such a person's experience, a natural step in preserving his psychic equilibrium. Many continued to think of baptism as a talismanic aid. Regarding Christian ceremonies as parallel to Huron rituals, they wanted to use both forms of shamanistic power as surety against misfortune.[19] Converts would have increased rapidly had the Jesuits accepted everyone who requested baptism for such reasons. However, they baptized only those who manifested a steadfast determination to follow Christian precepts, making exception only for those about to die from illness or execution.

Huron converts did not submit passively to wholesale changes in their cultural orientation. Rather than capitulate to an entirely different set of ideas and actions, they borrowed Christian elements selectively to enhance a native life-style without suffering complete disintegration in the process. Their own economy, kinship, language, architecture, and dress remained substantially intact. But converts abandoned shamans; biblical cosmology largely replaced the world of Aataentsic; totems and oki gave place to saints and angels. Compared with many other native groups, the Hurons enjoyed a strong cultural nexus that allowed for conversions manifesting a New World expression of the Old World faith.

Huron Christians were hardly less Indian in their overall life-style than their traditionalist brothers, but they differed enough to cause factionalism in the villages and tribes. As an indication of their changed perspective, they resisted participating in curing ceremonies. Tribesmen customarily presented gifts and performed acts required for the fulfillment of dreams or the efficacy of shamanistic healing rites. Refusals were considered antisocial and possible evidence of witchcraft. But Christian Hurons began to reject this kind of cooperative participation, and this caused the others to suspect that they no longer cared for the village's corporate well-being. Converts also seemed corrupted by European notions of private property. Protesting Christian loyalty as an excuse, they often refused to participate in festivals and contributed nothing to common meals or gift exchanges. The new religion appeared to make them selfish because they did not share their property by entertaining neighbors and giving them presents. While hoping to gain materially from traders in New France, many Christians exacerbated ill-feeling in the tribes by not distributing their wealth according to the time-honored ways of acquiring prestige.

A more drastic sign of cultural tension in Huronia appeared when baptized Indians anticipated the next Feast of the Dead. By the early 1640s many of them stated that they did not wish to be buried alongside non-Christians in the traditional ossuary.[20] Mingling the bones of deceased tribesmen was the supreme expression of Huron cohesiveness, and traditionalists charged baptized Indians with rejecting the very heart of community solidarity. But the converts remained adamant and insisted that, if others wished to retain the corporate identity, they could accept baptism and be united with regenerated Indians in Christian burial. The Jesuits encouraged converts to believe that their destiny was different from that of their former associates; rejecting traditional burial practices simply acknowledged that fact unequivocally.

Until great numbers of Hurons converted, the Christians had to live in two worlds, integrating aspects of each into some workable system on their own. The resulting psychological tension often caused some degree of personal insecurity while disrupting social relationships up to the confederacy level. Converts reflected the strain by depending on their Jesuit mentors for help with daily de-

cisions and future plans. But when that problem eased,
other events intervened to create more problems. Such
conditions made it impossible for the confederacy to make
united decisions; more important, it opened a fatal breach
in the group's ability to defend itself.

However, death from disease probably destroyed
Huron cohesiveness more than any other single factor.
The Jesuits recorded only 22 baptisms in 1635 and no
more than 100 the following year; but after 1637, when
the Huron population fell by more than half, conversions
began to snowball. By 1646 over 500 Indians had been
baptized; an equal number was added the next year and
another 1,700 in 1648. Such statistics indicate that converts were developing a momentum away from cultural
self-sufficiency. By the summer of 1648 one Huron in five
had adopted new standards of thought and conduct by
declaring himself Christian. Then disaster struck. As the
crisis deepened, only a minority of natives refused to accept Christianity. But missionary work could not be called
a successful enterprise by then because the confederacy
had ceased to exist as a cultural entity.

In mid-1648 it seemed that the missions would succeed
in building a model Christian state with increasingly com-
pliant natives. Twenty-two Jesuits lived in various towns
and used forty-six lay assistants to expand their effectiveness. But in July of that year the Iroquois League launched
a military campaign of unprecedented scope and duration.
Until then, small contingents of warriors had customarily
raided Huron towns, collected available goods and prisoners, and then returned home before defensive forces could
repulse them. The year 1648 brought a change in these
tactics, based on a revised strategy. Instead of just harrass-
ing the Hurons, the Iroquois meant to annihilate them
because they constituted too dangerous an opposing force
and occupied territory needed for Iroquois expansion. If
Huron influence were obliterated, the League could fill the
vacuum and divert the lucrative Ontario trade to its own
markets. Such plans called for a concentrated military

offensive, and thousands of warriors massed for an attack that defined conquest, not pillage, as its objective.

The Iroquois forces destroyed one town after another in the eastern Huron territory during the late summer months. The villagers fled west to safer towns, sometimes abandoning their homes in panic if it was merely rumored that Iroquois were in the area. In its disoriented condition the Huron confederacy was unable to meet the enemy with a united front. Instead of sending all warriors to fight on the eastern frontier, the villages kept them at home to protect the local precinct. The Iroquois armies thus picked off the Hurons village by village, driving steadily to the inland sea. Within six months they had demolished all but the largest, best-fortified Huron towns. Thousands of people died, and prospects were bleak for the survivors, because they had lost most of their food reserves. Local defenders apparently did not realize that they were involved in a war of extermination. Headmen and Jesuits alike thought the fighting was just another of the traditional conflicts that had always affected native life. They continued the village routines and chapel services, trading and baptisms, council debates and catechism classes, as normally as straitened circumstances allowed.

When the enemy mounted new attacks in early 1649, the Jesuits heard too late that their most experienced colleague had fallen, a casualty to the war. Before dawn on 16 March, Iroquois warriors captured the town known as Saint-Louis. Jean de Brébeuf and Gabriel Lalemant refused to save themselves by leaving their friends, so they were seized while ministering to Huron villagers. Instead of killing them on the spot, the triumphant Iroquois braves decided to save their prisoners for ritual slaughter, stripping them naked in the meantime and tearing out their fingernails. After marching them to Taenhatentaron (Saint-Ignace), a nearby village that served as a staging area for their campaign, the Iroquois warriors beat the Jesuits repeatedly and forced them to run the gauntlet. Brébeuf endured the usual tortures with awesome for-

titude; consequently, the Iroquois concentrated most of
their fury on him to break his spirit. But rather than flinch
or cry out, he showed concern only for his fellow victims
and exhorted his captors to repent. All the mutilation,
burning, and abuse that the Iroquois executioners heaped
on him could not make the missionary beg for mercy. His
infuriated tormentors redoubled their efforts, and, as a
result, Brébeuf died that afternoon. Those who killed him
were so impressed by his bravery that they ate his heart
and drank his blood to acquire the courage he had so
magnificently displayed in his death. Lalemant experienced
more regulated tortures and died the next morning.

The news reached the other Jesuits at Sainte-Marie several days later. In due time they celebrated not a requiem
Mass but one of thanksgiving, expressing joy that God had
allowed two of their number to die in His service. In subsequent years stories clustered around Brébeuf's name,
and his image accumulated the characteristics Catholics
expect of saints. Canadian testimonies regarding his piety
finally resulted in his canonization in 1930. Jesuit concern
for their brother's suffering and martyrdom probably kept
them from noticing that Brébeuf also died like a Huron
warrior. After living so long amid a people who valued
unflinching courage in the face of death, his final actions
conformed exactly to indigenous expectations. He may
have died with Christian prayers on his lips, but he also
embodied a stoicism consistent with Huron cultural values
that his torturers could not intimidate.

By late spring, both Huron leaders and Jesuit missionaries finally admitted that their position was untenable.
Manpower kept shrinking; prospects for new food crops
were bleak; the confederacy was broken. Two months
after Brébeuf died, the Jesuits abandoned Sainte-Marie,
their stronghold for evangelical operations, taking the surviving Hurons with them. They preferred to burn what
they could not carry rather than leave anything for the
invaders to enjoy. Attempting to escape repeated attacks,
the refugees fled en masse to an island called Gahoendoe

(Christian Island) in Georgian Bay. The winter of 1649–50 was a desperate time. Hunger presented constant problems, and fear of Iroquois assaults across the ice made them realize that Gahoendoe was a death trap. As soon as the lake thawed, foraging parties set out to find badly needed supplies, but many canoes capsized before reaching the mainland. Those who did touch shore were cut down by implacable Iroquois, who had waited to inflict more damage on their shattered foe. By June 1650 only one alternative remained: dispersal in small groups, with each band intent on saving itself.

So the land of the Hurons became a no-man's-land, its people scattered in every direction. The Tobacco tribe absorbed some of the homeless wanderers, while, ironically, the Seneca adopted others, who then lived amicably with their former enemies. Additional Huron units moved farther west, settling on Shawnee and Ojibwa lands in Ohio and Michigan. When Yankee frontiersmen later met tribes called "Wyandot," they were actually dealing with isolated fragments of the once proud Wendat Confederacy.

Christian Hurons remained with their Jesuit leaders. Not surprisingly, converts increased rapidly as their culture declined from demoralization to total disintegration. Between March and August of 1649 the Jesuits baptized more than 1,400 people; during the next seven months another 1,600 received the sacrament, most of them after moving to Gahoendoe. We do not know how much the Jesuits relaxed their probationary rules about testing a convert's interest in religion. It is possible they offered the rite to everyone as a consolation for the dangers continually threatening them.

By the summer of 1650 their spiritual mentors invited surviving Christian Indians to move north and settle in the protected Saint Lawrence Valley. Over several decades they found temporary placement around Quebec, at Sillery, and on the Ile d'Orléans. But the strongest Huron town was Jeune Lorette, founded in 1697; here they sustained their chosen faith with an essentially precontact life-style and subsistence patterns. Descendants of that community have survived to the present, but their assimilation of technological culture now evinces a way of living far removed from independent Huron civilization. The Iroquois victory and Huron diaspora prevent us from knowing what might have been achieved in the free Christian state that the Jesuits originally envisioned.

4 Northeastern Indians, English Missions

The Massachusets

The Northeast Woodlands constituted a large culture area between the Atlantic Coast and the Mississippi River, bounded also by the Great Lakes and the Ohio River. In that large territory many different peoples flourished; that is to say, their languages and customs varied greatly. Nevertheless, the woodland tribes shared conditions that shaped their economy, architecture, sociopolitical institutions, and religious ceremonialism along similar lines. Two of them, the Massachusets and Wampanoags, both of them Algonkian-speaking, occupied land around Boston Bay and Narragansett Bay, respectively. They were among the first native Americans to experience prolonged contact with English settlers. Many generalizations about the Massachusets and the Wampanoags pertain to other native peoples who occupied the same geographical area—what is today southeastern New England—but most of our anthropological data derive from these two groups.

Population estimates are tentative and sketchy, but possibly 150,000 natives inhabited the region before the whites arrived. The Massachuset tribe, with all its affiliates, contained approximately 21,000 people, the Wampanoag perhaps another 21,000. These figures are based on estimates made in the early 1600s.[1] Debates about such statistics are largely academic because, whatever the tribal

THE ALGONKIANS

Atlantic Ocean

Nantucket

Cape Cod

Martha's Vineyard

Boston Bay

Roxbury Bay

Plymouth

Punkapaug

Taunton

Boston
Roxbury

MASSACHUSETS

WAMPANOAGS

Narragansett Bay

Wamesitt

Nashoba

Natick

Magunkaquog

NIPMUCKS

Hassanamasitt

R.I.

NARRAGANSETTS

Lebanon

PEQUOTS

Mass
Conn

MOHEGANS

Connecticut River

populations may have been in precontact times, European
diseases reduced it drastically. Between 1600 and 1620
more than half of all the natives of eastern Massachusetts
and Rhode Island succumbed to fevers, pox, and other
maladies of which they had had no previous experience.
The years of greatest suffering were 1617–19, when an
unknown infection swept the area and wrought irreparable
damage. By the end of that period, just when the Pilgrims
were starting their small colony at Plymouth, the local
tribes had suffered tremendous attrition. Thus the Massachusets and Wampanoags were not at optimum strength
during the initial period of intercultural contact.

These native Americans had long prospered on a diet
fairly evenly divided between agricultural items and the
products of a hunting-gathering economy. Their domesticated plants included corn, several varieties of beans,
squash, and pumpkins, raised as food items, sunflowers
(used for oil), and tobacco. These plants provided the
staples, but the Algonkians also depended heavily on meat
acquired by hunting. Deer, bear, turkey, and many smaller
animals taken in the chase supplied much of the fare.
Shellfish, eels, and various types of freshwater fish provided additional protein. Berries, roots, nuts, and other
wild seeds supplemented a diet that was both substantial
and well adapted to its natural setting.

Many commentators have erroneously described the
New England tribes as nomadic huntsmen, totally dependent on the results of foraging through woods and
coastal marshes. The Massachusets did rely on wild game
to a great extent, but it is wrong to think that their dependence on hunting excluded other major resources. Cultivated fields were an essential feature of Algonkian subsistence, and annual crops constituted a strong element in
local economic patterns.[2] Compared with other groups in
North America who farmed extensively, such as the Hurons in Ontario and the Pueblos in New Mexico, the New
England Algonkians did not rely as heavily on planted
crops, but they cultivated substantial food supplies and

possessed technical capabilities plus the practical wisdom to grow staple crops as part of a feasible economic system.

Massachuset living patterns were intentionally diffuse and mobile, geared to fit their manner of coping with their natural surroundings. Villages hardly ever remained at a single location for an entire year. If some did, dominating their area in strong palisaded locations, they seldom contained their full complement of residents through all seasons. Algonkian life was more given to regular movement within restricted geographical limits, being neither truly nomadic nor rooted at permanent sites. A standard pattern would find perhaps thirty to fifty families living in mutual support of each other at one place. When spring came, they planted crops in cleared fields and then moved to the seashore or to streams where fishing promised to be good. Then some or all of them would move to places where berries and nuts grew in abundance. By autumn they congregated at the first site again to harvest their fields and store food for the winter. Later, in the cold season, small family units scattered to favorite hunting stations to make feeding easier. The cycle began again when the groups reunited for another springtime planting.

The housing construction was admirably suited to this peripatetic way of life, with its multiple residences. The basic dwelling was a lodge shaped like a rounded cone, formed by a circle of poles tied at the top and covered with overlapping shingles or strips of bark. These *wigwams* were easy to build from local materials. They provided shelter from the elements, and their construction did not require time or energy out of proportion to their transitory usefulness. When it was time to move, after a few months, the natives abandoned the old wigwams and built new ones at the next site. Economy, village location, and architecture thus formed a coherent pattern in the Massachuset life-style. While there was little in it to convey a sense of permanence, it possessed a diversified regularity that coped with natural rhythms and sustained participants with a sense of accomplishment.

The kinship structure tended to include relationships
beyond the nuclear family, but many variations make it
difficult to rely on a single category like "clan" to cover all
types. Still, the general point is that each member of an
extended family gained an enlarged sense of identity by
belonging to, and sharing mutual responsibilities with,
many people. These extended families also functioned as
intermediaries between individuals and tribal ruling
structures. They were a source of psychological support in
personal development, a medium of expression in political
activity, and a focal point of loyalty in times of crisis.
Among Massachusets and Wampanoags such extended
family groups tended to be patriarchal. Not all Algonkians
defined identity and inheritance through the father, but
quite often the basic lines of authority in each wigwam and
in villages as a whole followed patterns dominated by
males.

It is difficult to say whether a strong reliance on
hunting—an activity monopolized by the men—
contributed to male dominance in kinship relations. We
know little about the extent to which Massachuset women
supervised agricultural activities, owned land, or participated in guiding family units. It could be that local villages
were evolving toward greater acceptance of female contributions to family, clan, and tribal affairs. In other tribes
male dominance seems to have diminished when their
economies developed from hunting to greater reliance on
agriculture. Such farming cultures allowed women a more
integrated place in native life. But this is speculation. All
that we can do is acknowledge that in 1620 most New
England tribes were patriarchal in authority and patrilocal
in residence patterns. Basic elements of identity and inheritance devolved patrilineally.

As in most Indian cultures, the Massachusets, once they
had defined clans, forbade marriage within them, for such
marriages were commonly held to involve incest, a crime
that offended the totem, the mythic grandfather of all clan
descendants. Marriages were usually monogamous, but

there was little to prevent either partner from terminating the relationship for numerous reasons. Divorce and re-marriage were prevalent features of tribal life, and clans accommodated them without much damage to adults or children. Vocational training and role models survived the disruption, too, because clan members other than parents supervised child care. Exogamous clans afforded the most important nexus for maintaining personal identity, and they facilitated cooperation on larger social issues, where men exerted most of the leadership.

The northeastern Algonkians organized larger social units under headmen called *sachems.* Authority structures differed widely throughout the culture area, but sachems generally exercised control over units made up of multiple clans. These individuals were not equal by virtue of their office; their influence varied according to their diplomatic skill, their personal charisma, and their prowess in warfare. Most held office all year long—in fact for life, unless some serious mistake discredited them and caused the people to seek a new leader. Despite the fact that English chroniclers often used the word "king" to describe them, they did not wield such extensive authority. Each Massachuset and Wampanoag sachem influenced a segment of the tribe, but none controlled the entire population. Occasionally a strong sachem would extend his sway to several villages, and his words received special deference in great councils. But that kind of power came from individual attributes, not from laws defining a traditional office. Each sachem's power fluctuated with popular opinion and changing cir-cumstances. At bottom, then, local institutional authority did little to ensure loyalty to headmen once the whites had introduced alternative social patterns.

The Massachuset and Wampanoag political structures remained in a generally balkanized state because the people idealized personal initiative as much as they did group conformity. They based social values on corporate consciousness, but within that cohesive framework there was great latitude for individuals to act on their own.

Young men were encouraged to seek personal distinction in woodcraft ability, successful hunting, and physical endurance. When one of them excelled at games or in other competitions, his honors were won at the expense of other tribesmen, but competitive activities always occurred within the ego-sustaining camaraderie of village geniality. In warfare, an individual's capacity to act bravely, to lead warriors in the forefront of an attack, and to vanquish enemies were stressed. Kinsmen also urged individuals to pursue additional honors, recognized in the greater world beyond the village campfire, by discussing tribal affairs and by representing the tribe in diplomatic missions to other territories.

English accounts of Algonkian life frequently emphasized the disorganized character of village occupations, particularly the "lazy" habits of the men. What these observers failed to recognize was the great respect for personal initiative that undergirded and encouraged such behavior. It seemed dissolute and badly organized to whites because most of them valued systematically industrious activity. They thus judged natives to be indolent, but in fact the Massachusets were simply free to choose among objectives and set their own pace for securing them. They could hunt or not as their mood dictated. They were not required to take part in village councils or diplomatic missions. The social and political spheres were open for participation as people wished; it was entirely a matter of personal choice whether someone exerted himself or not. Once engaged in such tasks as hunting, trapping, canoe-building, or dozens of other pursuits, however, the natives accomplished their work with an energy and self-denying concentration that belied all thoughts of laziness.

Even warfare was voluntary. It is impossible to imagine anyone refusing to defend his own village when attacked, but aggressive raiding parties were another matter. They included only those who had volunteered to support the venture, and no social opprobrium attached to those who remained at home. The leaders of these aggressive forays

announced their intention of making war on some enemy
target; other warriors responded positively or negatively as
their feelings led them. Young men almost always
accepted invitations to participate because they wanted to
acquire prestige and the higher social standing that came
with military glory. Others, young or old, might remain
aloof and decline the invitation without dishonor. No sachem or war captain could forcibly assemble braves for any
given campaign because native respect for individualistic
behavior overruled coercive recruiting. The usual pattern
of local warfare, then, was a series of small-scale attacks
and retaliations in which individuals could display personal
valor. When exceptions to this voluntaristic warfare
occurred—as in 1675, when the great majority of Wampanoags formed a single strike force—the effect on the
English settlements was devastating.

Another deeply held aboriginal value had to do with
land and attitudes about owning it. The Massachusets and
Wampanoags considered the land a basic part of their
nurturing environment, part of a universally shared
created order. It was not a commodity to be parceled out
in separate allocations with no regard for corporate use.
For all the latitude granted to personal initiative in other
kinds of behavior, these native Americans never seriously
thought an individual could own a plot of land for his
exclusive benefit. Each tribe was identified with specific
portions of the landscape that encompassed routine existence, and within that territory the sachems could assign
areas for temporary use by specific groups. But they could
not transfer land to an individual in fee simple or let someone sell it again in a private transaction. The idea of someone's claiming irrevocable title to the land, distinct from
tribal possession, was as absurd as trying to own air or
sunlight.[3]

It would be wrong to think that the Indians were selfish
about the land, that initially they were reluctant to share
territory with the whites. When the English first arrived,
the Wampanoags and then the Massachusets met them in a

manner consistent with their code of hospitality. They
charitably gave choice locations for houses and allowed the
newcomers the use of fields for planting. But when they
discovered that the Puritans wanted to keep these tracts
exclusively for themselves, without title ever reverting to
those who had originally loaned it, the Indians grew bitter.
They were unable to understand the European pattern of
land ownership because their experience envisaged nothing like it. Land was part of the sacred universe, an aspect
of the divine order of things held in trust for posterity. It
was inconceivable to them that anyone would dare restrict
a part of that universe for his exclusive use.

Massachuset folkways relied on ritualized behavior to
clothe daily activities with a sense of propriety. The shaman, usually called a *powwow,* was the primary leader in
these religious ceremonies. The Massachusets believed
that shamans could enter trances in which their souls left
the mundane sphere to commune with spirit beings; then,
when they revived or became whole again, they relayed
messages from the divine powers to designated individuals
or to the entire group. The powwows also interpreted
dreams and predicted the future; some of them even
claimed the ability to discover secrets or carry messages by
assuming the form of various animals. They were also
thought to have the power to cause illness by "shooting"
alien objects into other people's bodies; by the same
token, they could diagnose what an enemy powwow had
done to harm a fellow tribesman. Local powwows often
cured what today might be called psychosomatic illnesses
by extracting shells, bones, hair, or feathers from their
patients.[4] Their power, whether sought or feared, was paid
great deference in precontact value systems.

Yet, for all their significance as religious figures, the
powwows' influence was limited; for success, in the Massachuset villages, depended on individual performance and
constant validation—on meeting each new challenge as it
arose—and for these tests there was no priestly brother-

hood to bestow religious powers through ordination, nor
did a society of powwows support individual practitioners
in their spiritual efforts. Many shamans engaged personally
in preparatory rituals, such as fasting, sitting in the sweat
lodges, and practicing sexual abstinence, but in doing so
they followed no uniform liturgical rules. Each seer's
behavior depended on personal choice and personal innovations; his successes stemmed from pragmatic ingenuity, not inherited formulas. Such religious individualism illustrates in another sphere how New England
natives allowed wide latitude for private initiative.

A second factor suggesting the tentative nature of the
shamans' influence is the fact that their religious powers
differed from those held by common people only in degree. Powwows could accomplish more easily and frequently what everyone else could do—at least at certain
times in their lives. They differed from their fellow villagers
simply by having a greater personal facility for visions,
trances, and prophecy. Since the Indians prized such experiences, they freely consulted those who had a better-
than-average capacity for communing with spirits. But
such consultations did not imply that the shamans possessed a religious power different in kind from that of their
kinsmen and friends.

Another restriction on a powwow's authority was the
fact that the popular support he received was voluntary.
The villagers could back a shaman or seek another's help
whenever they chose, and so his influence survived only as
long as he earned it. Thus, in contrast to the sociopolitical
office of sachem, which remained fairly stable in New
England, the powwows' leadership base was not institutionalized. Their influence expanded or contracted according to the practical benefits they could provide. Native respect for the institution itself did not prevent
once-influential powwows from sinking into obscurity if
popular acclaim shifted to new individuals who performed
spiritual tasks more successfully.

The Massachusets and Wampanoags were relatively free
to vary from loose norms regarding dress codes, civic responsibility, military conduct, and religious expression.
Their respect for individualism pertained especially to
religion because they acknowledged that divine-human
encounters could take many different forms. They usually
consulted powwows during personal emergencies or when
village interests were at stake. But many other occasions
called for private visions—for direct communication between the seeker and a guardian spirit who chose to reveal
itself uniquely. Youths were expected to establish such
contact with the supernatural world, especially at puberty.
To achieve that goal, they resorted to prolonged fasting,
isolation in sweat lodges or wilderness seclusion, sexual
abstinence, and sleeplessness. These mild physical
deprivations often resulted in a dreamlike state in which
they saw divine beings and communicated with them on a
personal level. These visions confirmed the natives' general sense of living harmoniously with spiritual powers;
they also determined quite specifically the direction and
content of the participant's subsequent life-style.

In visions, divine beings usually appeared to humans as
an animal or some other transfigured phenomenon.
Dreams also had a place in directing personal behavior.
The natives valued unanticipated clairvoyant experiences
because these provided goals and a sense of proper orientation; but they stressed prolonged visions, those deliberately and carefully sought, because these formed the
core of private religion in precontact times.[5] Spiritual communication with animalistic forms gave sanction to local
folkways when each generation participated in them; at the
same time, it also allowed for modifications in ritual.
Among the Massachusets what mattered was not preserving or altering old patterns but basing current actions on
the validating experience of genuine spiritual communion.

Spirits who appeared to individuals in animal or other
natural shapes did so when they chose to favor those
seeking visions. Whether they appeared periodically or

once in a lifetime depended on their inscrutable will. Those seeking communication could influence their private gods somewhat through sincerity and persistence, but in other areas there were more formalized rituals for dealing with divine powers. Hunting was one sphere in which the Massachusets were especially careful to treat spirit beings with reverential ceremony. They thought that animal spirits were easily offended by menstruating women for instance, and hunters therefore rigorously avoided females in that condition. Successful hunters often performed simple rituals over fallen animals, too, apologizing for having taken their life and wishing their souls a safe journey back to the spirit world. Failure to act with propriety could anger all animal spirits and cause them to leave the hunting grounds. Disrespect shown to an animal's bones could also offend spirits. Hunters were particularly careful not to mistreat a bear's bones, never burning them or letting dogs eat them. By observing all of these proprieties they hoped to preserve the good will of the spirit powers who provided a great portion of their subsistence.

This variegated, complex pattern of ritualized behavior among hunters is the best example of a trait that appears countless times in native American religions. The Massachusets and Wampanoags treated their environment with a reverence born of knowledge that all phenomena—animals and plants, mountains and rivers—possessed supernatural qualities. Just as cordial relations between humans called for courtesy and mutual deference, it was equally necessary to show proper respect for other forms of life. Much of Indian religion consisted of rituals that expressed such an attitude. The Massachusets hoped to maintain a correct set of relationships with the other inhabitants of the cosmos, securing cooperation through ceremonies appropriate to the various personalities.

The Indians of southern New England recognized that many different powers surrounded their own level of existence. They demonstrated this whenever someone

asked for safe passage on a journey, placated a menacing
spirit at some dangerous locality, invoked aid before a
battle, apologized to the bear spirit for an actual kill, petitioned earth spirits at planting time, or uttered hundreds
of other prayers about the outcome of life's experiences.
Effective action in every sphere of life involved ritual action as a basic component. Activities related to home life,
food gathering, community solidarity, and dealings with
enemies all involved religious ceremony as well as practical
skills. Natives who ignored ritual duties were bound to fail
in life because they disregarded the larger context of reality
and risked offending a great number of ubiquitous personalities. Those who observed the proprieties faced their
environment confidently, knowing that their ceremonious
acts conveyed the deference and cooperative respect demanded by higher powers.

The Indians' sense of group, place, and ritual propriety
confirmed their overall view of reality, which in turn
made their daily activities meaningful and appropriate.
Algonkian rituals provide us with a better understanding
of their religion than their mythology does because their
myths are quite diffuse and contain varying details. This
diversity is somewhat puzzling. Either Massachuset and
Wampanoag worshipers did not emphasize narrative explanations, stressing immediate contact with divine powers
instead, or else the whites obliterated most of the mythological record. All we can say now is that there is no evidence of a normative creation story to shape Algonkian
thinking, no general account of origins regarding the cosmos, environment, animal and plant life, or humanity.
Different Algonkian stories abound, but they do not con-
stitute a unified canon that dominated the minds and controlled the activities of those who told them. Such tales
offered a variety of explanations about origins and meaning in the world, but no one depended on an authoritative
text. Stories were not systematized, and multiple answers
to a single question were accepted as equally satisfying

accounts of universal themes. Activities described in
mythic narratives suggested norms for behavior, but there
was no resulting uniformity. The Algonkians did not insist
that all should act the same way any more than they were
supposed to think alike. Although myths supplied a loose
rationale for Massachuset religion, they afforded little
binding content; their diffuse focus permitted serious intellectual reflection, but those who used them thought
personal religious encounters were more determinative.[6]

The mythological narratives that survive reveal a religious consciousness attuned to sacred qualities in all forms
of life. The most striking Algonkian term for godly power
was Manitou, but it is impossible to say whether this word
denoted an exalted monotheistic deity in precontact times.
After the whites arrived, Manitou apparently came to resemble Jehovah as a local counterbalance to Christianity.
But before those changes, Manitou was generally associated with heaven, sky, or the sun, often with other life
rhythms too, a concept conveyed by translating the divine
name as "Great Spirit" or "Master of Breath." In their
actual religious practices, however, the Massachuset and
Wampanoag peoples believed in countless beings, *manitowuk,* who inhabited the local surroundings and directed
the course of daily affairs. Without distinguishing between natural objects and the spiritual power within them,
the Algonkians treated all aspects of their world as living
personalities. All phenomena were alive, imbued with in-
telligence and supernatural force. Divine power was
everywhere, and encounters with spirits had to be expected at every turn. These New England Indians placed
no strong reliance on one god with multiple capacities, nor
did they develop a clearly defined hierarchy of deities who
controlled different spheres of life. Each daily activity and
objective had its own sacred aspect. For the Massachusets,
this fragmented but homogeneous view of the world was
more realistic than generalized explanations. The ubiquitous, localized presence of thousands of manitowuk fit well

with a religious behavior that stressed individual responses to the spirit beings who directed each person's experiences.[7]

One further common denominator among the Algonkian myths bears mention. They did not often speak of creators or malicious personalities, but they commonly included the paradigmatic actions of a culture hero. Such tales depicted facets of the culture hero's life to explain how the present world came to be the way it is: why rivers flow downhill, for example; why corn is an important plant; how fire originated. Names for this culture hero differed from one tribe to another, but a favorite was Wetucks (var. Moshup), who was believed to have existed since early times, when the people were learning how to master their environment. Wetucks aided them by creating conditions for their corporate benefit and by teaching them the skills necessary for successful ecological adaptation. Apparently the culture hero was not worshiped as a god, though his activities clearly exhibited superhuman knowledge and ability. His chief function in tribal lore was to legitimate present conditions, explaining them in terms of narrative antecedent conformable to both dawn-time precedent and contemporary psychological mindset.

An enigmatic alter ego, sometimes a twin brother who produced the opposite kind of results, often accompanied Wetucks. Whether through spite or, more frequently, through a sense of prankish mischief (occasionally because of sheer bungling), the work of this trickster figure accounted for the less pleasant features of life. Wetucks caused many good things in human existence; his opposite number was responsible for failures, hardships, and death. In some Algonkian groups a single mythological figure, termed "Great Hare" or "Rabbit Man," combined both positive and negative qualities as the author of both good and bad in current conditions. But regardless of whether circumstances stemmed from two individuals or from contrary impulses in one figure, the Algonkians' worldview posited no sharp dichotomy between good and evil.

They acknowledged life to be a mixture of joy and pain,
triumph and suffering, and thought that no particular design was present. Good and evil were simply different aspects of a single reality, where positive and negative forces
operated beyond human control. Algonkian views of the
world thus avoided dualism but remained ambivalent
about the relative worth of moral options and the ultimate
meaning of life.

In rough outline, such components of Algonkian
mythological thought gave cognitive structure to the
Massachusets' world-view. Together with corporate rituals
and private spiritual communion, these supernatural reference points justified the reality of everyday activities.
These Indians were generally satisfied with life as they
understood it. When death inevitably occurred, they were
confident that the basic features of their present-day existence would continue beyond the grave. Like most other
native Americans, they did not stipulate a place of
punishment for the wicked and another of reward for virtuous citizens. They looked forward to residing in a new
land, where everyone would be reunited after death, inhabiting the same type of villages and pursuing the same
kind of life-style as before. Their way of living and general
view of reality were compatible enough to reinforce each
other, affirming the practices with which they met environmental challenges. They accepted such conditions as
essentially supportive, and they pursued a life of adaptive
cooperation as the proper approach. Death posed no ultimate threat because it did not terminate the exuberance of
living. The Massachusets expected to triumph over death
by finding new opportunities in another realm, beyond the
grave, where individual accomplishments could flourish
again with undiminished vigor.

The Puritan Missions

By the early 1600s many English Reformers decided that
emigration was the only effective way to avoid religious

corruption in their homeland. Both the separatist Pilgrims
who settled Plymouth Colony (1620) and the non-
separatist Puritans of Massachusetts Bay Colony (1630)
came to the New World hoping to build model communities of godly living. Another principal end of their
colonizing effort, stated quite early in the course of events,
was to win the natives to a knowledge of and obedience to
the Christian faith.[8] The Puritans declared missionary
work to be a central justification for establishing towns and
also for expanding westward, though efforts toward that
end languished for more than a decade. Practical considerations seem to have preempted any altruistic sharing
of the gospel message. Initially the Puritan statesmen
and clergy spent most of their time shaping a government that would conduce to the best form of Christian civilization. Their priorities centered on achieving
righteousness for themselves and building new plantations, not on converting those who already occupied the
territory.

The earliest sustained missionary program was inaugurated by Thomas Mayhew, Jr., among Algonkian-
speaking Indians who lived on Martha's Vineyard. When
the elder Thomas Mayhew acquired proprietary rights to
the island, young Thomas began (in 1642) to converse
with the natives in their own language about religious
matters. Through patient effort and the fact that few other
whites interfered with his work, he recorded some notable
conversions by 1657. In that year, however, he perished
when the ship on which he was traveling to Europe disappeared at sea. Thomas Mayhew, Sr., then continued the
work begun by his son in the territory he monopolized as a
feudal domain. His grandson followed suit, and, eventually, five generations of Mayhews gave Christian guidance
to Indians on Martha's Vineyard and Nantucket for the
better part of two centuries. Their evangelism probably
harbored some patriarchal condescension, but it also produced undoubtedly beneficial results among the people
who responded.[9]

Several other New England ministers became interested
in missionary work during the seventeenth century,
though their efforts did not convince many of their fellow
clergymen that native Americans needed the gospel. No
more than a dozen Congregationalist ministers tried to
reach out to Indians in this initial period, and none of them
devoted himself exclusively to missionary work. Only a
handful produced noticeable results, and none of their
work can be termed outstanding. If we judge from their
promotional rhetoric, the English seemed to be as committed to Christianizing the Indians as were the Spaniards
and French, who occupied other parts of the continent;
however, the English colonists actually produced the
smallest number of missionaries and allocated less financial
support to their work and exhibited greater indifference
toward it than did the other Europeans. In spite of the fact
that some Puritans acquired fame as evangelists to the Indians, most of their fellow colonists ignored their special
concern for Indian souls. In missionary work in early New
England there was thus a wide gap between declared intentions and actual accomplishments.

The reasons for this neglect of what they had announced
as one of their primary concerns go deeper than a general
English sense of cultural superiority over the native
Americans. All whites—Spanish and French, Dutch and
Portuguese, as well as English—looked down on the Indians because European technology produced better tools
than native artisans could make. But it was the English who
seemed the most arrogant about this fact and the least
concerned to preserve any aspect of native civilization.
Few Englishmen cared to save aboriginal peoples even if
they could persuade them to adopt the values, habits, and
materials of a superior culture.

One factor that accounts somewhat for the scornful English attitude toward Indian cultures has to do with their
prior attitudes toward the Irish. Since Elizabethan times
the English had viewed the truculent Irish, who followed a
separate religion and culture, as barbarians who would not

accept the manifest advantages of British control. In
America that preconception transferred easily to the Indians, who indicated a similar reluctance to acknowledge
the superiority of English life.[10] Then, too, these English
were Puritans. Having left Old England because of an
unwillingness to compromise on matters of belief and
conduct, they were not about to tolerate deviant customs
in a setting they controlled. The Puritans were religiously
and culturally aggressive, against all forms of behavior they
considered ungodly. They were as intent on managing the
lives of whites in Boston as they were on changing the
customs of Massachusets warriors. Their zeal had brought
them to the New World, and they were resolved to build a
holy commonwealth for those sharing their confessional
viewpoint. As a persecuted minority fleeing from episcopal interference, they were more interested in
establishing security for their own "tribe" than in extending its benefits to others.

Such cultural factors may explain why the English were
not generally disposed to accept the Indians as equals, but
it does not show why so few of their clergy tried to convert
natives and bring them "up" to white cultural standards.
One cannot accurately say that Calvinism itself was the
source of their religious exclusivism or posture of cultural
superiority. The Puritans genuinely believed in the arbi-
trary nature of God's inscrutable will, His freedom to grant
some individuals redeeming grace while withholding it from
others. They affirmed that salvation depended on divine
foreordination and not on human attempts to influence
God's predetermined decrees. This conviction was the
sobering prerequisite to a type of thinking that kept believers humble before a sovereign deity who moved in
mysterious ways to accomplish His purposes. The predestinarian aspect of Puritan theology often produced a
sense of self-assurance among those who felt chosen by
God's grace. But English divines did not include all members of a nation, socioeconomic class, or racial group within

their spiritual elitism. Their respect for divine sovereignty
was too great for that. They admitted that the Almighty
could affect Massachuset souls with the experience of
saving grace as freely as He had apparently redeemed a
large number of Cambridge graduates. So there was little
in their theology to account for their inadequate missions.[11]

An additional factor pertinent to missionary inactivity
on the part of the Puritans has to do with their conception
of ministerial status. If someone studied theology, passed
doctrinal examinations, and preached acceptably, he could
be ordained a Christian minister, but he achieved the legal
designation of clergyman and won community acceptance
as such only while actually serving in a ministerial capacity.
If he terminated that responsibility for any reason other
than moving to a different church, he no longer kept his
clerical status. The number of ministers in the Puritan colonies thus corresponded to the number of churches, the
total growing in tandem with increased population and the
formation of new congregations. Association with a
specific church defined a minister. Former ministers joined
the ranks of pious laymen who contributed to the general
pattern of religious activities. Since a minister needed a
parish to legitimate his existence, and since the community
did not think it proper for someone to be ordained as a
minister and preach only to Indians, few clergymen devoted much time to their neighbors, the Massachusets;
what time they did give had to be appropriated from their
primary duties as pastors of white churches.

These brief considerations help to explain why the
seventeenth-century English missions were so meager.
Even when full weight is given to such factors, however,
the fact remains that the English in general did not respect
Indians as persons having value in their own right, and the
Puritan missionaries pretty much shared this general cultural bias. They saw the unregenerate, whether red or
white, as alike sinful, deserving of censure, yet eligible for

salvation. They agreed that the Indians, though depraved
and uncivilized in their natural state, could respond to
grace, change their habits, and qualify as members of
covenanted communities. Still, they made only minimal
efforts toward enlarging the Kingdom of God with native
converts. Compared with Spanish and French missionaries
in similar situations, the Puritan clergymen were not
energetic or self-sacrificing. The Spanish Franciscans and
French Jesuits, often among the first Europeans to come
into contact with native peoples, lived with or near the
tribes they wanted to convert. Puritan ministers never
lived among their native charges during the seventeenth
century, and their contact with them occurred long after
other Englishmen had pioneered in general patterns of
cultural exchange. In short, they trailed behind almost
every other participant in red-white interaction instead of
being on the leading edge of the social process. By the
time English ministers began preaching the gospel to
Massachuset and Wampanoag tribesmen, English explorers, soldiers, land speculators, traders, and farmers had
already established many contacts with native cultures.
Whether through preference or circumstance, Puritan
evangelical work seems generally to have been an after-
thought, not a primary motivation in colonizing the New
World.

Among the few ministers who did attend to Indian missions were such notables as Richard Bourne on Cape Cod
and John Cotton, Jr., at Plymouth. Samuel Treat preached
to Indians around Eastham, adding his spare hours to the
effort as well. But of all those who worked to evangelize
the natives, none matched the reputation of John Eliot,
"apostle to the Indians." In 1631 Eliot joined other Puritans who sought freedom in the New World. Sailing
aboard the *Lyon,* he landed at Boston in November and
served for a time as teacher in the church there. The members asked him to continue as their associate pastor, but in
1632 Eliot honored what seems to have been a prior

agreement and became minister at Roxbury, a post he held
for more than fifty-seven years. He also taught school to
augment his salary, providing secular education as well as
religious nurture for two generations of Roxbury townspeople. It was during the Pequot War (1636–37) that Eliot
for the first time became really aware of the Indians in his
region. It may be that his interest in converting them
began that early, but he did nothing about it for another six
years. Finally, in 1643, he began learning to speak Massachuset, and within three years he was able to preach
elementary sermons in the local dialect.

Over the course of time Eliot endeavored to place
Massachuset among the literate languages. He compiled a
dictionary and grammar, perhaps more for his own aid
than for that of ambitious natives. In 1654 he printed an
Algonkian translation of the Shorter Catechism and seven
years later published the New Testament for Massachuset
converts to read in their own tongue. Finally, in 1663, the
complete Bible appeared, *Mamusee Wunneetapanatamwe
Up-Biblum God.* Eliot produced other literary works to
edify the tribesmen, translating Richard Baxter's *A Call to
the Unconverted* (1664), Lewis Bayly's *Practice of Piety*
(1665), and several shorter religious tracts. In Indian
settlements where Eliot had any influence the schoolmaster was as prominent as the minister, and in 1669 his
helpful *Indian Primer* appeared as a means of starting
young minds on the road to intellectual as well as spiritual
enrichment. Most of Eliot's other writing was in English,
proclaiming to British readers the success of his missions
while soliciting funds for continued progress. In 1649
Parliament created the New England Company and authorized it to collect money in Britain for Indian missions.
Eliot began receiving a stipend shortly thereafter, and in
subsequent decades several ministers acquired supple-
mental income through the Company, which lasted for
more than a century.[12]

In 1646 Eliot began preaching in the Massachuset lan-

guage, at first haltingly but with increasing ease over the
next forty years. His initial attempt in September was little
short of a disaster. Addressing some natives who lived
near Dorchester under a sachem named Cutchamekin, he
tried to explain simple biblical truths. Instead of responding
to the point of his message, the natives asked him to explain
the cause of thunder, where winds came from, and why
tides operate regularly. Daunted by failure to communicate
his theology, Eliot withdrew for more preparation. Then,
on 28 October 1646, he met with greater success. He spoke
to a small gathering of men, women, and children assembled at the wigwam of Waban, a petty headman who lived
at Nonantum, near Newton. For more than an hour he
preached about. the sinfulness of all mankind. After
dwelling at length on Christ's sacrifice and the coming
judgment, he ended by describing the blessed estate of
those whose Christian faith yielded joy in heaven and by
depicting just as vividly the horrors of hell in store for
wicked unbelievers. The natives did not immediately accept ideas so unfamiliar to them, but Eliot's preaching at
least started the process by which some Indians eventually
embraced as genuine a form of Christianity as their white
coreligionists.

During these first contacts, Eliot and his fellow missionaries scarcely noticed compatible elements that would
have allowed them to meet the Indians on common religious ground. Both cultures were deeply conscious that
spiritual forces presided directly over all features of human
existence. A fundamental religious sensitivity was already
present among the Indians of New England before the
Christians began their missionary efforts. Massachuset
tribesmen readily acknowledged that the world was not of
their own making, and their native concept of Manitou was
analogous to Jehovah, for they usually identified him with
the sky or heavens, at least to the point of distinguishing
him from spirits of the forest and subterranean regions.
One should not, however, press the common recognition
of a "god above" too far. Still, a compatible idea did exist

here, and it could have served as an avenue to mutually
profitable religious discussion.

Another area of general agreement lay in the affirmation
by both groups that supernatural power affects everyday
experience. Regardless of whether blessings or hardships
came their way, individuals in both religions attributed
their daily lot to the wills of divine beings who directed
events according to higher purposes. Though the Indians
called them manitowuk, while the English referred to
angels as agents of supreme Jehovah, a common pattern
held in both cultures, and people were expected to cooperate with the immortals who influenced their lives. Both
groups interpreted good harvests, successful hunts, and
military triumphs to be the result of their collaboration
with spiritual forces. They saw personal misfortune, natural catastrophes, and national defeats as punishment for
human wrongdoing. In this common framework of supernatural dominion over mundane affairs, both Indians and
Puritans invoked the aid of higher beings, and both
thought that private prayers as well as communal ceremonies were effective means of approaching them.

There were also many contrasting elements in the two
religious orientations. The Puritans were strict mono-
theists, and they condemned worship of lesser beings as
idolatry, impediments to adoration of the one true God.
Drawing upon a stern prophetic tradition, they denounced
multiple holy figures because such an array detracted from
single-minded devotion. They thought it was unalterably
wrong to deify natural phenomena or imbue material objects with independent life. Whether the Indians had developed a highly articulated polytheism or simply recognized specific localizations of supernatural power, their
spiritualism contrasted sharply with the Puritans' rigorous
monotheism.[13] Another antithesis lay in the fact that
Puritan ideas derived from specific biblical traditions,
while Algonkian religion had a rather flexible ideological
content. Christian leaders tried to determine proper conduct according to normative theological standards, which

they considered valid for all circumstances. The Indians
defined their behavioral guidelines more pragmatically,
considering both group interests and individual needs
whenever conditions presented problems needing expe-
dient solutions.

In keeping with their grimly predestinarian version of
Reformed thought, the Puritans also emphasized the
depravity of human nature and the need of divine grace for
regeneration. The Indians did not perceive human life as
congenitally wicked. Of course they distinguished between good and evil according to their own definitions, but
they did not see human failings as symptoms of a per-
verse appetite. It never occurred to them to threaten death
and damnation to those who transgressed community expectations. The Puritans viewed natural man as incapable
of living up to God's righteous demands; the Indians considered everyone capable of interacting harmoniously with
the divine powers who regulated their universe. The
Puritans put a premium on deliverance from humanity's
endemic corruption; local tribesmen found it hard to appreciate salvation because they saw no need of being rescued from a positive existence and its practicable means of
enjoyment.

It was difficult enough for the Indians to understand
Puritan convictions about sinful humanity, but the in-
tricacies of how divine grace operated to redeem sinners
created even greater problems. After trying to digest the
unsettling news that they were indeed depraved and without hope except for heavenly forgiveness, they were probably more disconcerted to hear that they could do nothing
at all to influence God's decision about their fate.[14] But if
they felt stirrings of unmerited grace within them, the missionaries insisted that they should respond in specific ways
to obey the Savior's will. Efforts to lead a sanctified life
stemmed not from attempts to cause salvation; Christian
propriety sprang from a sense of joyful duty, which only
the chosen few were privileged to realize. All those lacking
the experience of grace were doomed to everlasting

punishment, a fate their inherited proclivities and mis-
directed actions made them richly deserve.

Massachusets and Wampanoags had probably never
thought of a hell for tribesmen whose misdeeds called for
retribution. They thought the gods would punish sac-
rilegious acts almost immediately, just as socially destructive behavior met with swift communal justice. But
they assumed that everyone would eventually reside in the
same place after death. Christianity threatened to destroy
that aboriginal understanding of community. It menaced
tribal solidarity by declaring that only certain individuals
would be saved. The new faith separated chosen saints
from all those who did not share redemptive grace. This
disruption of corporate identity stemmed from the fundamental Puritan belief that Indians, like all human beings,
were permanently separated into the elect and the non-
elect, destined by God never to see each other again after
this life.

It is also important to note that the type of religious
leadership utilized in the two traditions was strikingly dis-
similar. Puritanism received its specific content from pro-
fessional specialists who defined churchly standards in
terms of their own culturally conditioned perceptions of
biblical tradition. The New England clergymen were
highly trained, and they seriously tried to meet their responsibility of monitoring every citizen's deportment.
Their work focused on exhorting church members to
greater approximations of Christian virtue, but it also extended to advising magistrates on most civil affairs. Religious activity among the Massachuset Indians had a much
less uniform structure and little authoritarian guidance.
Puritan ministers could demand a modicum of respectable
conduct from everyone within their sphere of influence;
shamans provided religious leadership when consulted
about specific problems, but they did not occupy a place of
sufficient spiritual eminence to provide stability and
cohesiveness for Indians inclined to follow the missionaries. The two religions thus differed significantly, not

only in their views about human nature and ultimate destiny, but in the leaders they had, who affected daily conduct along very different lines.[15]

In actual practice the Puritans made little use of the compatibilities that existed between the native religion and their own. They did not emphasize common ideas or encourage Indians to use them as bridges for crossing over into Christianity. They chose rather to heighten the contrast between Indian religiosity and their own by denouncing all precontact activity as devil worship. With few exceptions they censured Indian practices as "barbarous," "heathen," and "uncivilized." They shared the Englishman's general sense of cultural superiority, but they added moral indignation to it. They looked at the Indians and saw only laziness, thievery, drunkenness, blood lust, nakedness, sexual promiscuity, and a congeries of religious superstitions.[16] The handful of ministers who visited the native villages may have been moved by compassion for the depravity they saw, but their message was primarily one of condemnation, a warning of God's wrath, and a prediction of eternal torment for those who continually flouted the Almighty's law of righteousness as found in Scripture.

Surprisingly, this denunciatory stance, which Eliot and other New England missionaries adopted, did produce a few converts over the years. According to reports meant for British consumption, some Massachusets acknowledged themselves to be sinners and showed signs of genuine repentance—evidence to Puritans of divine grace. The preachers thought that their gospel efforts had shed enough light to call it the daybreak if not the sunrise of Christian hopes for New World inhabitants. While we cannot ignore the possibility that the Indians really understood Puritan theology and sincerely confessed the operation of grace in their souls, other factors played a part as well. Early missions yielded few positive results in places where native cultures were still relatively intact (like the

Wampanoag) and strong enough to resist. But after the
fiber of precontact culture had been weakened by disease,
loss of land and manpower, and increased dependence on
European trade, conversions increased considerably.[17]
Many who chose the new way of life were actually indicating the impossibility of maintaining their traditional
life-style under English domination—politically, econom-
ically, and now religiously. The missionaries had made
contact with the Indians later in the overall sequence of
red-white interaction than many other English participants. They did not instigate native decline and never
self-consciously based their evangelism on a policy of
eradicating all precontact customs; but, despite whatever
altruism they possessed, they depended upon, and probably accelerated, the pace of Indian cultural disintegration.

Even in conditions of political fragmentation and cultural disorientation, not all Indians adopted the white
man's religious perspective. They accepted new material
goods rather easily, but the deep psychological roots of
their religious loyalty were less susceptible to change.
Some were willing to add the white man's deity to their
pantheon, just as they had assimilated kettles, hatchets,
and blankets into their established subsistence patterns.
Others adopted Christianity under crisis conditions; for
example, when a general sickness swept Martha's Vineyard
in 1646 and fewer Christian Indians than scoffers fell sick,
many natives concluded that the monotheistic faith had
better protective powers, and a number of them continued
to regard baptism as preventive medicine. Still others
came from the ranks of once-influential sachems and powwows who accepted new behavioral standards in order to
retain some of their old standing. In 1651 Cutchamekin,
Eliot's early opponent, accepted rulership in a Christian
Indian town primarily to keep a modicum of his diminish-
ing eminence. Such factors as these, secular and religious,
operated during the complex processes termed "conversions." Whatever motives came into play, some Indians

did respond favorably to Puritan preaching, and they emerged as a distinctive entity known as "Praying Indians."

Given the Puritans' strong emphasis on doctrine—and the concurrent stress on such cerebral activities as sermons, study classes, and reading—many converts showed remarkable sophistication in adapting to new religious norms. The missionaries insisted that understanding had to precede confession, that rational assent prepared the way for ritual participation. One exception to this rather thoroughgoing religious imperialism was the fact that Eliot and others used the native language rather than English to communicate their evangelical program. That single concession to precontact patterns allowed Christian Indians to preserve some of their old identity while they changed in most other categories. Under Puritan tutelage many learned to treat religious propositions with the gravity of systematic theologians. The importance of such behavior is not that Indians could make what some whites considered rudimentary steps toward theological comprehension. Its real significance lies in the fact that Indians were willing to accept a new conception of religion, one that gave almost exclusive priority to cognition. The Puritans made little use of pictoral art, dance, rituals, dreams, or private communion with spirit beings. The Algonkians had customarily utilized all these forms, and it is a measure of their inner change to see that they abandoned virtually all such practices, conforming to the Englishman's narrow definition of true religion.

By preaching the Word of God, the Puritan missionaries thought they served as avenues through which divine grace could touch the souls of those predestined to live among the saints. The fact that some natives responded positively to their exhortations confirmed the whole Calvinistic order of things. Unlike Catholic missionaries, who relied on the efficacy of sacraments, the Puritans insisted that baptism did not convey salvation to the recipient; Indian converts in New England were thus baptized as a sign of grace already experienced inside them. The ritual only symbolized an internal regeneration wrought by divine agency; it did little to improve the quality of daily conduct. Those who accepted the new view of cosmic order and its omnipotent triune deity then strove to develop habits of Christian virtue. As an alternative to sacraments, the non-literate natives were taught to read in their own language. Once the Praying Indians had reached that crucial plateau, they could read edifying tracts, books, and especially the Bible to improve their behavior. Reading was the chief Puritan means of acquiring practical guidelines for spiritual improvement.

The cognitive features of the Reformed tradition were the marrow of Puritan divinity, and native converts accommodated to it with a fair degree of competency. On the tangible level, however, the missionaries required Praying Indians to adopt an equally thoroughgoing set of behavioral changes. They took great pains to define specific activities expected of Christian believers. Much has been written about how the Puritans wished to destroy Indian customs and let their superior ethical standards fill the resulting vacuum.[18] But this is generally true of every proselytizing effort, because most proselytizers associate their faith with the dominant ideas and behavioral norms of their own culture. The Puritans were no different in this cultural self-assurance from European Catholics or from native American groups, and in this larger context we can more readily understand what Eliot meant when he said that Indians had to be civilized before their conversion was complete. He considered them to be on the path to salvation if God chose them, but he insisted that they follow that path by conforming to Puritan moral standards. He was neither unique nor devious in thinking that converts should repudiate their indigenous culture and adopt an essentially English way of life. Still, such Puritan ideology led to complicity in the deterioration of native cultures and their wholesale replacement with English patterns.

The key to understanding the cultural impact of Puritan

missions is a theological one. Ministers emphasized that
the sanctified life followed regeneration as a secondary but
essential component of the salvation process; once a person had experienced justification through faith, additional
grace helped him to achieve outward righteousness. Puritans insisted that godly living had to follow as a tangible
sign of the inner miracle wrought by God's regenerative
forgiveness. High moral standards without grace could not
save anyone, but Puritans also rejected the antinomian
suggestion that internal experience by itself was sufficient
for salvation. Christians were not free from the obligation
to follow a strict code of sanctified conduct. Ministers
exhorted all believers to moral probity, insisting that
God's people must fulfill the biblical requirements of a
righteous nation. Puritan action among native converts
stemmed from the same theological drive that admonished
whites to mend their faulty habits and achieve virtue with
divine help. The Puritan missionaries did not want to destroy Indian culture because it was Indian; they simply
considered foreign standards displeasing to God. Puritans
sought to transform the customs of everyone who fell
short of biblical precepts, and this zeal applied as much to
Stuart courtiers, Anglican prelates, and common English
yeomen as to the natives of the New World.

When Puritans gave specific content and direction to
their ethical precepts, they inevitably drew on historically
conditioned mores. In teaching Indians how to live a full
Christian life, they were therefore teaching them in fact to
act like Englishmen. Thus they helped to destroy native
cultures. But they did not direct converts' lives in new
directions for economic benefit or for their colony's political advantage. Eliot and his confreres were basically religious leaders who sought to save souls by shaping both the
inner and outer lives of their converts. In retrospect we
can see that they mixed their own customs uncritically with
biblical teachings. While they thought such standards transcended limitations of time and culture, they were wrong,
and that is one of the ironies of missionary history. Con-

version to Puritanism necessitated changed beliefs and behavior in both red and white individuals who accepted the
yoke of salvation, but the changes required of Indians
were far greater than those required of other recipients of
Puritan evangelism.

One of the major transformations in store for Praying
Indians was settlement in a permanent home—a prerequisite to other modifications the evangelists desired to make
in their converts' lives. Beginning with his early sermons
to Waban, Eliot urged natives to accept the related links of
Puritan religion: trust in God's unmerited forgiveness and
obedience to His will through communal discipline. By
1650 he had persuaded his followers to end their semi-
nomadic subsistence patterns and locate for all seasons at
Natick. Over the next quarter-century he was instrumental
in establishing fourteen such towns. In addition to Natick,
the principal ones were Punkapaog, Hassanamasitt,
Okommakamesit, Wamesitt, Nashobah, and Magunkaquog, all located an average of twenty-five miles from
Boston. Perhaps settled towns made it more convenient
for preachers to find listeners; they certainly made it easier
for Indians to pursue Christian virtue without the dis-
tracting influence of unconverted tribesmen. Whatever the
reason, Eliot's enthusiasm for nurturing Indian Christianity at permanent locations set the stage for a comprehensive alteration of precontact behavior.

The Massachusets had customarily relied heavily on
hunting and gathering to feed themselves; settlement in
towns made such an economy virtually impossible. They
were still able to hunt occasionally—Natick comprised
6,000 acres, Punkapaog had 8,000—but confinement inevitably pointed to intensive agriculture as the new economic base. In addition to planting larger gardens, Praying
Indians developed orchards and began raising cattle to
supplement their diet, becoming incipient capitalists into
the bargain by selling surplus crops. Instead of living in
wigwams, many at Natick learned enough carpentry to
build solid houses of English design. They also laid out

three streets, built a bridge, and constructed a combination meetinghouse and school. In a strictly physical sense, Praying Indians accepted many changes in daily conduct. They became familiar with mattocks, spades, crowbars, and hammers. They were urged to cut their hair, wash off the bear grease that protected their skin, wear European clothes, and dwell as nuclear families in separate houses. In perhaps the most striking contrast with traditional Massachuset practices, they also erected fences to enclose plots of land for private use.

Social values changed along with physical arrangements as the converts conformed to the Puritan ideal of proper conduct. They modified their attitudes toward lineage and other tribal institutions that had provided a secure matrix for personal identity and individual initiative. New loyalties, especially to the church as a new identity-giving structure, replaced former reliance on kinship patterns. Natick and other towns contained converts from many bands, and the familiar basis of native political authority rarely survived transition to the new scheme of things. Visiting ministers and local exhorters or elders were the real leaders now, superseding the sachems by virtue of their seniority in the new faith. Powwows were hardly welcome at all, but if one converted and asked admission to a native church, he renounced all his former powers as marks of a degenerate past.

The old Indian respect for individual initiative in warfare, councils, vision quests, and displays of valor gave way before Puritan strictures. Eliot set a precedent at Natick by supplying rules for what he hoped would become a model Christian community. Basing its constitution on what he saw as a biblical prototype (Exodus 18:25), he drew up rules to promote virtue and discourage vice. The Indians adopted these requirements in order to approximate the ideal sanctification all converts longed to embody. Personal freedom gave way to new standards of piety that stipulated fines and flogging if Praying Indians broke the rules. Many Massachusets also altered their psychological attachment to the land. Since they often broke ties with clan and tribe to accept the new faith, they usually felt closer to fellow confessors who had moved to Christian towns as a result of similar experiences. Church congregations replaced native adherence to kinship structure, and Praying Indian townships gave converts a new sense of locality to replace their earlier regional consciousness.

Except for retaining their original language, Massachuset converts seem to have permitted a rather thoroughgoing behavioral metamorphosis. In attempting to explain their vulnerability to change, we must recognize that they did not have a strong framework of social institutions to help them resist missionary demands. This was particularly true in the area of religious leadership. When the missionaries increased intercultural tensions, the Massachusets had few precontact organizational forms to sustain them in their customary beliefs. Individuals had to deal with such tensions by themselves, and some decided to accept the white religion as well as the white material culture. To be sure, sachems and powwows resisted change because it eroded their status. But since their prestige depended on others' voluntary recognition of their power, they could not prevent individual decisions to accept a new way of life. Once converts began adopting English usages, momentum toward complete accommodation to new standards began.

Another factor explaining the unusual degree of change among these Indian converts is Puritan zeal. The Puritans were a religious group still battling to establish themselves on the Christian map, and they resolved to control their part of the world with stern measures. This grim reformist determination was inspired by a need to succeed as well as by the omnipotent deity who supposedly demanded it. The combination of weak aboriginal institutions and vigorous pressure from Puritan missionaries as well as magistrates makes cultural collapse among these converts more easily understandable. Compared with other native American groups, the New England Indians possessed relatively limited means of preserving their cultural integrity. This is nowhere better exemplified than by the Praying Indians, who, in conforming to English notions of proper human existence, accepted a radically different world-view and ethos. For some, the transformation was complete, and they became red Puritans.

It would be wrong, however, to think that all members of the Massachuset nation accepted Christianity, lived in model towns, and subjected themselves to the virtues enforced there. In its early days Natick comprised no more than 30 families, or about 145 persons willing to inquire further into Christianity. At the high point of mission success in 1674, only 1,100 natives lived in all of Eliot's fourteen towns. Missionaries in Plymouth Colony reported a total of some 500 converts in their area; Martha's Vineyard and Nantucket claimed up to 600 families. These figures represented scarcely 10 percent of the mainland native population, and, even then, most of those residing at missionary sites were only potential Christians, as yet unbaptized. For example, of the 1,100 in Eliot's missions, no more than 119 were baptized, and only 74 of these were full communicants in covenanted churches: 50 at Natick, 16 at Hassanamasitt, and 8 at Magunkaquog.[19]

Statistics alone are not an adequate measure of successful missions. Over the years many natives came to resemble the ideal kind of witness Eliot labored to produce. Several taught regularly in Praying Indian schools; twenty-four served as ordained ministers, some of them even administering communion to nearby whites on stated occasions. For a time it seemed that a burgeoning native Christianity might gather strength, expand its influence, and develop through indigenous leadership. Whether this might have happened we cannot know, for events beyond the missionaries' control ruined all chances for what might have become a flourishing native church. King Philip's War, which broke out in 1675, destroyed much of what

Eliot had tried to nurture in these isolated Christian communities.

The downward spiral of red-white relations in New England had actually begun with diseases introduced before
the Pilgrims landed at Plymouth. After their arrival, some
of the Pilgrims tried to deal fairly with Indians in land
purchases and legal administration (according to white
standards, of course), but the natives generally resented
English insistence on conformity to English legal standards. White expansionist pressure and political intrigues
eventually led many tribes to rally around a Wampanoag
sachem named Philip because he symbolized an attempt
to save their cultural autonomy. Philip was not an organizational genius who designed a pan-Indian alliance to push
all whites back into the sea. His war started prematurely
and was conducted sporadically, but those who flocked to
him succeeded in waging one of the most devastating and
costly wars in American history. During the conflict
known as King Philip's War, the natives damaged half of all
white settlements and inflicted casualties on more than 6
percent of the population. By the time Philip was killed in
August 1676, mission work had also been irreversibly
damaged.

The war greatly affected missions by stimulating the
colonists' latent animosities toward all Indians. When
Wampanoag raiders first struck outlying settlements in
Massachusetts and Plymouth, the trouble seemed minor
because only one tribe was involved. But various bands of
Nipmucks came into the fight too, adding enough man-
power to make the colonists fear they were surrounded
and outnumbered. Some Nipmucks had lived in Christian
Indian towns in the early 1670s, but most of them joined
Philip to end further white encroachment on their territory.
Some Massachuset warriors also left Eliot's missionary res-
ervations to join the Wampanoag army. But most Praying
Indians remained peacefully in their towns, even when this
docility exposed them to attack from marauding Indians.
As it turned out, however, they had less to fear from

enemy forays than from the siege mentality developing
among the whites—whose cause the Christian Indians
espoused and wished to defend. Fearful whites ignored
this loyalty and concluded what they had suspected all
along: that no Indian could ever be trusted. Contagious
fear led to blanket condemnation of all natives; the missionaries could not counteract the anti-Indian prejudice
fed by wartime hysteria.

By June 1675 the authorities ordered all Praying Indians
to concentrate in five towns "for their own security." They
then confiscated the Indians' weapons and forbade them to
hunt. They also rejected the Indians' offer to join the war
effort. Eventually many did fight alongside the white
militia and were crucial to the colonists' victory, but in
October 1675 racial prejudice and wartime panic produced an extreme measure: the General Court established
what amounted to concentration camps for loyal Indians.
Many fled to escape incarceration, but the acculturated
natives—those most willing to internalize English
values—submitted to confinement on bleak Deer Island in
Boston Harbor. John Eliot, his protégé Daniel Gookin,
and others protested against these harsh tactics, but in
vain; in fact, the old missionary himself barely escaped
being lynched. In the end the missionaries could do no
more than alleviate some of the suffering of the Indians
who made common cause with their jailers.

Nearly five hundred Praying Indians endured the winter
of 1675–76 on barren terrain without adequate food,
clothing, or shelter. By late spring the colonial authorities
relocated them near Cambridge, but prison life and the
antecedent bullying had taken a dreadful toll.[20] After the
war the mission program was in shambles; Christian Indians rebuilt only four of their former towns. The missions
on Cape Cod and Martha's Vineyard hardly felt the impact
of the war, and many Massachuset refugees had fled there
for security. But Natick never recovered; as late as 1698 it
had only 180 residents, of whom 10 were members of the
church. Eliot continued to work with the remnant of his

congregation, but he was in his seventies by then, and no
young missionaries of his stature emerged to take his
place. A reservation system that lumped belligerents with
peaceful Indians superseded the old model of havens for
cooperative believers. The war crippled missionary work
because it unleashed the pent-up fears and hostilities most
whites felt toward Indians, converted or not.

The remarkable thing is that the Puritan brutalities did
not lead the Praying Indians to abandon Christianity
altogether. Almost half the Massachuset converts survived
the maelstrom with their faith intact, however disillusioned they may have become with their white coreligionists. Their constancy indicates something of the
power with which gospel precepts can sustain individuals
despite adverse conditions. But their low residual number
highlights the fact that the seventeenth-century missions in
New England were irrecoverably broken. Two decades
after the war, missionaries reported only seven Indian
churches and twenty preaching stations and schools. The
population at Natick resisted attrition better than other
mission towns, but its population declined to 166 in 1749,
to about 20 in 1797, and, in 1855, to 1 Christian Indian.
Elsewhere in the country, in the early eighteenth century,
the number of Indian converts increased when the Great
Awakening breathed new life into evangelical work; but in
New England, where white expansion relentlessly pushed
the dwindling cluster of adherents into cultural oblivion,
the missions never regained their former vitality.

5

Missions in the Eighteenth Century (1701–95)

By 1700 Indian missions were a familiar enterprise. During the eighteenth century several new denominations inaugurated missionary activity, and the traditional churches modified some of their tactics. Fresh efforts began in western New England and the Middle Colonies, and the evangelical programs behind them stemmed from various theologies, with corresponding motivations and methods; but as a whole these endeavors did not depart significantly from the earlier procedures. New tribes were brought under European domination, while the culture base of those already affected was further eroded.

One factor influenced missions in this period to a degree unprecedented in earlier times. As the colonies grew from tentative plantations to thriving components of European empires, events within their borders became part of overall imperial designs, for Spain, France, and Britain brought colonial activities within the orbit of their international rivalry. Economic, military, and often missionary activities in America thus became subsidiary to the interests of governments whose fundamental priorities lay on the other side of the Atlantic. Shifts of fortune in far-away royal courts affected trade agreements, mutual-defense pacts, and cultural relationships involving missionaries. This state of affairs often bewildered Indians who bargained in good faith, and it frustrated the many whites who dealt with them on a day-to-day basis.

Some evangelists, however, engaged in a parallel struggle for power in eighteenth-century international politics. The best example of a missionary organization that blended religious and nationalistic goals was the Society for the Propagation of the Gospel in Foreign Parts, founded in 1701 by the Church of England. Its originator, Thomas Bray, who had served the bishop of London as colonial commissary, thought that the SPG could reap a double spiritual harvest. First, it could spread the gospel among those who had never heard it before, especially American Indians and African Negroes. Second, the Anglican priests could counteract the influence the Congregationalists and Presbyterians had established along the seaboard and win dissenters back to the respectable religion maintained in England's national church. Bray advocated establishing artisan-mission outposts to Christianize Indians while civilizing them according to British standards. He hoped the colonial governors would support his plan, because it promised to extend their jurisdictions while placing a buffer between whites and the barbarous Indians who scorned their influence.

SPG agents in the event conducted few missions to American Indians. They gravitated toward less rigorous work among their white compatriots—parish work, which buttressed royalty and episcopacy, the twin foundations of proper civilization. An early exemplar of this pattern was Samuel Thomas, who came to Carolina in 1702 expressly to convert natives of the Yamasee tribe. Soon after arriving, he reported that the warlike Yamasees seemed "not at leisure" to attend his instruction. Concluding that it was unsafe to venture among them, he settled in a comfortable parish. Later he occasionally preached to black slaves, possibly to salve his conscience for failing to brave the hazards of Indian evangelism.[1]

During the eighteenth century a total of 309 SPG missionaries worked up and down the Atlantic Coast. None lived among the Indians; a few accepted native children in schools, where they taught them English habits of dress,

speech, and worship.[2] Most were content to ignore the
Indians and concentrate on the white population. Among
those who did concern themselves with Indians was John
Stuart, whose career demonstrates SPG priorities. In 1770
he arrived at Fort Hunter in Mohawk country. He tried to
make native youths literate in their own language, but the
Revolutionary War ended his ineffectual labors among a
dwindling number of pupils. Throughout that time he il-
lustrated the fact that SPG agents usually sought to serve
the crown while nurturing Church of England Christianity.
In dealing with Indians, they tried to manage them as a
power bloc against competing interests and enlist them as
dependable military allies, first against the French and later
against the republican colonists.

New England

White disdain for Indian cultures in Massachusetts grew to
smug complacency after King Philip's War had reduced
the native population to marginal status. The colonists no
longer feared the natives because, so few in number, they
posed no obstacle to agricultural and mercantile expansion. Those who gave any thought to saving Indian souls
now made it plain that religious benefits accrued only to
those who adopted English beliefs and habits. Cotton
Mather expressed this popular attitude in the following
words:

> The best thing we can do for our Indians is to Anglicize them in
> all agreeable Instances; and in that of Language, as well as
> others. They can scarce retain their Language, without a
> Tincture of other Salvage Inclinations, which do but ill suit,
> either with the Honor, or with the design of Christianity.[3]

Massachuset and Wampanoag independence had collapsed in classic patterns of forced acculturation. With
mounting confidence, third-generation Puritans simply assumed that their religion and culture were destined by

Providence to dominate the land. If the Indians were to
survive at all, and save their souls as well, they would have
to accommodate themselves to English norms. The old
missions founded by Eliot could hardly endure in that climate of opinion. By 1730 Natick church counted only
three full communicants and a larger membership of about
twenty-eight baptized Indians. Even though Oliver Peabody and his successor, Stephen Badger, struggled to
keep the work alive, it stopped completely in 1799, when
Badger resigned because there were so few Indians in the
neighborhood.[4]

At this time, Algonkian-speaking natives in western
Massachusetts still maintained their aboriginal cohesiveness. White complacency about cultural supremacy did not
yet apply to such groups as the Housatonics, a branch of
the Mahican tribe. In 1710, the same year in which Cotton
Mather made his self-satisfied pronouncement about native capitulation, the person who as an adult would in-
augurate missionary work among the Housatonics was
born in New Jersey. John Sergeant hailed from Newark,
but he came from New England stock and returned there
for school, graduating from Yale in 1729. He tutored at
his alma mater until 1735, when the New England Company commissioned him for evangelical efforts in the
Berkshire Hills. After being ordained a Congregationalist
minister that summer, he spent the remaining fourteen
years of his life among the Housatonics. Within a few
seasons he persuaded different bands to settle in one
place, and the Massachusetts General Court set aside a
tract of land six miles square around the mission for Indian
residence. The government also paid for a meetinghouse
and a school to facilitate Sergeant's program among his
charges at Stockbridge.

Early in his missionary career Sergeant learned to speak
the local Algonkian dialect. In addition to preaching in it,
he translated prayers, Bible lessons, and an elementary
catechism. Beginning with the small nucleus of Stockbridge residents, he slowly increased the number of

Housatonics willing to entertain Christian precepts.
Within a short time he reported forty baptisms and
another forty children in school. During the day he concentrated on teaching the young ones to read; in the evening he instructed the adults through communal singing.
But, true to the predominant missionary practice, his chief
interest lay in convincing the Indians to accept the central
characteristics of white culture. For years he tried to instill
"civilized" habits by persuading them to accept English as
their first language. Moreover, he tried to supervise the
usually carefree days of young Indians by alloting time for
manual labor and study. Hoping to instill the virtues of
industry, obedience, and restraint, he taught girls as well as
boys that proper work habits would rid them of both indo-
lence and ignorance. Toward the end of his life he counted
129 baptized believers in a church containing 42 communicants. He was clearly making headway with his acculturation program, but in 1749 an early death put an end
to his work.

The Housatonics did not revert to their aboriginal ways
after losing their first missionary. In 1751 they received
another clergyman, Jonathan Edwards, who recently had
been dismissed by his Northampton congregation as the
result of disputes about ecclesiastical discipline and
ministerial authority. Edwards preached in the Stockbridge church for seven years through an interpreter, but
he spent most of his time composing theological treatises
for whites, not for natives. In 1754 the French and Indian
War dealt Stockbridge a severe blow. Many Christian Indian males died while fighting alongside the British ex-
peditionary forces, and the settlement dwindled appreciably because it was situated on one of the main French
invasion routes from Canada. Much later, in 1775, John
Sergeant, Jr., assumed care of the remaining Stockbridge
community. He provided ministerial guidance for a decade
in the old location and in 1786 followed the Indians to
New York, where they established New Stockbridge. Finally, receiving ordination in 1788, he continued to serve

in his father's place until he died, after a protracted illness,
in 1824. By that time most Housatonics had merged with
remnants of other Algonkian tribes in a collective movement westward to escape the greedy white men.

While resident missionaries were contributing their part
to eighteenth-century evangelism in New England,
another Congregationalist minister was pursuing a different approach at his home in Lebanon, Connecticut.
Eleazar Wheelock, Yale graduate in 1733 and minister of a
white congregation since 1735, expanded his social usefulness by preparing indigent young men for college.
Naming the project Moor's Charity School, after its chief
benefactor, Wheelock taught there for several years before it occurred to him that the institution might serve
missionary purposes. In 1743 he accepted a young Mohegan, Samson Occom, who expressed a great desire to
acquire the skills needed for a gospel ministry. Occom
proceeded through his studies at a remarkably fast pace,
unfortunately impairing his eyesight in the process. The favorable impression he made inspired his teacher with a
vision of educating many Indians and sending them to
spread salvation among their respective tribes.

If his plan was to succeed, if he was to reach the Indian
nations through native graduates who personally embodied Christian civilization, he felt that he must first
protect his young candidates in their formative years from
shamans and their senseless rituals, from woodland life and
its permissive behavior, and, more than that, from the
temptations offered by unscrupulous white traders and the
liquor with which they so often debauched the unwary. He
hoped to produce scholars and farmers, housewives and
schoolmistresses, who would spread Christianity in scattered Indian settlements without relying on the continual
presence of white preachers.

He therefore created a boarding school where he could
isolate Indian youths from their native surroundings for
months at a time and so expose them to a strictly controlled moral environment. Perhaps more important than

specific knowledge, special skills, or doctrinal orthodoxy, Wheelock sought to inculcate his young charges with positive attitudes toward work and discipline. Compared with the free life of Indian camps, where adults rarely scolded or punished children, the missionary schoolmaster advocated restraint and industriousness. In 1764 he admonished a recruiting agent to "be sure you let all the Children, whom you bring, know that they dont come here without Government, nor to live a lazy sordid Life, but to be fitted for Business and Usefulness in the World."[5] Pursuant to that goal he required all pupils to be ready for morning prayers, clean and decently dressed, before sunrise in winter and at six o'clock in summer. After the older boys had read portions of Scripture, everyone answered questions from the catechism. Then, after breakfast, they did chores on the farm or learned to use tools in the shop. During the rest of the day both white and Indian scholars learned to read Greek, Latin, and Hebrew; for whether his graduates planned to live at Hartford or in stockaded native villages, Wheelock made sure that each of them had thorough grounding in Virgil and the Greek New Testament. Disciplined habits, knowledge of the classics, and mastery in mechanical arts—these were the accomplishments by which Wheelock's students would demonstrate the advantages of Christianity and so induce their fellow tribesmen to acquire them too.

Despite hardships and disappointments, Wheelock kept at his original plan for twenty-five years. He welcomed Algonkian pupils from New England and even recruited several Iroquois, after obtaining endorsement from their adviser, crown official Sir William Johnson. A total of almost fifty Indians studied for various periods of time at Wheelock's school, and at least fifteen of them returned to their homes as missionaries, schoolmasters, or assistants to white preachers.[6] On the whole, however, Moor's Charity School made no lasting evangelistic mark. True to their early upbringing, most Indian children rebelled against

Wheelock's regimen. Few submitted to rigorous discipline
for very long, and most of those who did became ill or
languished in despair. Several died. Most showed a taste
for exactly the kind of life their mentor was trying to prevent. In 1768 Sir William, who earlier had endorsed
Wheelock's efforts, used the Fort Stanwix Treaty to block
further work in New York; he thought Wheelock was
more interested in acquiring land than in saving souls. That
same year Wheelock, admitting that his educational evangelism had failed, closed the Charity School at Lebanon.

Within two years, however, he launched a modified version of his school at Dartmouth College in New Hampshire. During its first decade the institution educated approximately forty Indians, fifteen of them coming from
Iroquois settlements transplanted to Canada. But native
Americans were only a tiny fraction of Dartmouth's total
student body, and they rapidly melted away. Most Protestant missionaries still thought that evangelism was an
educative process, a patient inculcation of spiritual truths
and virtuous behavior. They relied heavily on instruction
as a means of affecting the unconverted, regardless of their
cultural background. But Wheelock's quarter-century of
experiment indicated that education—given his didactic
methods and taste for the classics—was not a fruitful
means for nurturing Christian Indians.

Samson Occom proved to be the exception to that general rule, and he probably succeeded in spite of the fact
that he studied with Wheelock rather than because of it.
Born in 1723 a full-blooded Mohegan, a tribe that was a
fragment of the old Pequot nation, Occom became a
Christian during the First Great Awakening and decided to
enter the ministry. Under Wheelock's tutelage he demonstrated a facility for languages as well as private devotions.
Eyestrain coupled with precarious health made college
training impossible, but Occom held to his clerical goal
and received a Presbyterian license to preach shortly after
leaving Moor's Charity School in 1747. Within two years
he settled at Montauk, Long Island, and acquitted himself

well as one of the few Indians to achieve ministerial
standing in the eighteenth century. But despite his learning, zeal, and proven ability to reach native Americans, the
white authorities were slow to grant him full ecclesiastical
approval. In 1757 he passed the theological examination,
but the Connecticut ministers delayed accepting his request for ordination. Two years later he was finally ordained by the Presbytery of Long Island, which had
already benefited from his labors for a decade.

Though he must have chafed at the white clergy's delay
and apparent distrust, Occom met no serious resistance
among the natives of his widespread flock. He enjoyed
patriarchal status in a thirty-mile area between the settlements of Montauk and Shenecook. Long Island Indians
trusted him, and, as a transfigured shaman, he achieved
notable evangelical success. In addition to preaching regularly at several locations, he taught school, boarded
young students, performed marriages, visited the sick, and
conducted funerals. He also served the traditional functions of sachem by providing leadership and hospitality to
a steady stream of visitors. He acted as scribe for the un-
lettered and settled disputes among them, adjudicating issues and assessing rival claims. Many of these activities
exceeded narrow definitions of ministerial responsibility,
but as an Indian who knew what his people really needed,
Occom conducted practical evangelism that went far beyond perfunctory duties.

New England's missionary organizations gave him scant
financial aid during his fifteen-year residence on Long Island. White evangelists made little enough in that era, but
the red clergyman did the same work for less pay. He lived
in traditional wigwams, moving at least twice a year because of custom and the need to find more firewood. He
raised his own corn, beans, and potatoes and fed his
growing family also with fish and wild fowl. To pay the cost
of plowing and fees at the mill, eighteen miles away,
Occom utilized his native skills to make things for sale:
carved ladles and spoons, cedar pails and churns, even new

stocks for guns. Somewhere he learned rudimentary
bookbinding and restored old volumes for the residents of
Easthampton. Many Indians living a semiacculturated life
on the fringe of white society found it difficult to survive
by such means, but Occom never let these activities inter-
fere with his higher calling as a Presbyterian minister.

He maintained a constant round of preaching. Three
times each Sunday and again on Wednesday evenings he
gathered part of his flock for worship. The simple services
began with song, either psalms or stanzas from Dr. Watts's
hymnal, and a short discourse on their meaning. After that
Occom usually read a portion of Scripture and explained
how to apply its wisdom to everyday life. The service concluded with prayer and more singing. We know little about
his doctrinal position, the ideas he advocated, or the moral
exhortations he delivered to those who came to him for
counsel. Since he himself was the product of Great Awakening enthusiasm, he undoubtedly emphasized the need
for genuine religious experience of a deeply personal nature. That experiential religious perspective led him to
serve his people as the medium through which divine
grace could enter their lives and work its subtle transformations.[7]

Between 1761 and 1763 Occom enlarged his missionary
commitment by making three lengthy visits to Oneidas, an
Iroquois tribe who lived just west of the Mohawks in New
York. Eleazar Wheelock wanted to attract promising
youths from that sector for his school, and he used his
former pupil to advertise the establishment's attractions.
Occom had some initial success among the Iroquois, but
his last evangelical tour was aborted by the war known as
Pontiac's Rebellion. Turning to larger fields, he continued
to serve his old teacher as a willing agent. In 1766 he
traveled to England with a white companion and solicited
funds for the mission school. This tour was an immense
success. It lasted for two years, and the two men collected
over £1,200. Occom received great public acclaim in England. He convinced throngs of British supporters that the

gospel could transform native Americans into paragons of
scholarship and piety.

Severe disappointment awaited him when he returned
in 1768. To his dismay he found that Wheelock had abandoned his original missionary purpose, and, when
Wheelock later moved to New Hampshire and founded a
college, naming it after the Earl of Dartmouth, its chief
patron, Occom noted bitterly that most of the students
were white. Charging that he had been misled and that the
money he had collected was being diverted to unintended
purposes, Occom broke with his spiritual mentor and remained unreconciled for the rest of his life. After those
glorious years of being lionized in England, it must have
been difficult to settle into the old routine as a local
preacher and tribal consultant, but Occom swallowed his
disappointment and returned in that capacity to his native
Connecticut town of Mohegan. In addition, he became for
the next fifteen years an unofficial itinerant minister to
Indian groups who lived in Charlestown, Groton,
Stonington, Niantic, and Farmington. He also succumbed
to occasional bouts of self-pity and heavy drinking—
behavior that further identified him as an Indian in the
eyes of both red and white observers.

The Middle Colonies

By 1784 most of the Indians remaining in New England
found their position untenable. White pressure to acquire
their land made it clear that westward emigration was the
only way to preserve their remaining integrity. Occom labored mightily for his people toward that end. He also
welcomed the task as a way of rising above the monotony
and discouragement that marked his later years. Even earlier, in 1773, a group of young Indians had decided to
move west and had secured permission from the Oneidas
to settle in their territory, in New York; but the Revolution had postponed these hopes of starting again in a new
land. After weathering the war years in Massachusetts, at

Stockbridge, these pioneers finally managed to found a
settlement in New York, which they named Brothertown,
and in 1784 Occom led the first contingent of parishioners
from their ancestral homes to what they hoped would be
peaceful seclusion.

Housatonic Indians also moved to New York after the
war and founded New Stockbridge, six miles from
Brothertown. Occom resumed itinerant preaching, and
unforeseen circumstances augmented his position in the
new territory. The Brothertown communicants chose him
as their minister, and in 1787 a faction at New Stockbridge
did the same, preferring him to their white minister, John
Sergeant, Jr. That turn of events must have strained relations between the two clergymen, but it was a tonic for
Occom, who thrived on acceptance among native brethren. From this new, strong base he traveled widely for two
purposes: saving souls and collecting funds to improve his
people's physical situation at Brothertown. He preached
and exhorted like a circuit rider through rural areas of the
state, often holding services six or seven times a week.
Since there were few ministers of any kind in these thinly
populated areas, the whites also gathered readily whenever
word spread that the Mohegan preacher would conduct
worship services.

Younger, stronger men found such activities wearisome
over extended periods of time, but Occom, though he was
almost seventy, continued to press for more conversions
while trying to preserve Brothertown as a Christian Indian
haven inside white political jurisdiction. Strangely enough,
he did not cultivate younger native leaders to succeed him
as minister of the exclusive Indian church. When he died
in 1792, his New Stockbridge followers united once again
with Sergeant, their former minister. The communicants at
Brothertown remained without a pastor and soon split into
factions, letting internal dissension fragment the solid
community that Occom had labored to establish. We do
not know how many baptisms he performed in his lifetime
or how many members his churches numbered, but his

labor on two continents remains an outstanding example
of missionary accomplishment and dedication by a native
American who took the gospel seriously.

Another missionary working in the Middle Colonies was
Samuel Kirkland, who spent most of his adult years among
the Oneidas near Brothertown. He too studied briefly at
Wheelock's academy in 1761 and then, at the age of
twenty, entered Princeton as part of its sophomore class.
Though he pursued the standard curriculum into his senior
year, he abandoned his studies when a missionary opportunity presented itself in late 1764. He never finished his
college work, but Wheelock persuaded the officials at
Princeton to grant him a degree at the 1765 commence-
ment. By that time Kirkland was living among the Senecas,
the westernmost tribe of the powerful Iroquois League.
His first mission lasted only a year, but he impressed his
native hosts with his aptitude for their language, his loyalty
to the friendships he made in their longhouses, and his
stoic endurance of the meager winter rations. Conditions
in the tribe were unsettled, however, because some of the
chiefs favored British imperial interests, while others
wanted to support the colonists' designs beyond the
Alleghenies. As a result, the Senecas were too much involved with frontier warfare to tolerate a missionary for
long.

Kirkland therefore left that unpromising field in May
1766 and returned to his native Connecticut. A month
later, while visiting Wheelock at Lebanon, he received
Congregationalist ordination and was shortly thereafter
commissioned a missionary by the Society in Scotland for
Propagating Christian Knowledge. Instead of returning to
the Senecas, Kirkland went to live among the centrally
located Oneidas in their principal town of Kanonwalohule.
From that base he was also able to influence the Tus-
caroras, a southern Iroquois tribe that had moved to New
York (1712–22) and constituted a sixth council fire in the
ancient League. Many natives suspected the missionaries

of having the same crass motives as other whites had,
thinking they wanted Indian land more than Indian conversions to a better way of life, but Kirkland soon made it
clear that Indian welfare interested him more than financial security. He refused to accept any land from them and
spent much of his SSPCK salary to alleviate need among
his tribal friends. Such generosity impressed the Oneidas,
but it caused a sharp controversy with Wheelock over the
way to conduct missions.

Wheelock envisoned Christian Indian communities
where missionaries and converts controlled all the surrounding acreage. Kirkland wanted to affect native lives
religiously; he wanted no socioeconomic alterations or
enforced cultural standards until the Indians themselves
requested such changes. After two years of wrangling over
missionary procedure, Kirkland dissolved his relationship
with Wheelock at the same time that Samson Occom also
broke with him. But Kirkland did not end his association
with the SSPCK. After disputing with Wheelock and other
Connecticut commissioners of the honorable society, he
traveled to Boston in 1770 and secured patronage from
the commissioners there instead.

Over the next few years Kirkland won a considerable
number of converts and vindicated his decision not to
intrude too much on native ways. Nevertheless, in his feelings about Indians, reproach was always mingled with for-
bearance. Even when reporting positive change he pro-
jected a negative attitude:

> I now rejoice that . . . in that dark corner, which a few months
> ago was a habitation of cruelty and gross paganism, there is
> now a blessed nest of Christians, and such as were not God's
> people must now, in the judgment of Christian charity, be
> called the children of God. There, in their little, despicable,
> bark huts, the true God is now worshipped in spirit and truth,
> and the poor, greasy, lousy, half-starved creatures are from
> day to day fed with the hidden manna, and a number of them
> rejoicing with joy unspeakable.[8]

So Kirkland urged white behavioral standards on converts willing to adopt them. Through persuasion rather than coercion he got the Oneidas to build a meetinghouse, a sawmill, a gristmill, and a blacksmith shop. He procured farm tools, seeds for diversified agriculture, and oxen for the heavy work around the gradually modernizing villages. He taught young natives how to cope with white material culture, but he remained true to his ministerial calling as well. He wanted to convince Indians that the white man's standard of living, though unequal in value to Christian beliefs, was worth accepting. In this approach he resembled other eighteenth-century missionaries, but his unobtrusive, patient, flexible methods had a more lasting effect than most.

During the Revolutionary War Kirkland discontinued much of his evangelical activity but did not entirely abandon it. He served as chaplain in the Continental Army, and Congress appointed him to negotiate with various Indian tribes. In that capacity he tried to secure native support for the new nation's cause or at least get a pledge of neutrality. Such assignments kept him away from the Oneida mission for extended periods of time, but he stayed in contact with his charges and at length settled again among them. The war and its aftermath caused serious deterioration in the Iroquois League. Many elements in the Six Nations had supported the British, and loyalist natives followed crown forces into Canada for resettlement. Those who stayed in New York had to face victorious Americans who wanted to punish all Iroquois because some of them had sided with the enemy. They also found themselves buffeted by westering citizens who wanted even friendly Indians removed as obstructions to the expansion of the new nation.

Such events demoralized Kirkland's Indian neighbors, and in light of their recent misfortunes it should come as no surprise that many turned to Christianity for relief. Conversions often multiplied when native cultures declined to a point where adopting the white man's religion

and culture seemed a wise alternative. The Oneidas conformed to that pattern after the Revolution. Kirkland reported a widespread revival among them in 1787. Most
Iroquois preferred to follow Episcopal or Catholic missionaries, who would baptize their children without demanding regeneration in the parents. Kirkland was a
rigorous Calvinist, and many natives did not like his stern
demands for doctrinal orthodoxy and upright behavior.
But this resistance diminished appreciably by 1786, and
the Oneidas accepted his teachings more widely than at
any previous time.

The war changed things in another way, too. In 1788
Kirkland accepted nearly 5,000 acres of Indian land within
the circuit of his old preaching stations. Sensing perhaps
that red-white relations had taken a downward turn because of the war, he agreed to accept the land when his
friends lost their independent status. This did not mean
that his evangelical zeal had faltered or that his hope for
conversions flagged; instead, he was trying to meet new
circumstances with new tactics. Kirkland hoped to protect
his converts' environment through his personal land-
holding; he also became financially well-to-do in the process. He continued to preach and to serve the remaining
Indians in a half-dozen villages, but in later years he built a
private log house and farmed extensively on what had
formerly been Oneida property. The once-altruistic missionary conducted three worship services every Sunday
and accepted visitors each evening to discuss various subjects. He advised them about plowing their fields, sowing
grain, and using other improved procedures to their own
advantage. And, as ministers have done in every pastoral
setting, he always visited the sick and comforted those in
need.

Another departure that marked a decline in native independence and Kirkland's recognition of their altered situation was the Oneida academy. Kirkland hoped that a
school would influence young Indians in ways that the old

sort of missionary activity could not achieve. In 1793 his academy received a charter to conduct classes where literate Iroquois struggled with white ideas and standards. White settlers who could afford to pay for education also sent their children to study alongside Iroquois youths. Kirkland donated 300 acres to support the school and helped give a solid economic foundation to what became Hamilton College in 1810. That aid, for both Indian and white students, was the missionary's last important contribution. After 1795 he was virtually incapacitated by ill health and financial difficulties, the latter exacerbated by the fact that the SSPCK terminated its relationship with him in 1797. Though he pursued some evangelical objectives until his death in 1808, Kirkland's later missionary work did not measure up to the accomplishments of his prime, when he lived happily among the Oneidas.

Farther south, in New Jersey and Pennsylvania, another group of Indians encountered eighteenth-century missionaries. Calling themselves Leni Lenape, "Genuine People," they clustered principally along a river the English named after Thomas West, Lord de la Warr, and thus received the name "Delawares." In precontact times the Delaware villages, extending from the Hudson Valley to Chesapeake Bay, contained more than 12,000 people.[9] Politically unorganized through the 1600s, they were divided into three territorial segments in which three distinct Algonkian dialects were spoken. The Munsis, "People of the Stone Country," lived in the upriver highlands and often took the wolf as their totem. The Unamis, or "People down the River," had the turtle as their totem and lived on central stretches of the Delaware River. The Unalachtigo frequently used the turkey as their sign and were known as "People Who Live near the Ocean." Native terminology indicated broad geographical distinctions, not self-conscious political entities. But when Swedish, Dutch, and English newcomers began taking over their land, the three linguistic divisions became rallying points as various subdivisions tried to preserve their identity. Displaced

Unamis and Munsis later clung to separate dialects and forged new conceptions of ethnic solidarity. The Munsis, for example, showed they were capable of unilateral action and declared themselves a separate tribe in the face of white encroachment. Pre-Columbian Delawares had developed a wide variety of customs in response to different physical environments, but the pressures of eighteenth-century international politics forced narrower and more deliberate cultural identifications.

The Delawares shared most of the aboriginal ethos and world-view of the northeast woodland Algonkians. They flourished on a diet of cultivated corn, beans, and squash augmented by game, fish, and various wild plants. Wigwams provided shelter, and social organization followed generally matrilineal kinship patterns. Sachems and counselors usually inherited their rank, but their effectiveness depended on demonstrated wisdom and practical accomplishments. Religious leadership came from shamans. Every Delaware could communicate with the spirit world, especially his own guardian spirit, but the shamans specialized in doing so. In addition to lesser manitowuk, all of the Delawares worshiped Gicelamukaong (var. Kitannowit), supreme author of life, whose benevolent concern directed all events. Their annual Big House ceremony recapitulated a vital link with that deity through elaborate symbolism and twelve days of ritual dances.[10] Ceremonial propriety and pragmatic behavioral standards helped define a basically confident pattern of native life. The Delawares cooperated effectively with different forces in their environment and expected to triumph over death because Gicelamukaong's care extended beyond the grave.

Of all the whites who met Delawares during early times, the Quakers dealt more fairly with them than other colonial authorities. Men such as William Penn honored treaties and hoped to convert local Indians because they thought everyone was capable of sharing the universal Divine Light. Their initial conversations with the Delawares confirmed their idea that the Good Spirit lived in all humanity, but few natives adopted the Friends' silent worship and English customs. By 1700 Quaker missionary activity consisted of little more than a willingness to allow outsiders to join in their worship services. They agreed to receive Indians at their meetings whenever they came to town, particularly on occasions "when our Governor is willing to speak to them."[11] In short, instead of reaching out to benefit others, they expected spiritual reform to occur through providential action; accordingly, they were prepared simply to welcome like-minded believers into their religious community after conversion had taken place.

Presenting a sharp contrast with this was the vigorous Presbyterian missionary spirit, represented in David and John Brainerd. David Brainerd entered Yale in 1739 to study for the ministry, but an argument with college officials over discipline led to his expulsion in 1742. Though greatly disappointed by this turn of events, he was determined to become a missionary, and by November he secured an appointment from the SSPCK's New York commissioners. After wintering on Long Island as a supply preacher, Brainerd began missionary work at Kaunaumeek, a Mahican station twenty miles west of John Sergeant's Stockbridge. He lived there for less than a year, studying the native language with Sergeant and trying his hand at elementary sermons. In the spring of 1744 he toured the upper Delaware region, returned to Newark in June for ordination, and then journeyed southwest to launch a singlehanded effort. Encouraged by the SSPCK, Brainerd hoped to secure land at a place called "Forks of the Delaware," where the Lehigh and Delaware rivers meet, and build a Christian Indian community, but the fraudulent Walking Purchase (1737) had already stripped the Indians of their holdings in that area.

Thwarted in this design, Brainerd spent his few remaining years trying to find another effective missionary approach. He spoke through an interpreter, Moses Tattamy, because Mahican was useless in communicating with

Delawares. While preaching to Unami bands who remained in the area, he nevertheless boarded with white
families and often ministered to white congregations.
Physically weak, he experienced frequent bouts of illness
and psychological depression. Because of these problems
he never stayed in the mission field for extended periods.
He either went on furlough or traveled to the Wyoming
and Susquehanna valleys, ostensibly to plan missionary
strategy there; but none of these fitful efforts was fruitful,
and by June 1745 he began to look for another place,
where his work might be more productive.

A small group of Delawares still held some of their lands
near Trenton, New Jersey, at two sites named Crossweeksung and Cranberry. By this time the whites had occupied much of the surrounding territory for over a century. The displaced natives led a marginal existence,
peddling homemade wares to their more prosperous
neighbors. Decimated as they were by disease and reduced
to poverty by whiskey traders, they presented Brainerd
with an opportunity for the kind of missionary contribution he longed to make. They welcomed him warmly,
but for some reason he left Crossweeksung two weeks after
arriving. It seems evident that he could never decide
where his real mission lay—in New Jersey, at the Forks, or
farther west, among a jumble of different tribes along the
Susquehanna. Perhaps he envisioned an overarching mission with bases in all three areas, but his desultory visits
did not lay sufficient groundwork for lasting influence in
any of them.

Returning in August 1745 to Crossweeksung with
Moses Tattamy, whom he had baptized a month earlier,
Brainerd recognized the signs of a religious awakening.
Meetings began to attract as many as seventy Indians at a
time, with some people traveling forty miles to hear him
preach. He baptized twenty-five converts, but then he left
on another futile venture into central Pennsylvania.
Meeting indifference there, he traveled constantly to
escape despair—to sympathetic whites in Newark and on

Long Island, for consolation; to dwindling camps at the
Forks and farflung Jersey villages, to establish new contacts. His congenitally pessimistic feelings about himself
soured his attitude toward the Indians, too, as this journal
entry reveals:

> They are in general unspeakably indolent and slothful. They
> have been bred up in idleness and know little about cultivat-
> ing the land, or indeed of engaging vigorously in any other
> business.... They have little or no ambition or resolution.
> Not one in a thousand of them has the spirit of a man. And it
> is next to impossible to make them sensible of the duty and
> importance of their being active, diligent, and industri-
> ous.... It is to be hoped, that time will make a yet greater
> alteration upon them for the better.[12]

Holding such convictions about Indians and beset by misgivings concerning himself, it is remarkable that Brainerd
contributed anything at all beneficial to missions.

Approximately twenty-five Jersey Delawares celebrated
their first Lord's Supper in April 1746, eight months after
Brainerd had begun his mission among them. Church
membership exceeded the number of communicants, but
distance prevented many from observing the ordinance. In
the intervals when Brainerd tended this flock, he usually
lived with white neighbors, though he planned to build a
separate cabin for himself. He also made another futile trip
to Pennsylvania, only to return in October, grieving over
his lack of tangible success. Sick at heart and weak in body,
he left Cranberry in November on yet another con-
valescent journey and died in 1747 at the home of
Jonathan Edwards, who memorialized the young missionary by publishing a sketch of his life. David Brainerd
held an SSPCK commission for four years and spent a total
of sixteen months in New Jersey, the scene of his most
productive labors. Converts totaled no more than fifty, and
they received communion from him only three times. Still,
his published journals inspired others to volunteer for

missionary endeavor, where he had hoped to accomplish
more than he did.

David's younger brother, John, held the Jersey mission
together and augmented it during the next thirty years.
After graduating from Yale in 1746, John Brainerd became a Presbyterian minister in 1748 and received an
SSPCK commission as a regularly constituted missionary
to the Delawares. Beginning work with them at Bethel, a
new settlement near Cranberry, he first studied his
parishioners' personality traits. He noted that many of
their characteristics impeded Christian behavior, the
greatest obstacle being an "almost universal propensity in
the whole nation of Indians to strong drink." Their weak-
ness for liquor was seconded closely by what he termed
"an indolent, wandering, unsteady disposition." Brainerd
did not excuse alcoholism as a by-product of white influence, nor did he recognize his judgmental opinions as
expressions of cultural prejudice. Holding to his convictions, he condemned both native habits and tendencies
"so riveted into their natures that it is almost as difficult to
reform them . . . as to change their color."[13]

But John Brainerd was mentally tougher and more tenacious than his brother. He did not let Indian faults discourage him; instead he struggled for decades to deal with
their special needs. After much reflection he decided that
the best way missionaries could influence native Americans was to treat them kindly and show that Christian
spokesmen genuinely wished them well. He defined
ministers as God's instruments, appointed to seek the
good of everyone in their care. That holy work should not
stem from a compulsion to atone for personal guilt or a
desire to manipulate others. In a discussion of evangelical
methods, Brainerd disclosed both altruism and a culturally
conditioned bias:

> we do not despise them for their color, but for their heathen-
> ish temper and practices; . . . when they become Christians,

and behave as becomes such, *they shall have the same treatment as white people.*[14]

Despite his condescending ambition to improve conditions among Christian Indians, social pressures outside the mission made it impossible to treat them the same as white people.

In 1749 land-hungry whites around Cranberry foreclosed on the Bethel property and forced the natives back to Crossweeksung. Nine years later New Jersey paid the Delawares £1,000 for all land claims in the colony and established the Brotherton reservation for them in the pine barrens of Burlington County. Meanwhile, Brainerd found it difficult for other reasons to stay with his flock. The SSPCK terminated its arrangement with him in 1755, and he was forced to work in Newark as a supply preacher for four years. Then the missionary society recalled him, and the colonial governor also asked that he act as Indian "superintendent and guardian" at Brotherton. Brainerd served in that capacity for most of his life, even though both agencies failed to support him financially. At its peak the Indian population at Brotherton amounted to about 300 persons. By 1774, deaths and departures had reduced that figure to less than 60, of whom no more than a dozen were qualified to receive communion. Since these few required little time, Brainerd expanded his missionary concern to include destitute whites in the surrounding area. He frequented seven preaching stations for whites scattered between Cape May and the Shark River, ministering gratuitously in a region so desolate that no other Presbyterian clergyman entered the area for a century thereafter.

The reservation never provided stable living conditions for the Indians, for John Brainerd, or for the struggling church his brother had begun thirty years earlier. Loss of their land and their cultural integrity demoralized the Indians and left them prey to whiskey and ancillary vices. Many young Indians left the church to fight alongside co-

lonial military units, hoping perhaps to recover the warlike
dignity that had ennobled their forefathers; most of them
perished in the French and Indian War—twenty-two in a
single action at Fort William Henry in 1757. Turmoil
during the Revolution then worsened the Indians' lot, but
Brainerd held fast to his friends throughout their fatal decline. In 1768 he had added a white congregation in
Mount Holly to his other responsibilities, and financial
need and poor health apparently caused him to reside
there. But in 1775 he was back on the reservation again,
dividing his time between the Indians and a church on the
seacoast. In 1777 he moved from Brotherton for the last
time and accepted the charge of a white Presbyterian
church in Deerfield.

During the last four years of his life Brainerd continued
to visit Brotherton while ministering to whites in many
locations. He founded seven new churches and preached
regularly at twenty other stations in the district, but when
he died, in 1781, no one replaced him at those places or at
the decaying Brotherton mission. In 1801 the last Jersey
Delawares sold their reservation and joined other refugee
Indians at New Stockbridge, New York. In 1824, deciding
that their position there was hopeless too, this group,
composed of remnants of the three old missions—
Sergeant's of Massachusetts, Occom's of Connecticut, and
the Brainerds' of New Jersey—moved to a tract near
Green Bay, Wisconsin. Eight years later the federal government moved them to the Indian Territory, beyond the
Mississippi River, where they tried to preserve the customs that made them a separate, creative people. The effect of John Brainerd's mission had faded by that time, but
his effort to improve the quality of human life was not
totally lost on the surviving religious community in Oklahoma.

Of all eighteenth-century Indian missionaries, the Moravians, or United Brethren, produced the greatest number
of converts and Indian communities loyal to Christian
principles. They thought that regular evangelism indicated

a vital faith, and so they established Indian missions shortly
after reaching this continent. In 1742 Christian Rauch and
Gottlob Büttner opened a station at Shekomeko, among
the Mahicans of eastern New York, but the colonial authorities soon closed it. In 1747 other Moravians set up a
blacksmith shop and preaching station at Shamokin, in
Pennsylvania's Wyoming Valley. A year later a young assistant named David Zeisberger joined them and began
the work that made him the country's most distinguished
missionary. Shamokin lay in a region then dominated by
the Iroquois League, and Moravian bishops concentrated
on converting them instead of satellite tribes. Zeisberger
was ordained in 1749 and returned to Shamokin, assisted
by the son of a Shekomeko convert. His work did not go
well; numerous visits north into Iroquois territory gave no
promise either. Onondagas adopted the young evangelist
in 1752, but the French and Indian War dashed his hopes
for a fruitful mission among them. By 1756 his superiors
called Zeisberger home to focus his energies exclusively
on the Delawares.

Because of the unsettled conditions produced by border
warfare, Moravian evangelism was stalled for the next six
years. Indian converts fled from raiding tribesmen and
sought refuge among German Christians at Bethlehem,
but white prejudice against all natives made life hard for
them. Zeisberger led a group of Delawares back to
Gnadenhütten, their former village on the upper Lehigh,
after the European powers had signed a preliminary peace
agreement in 1762. But hostile Indians continued to
wreak violence and destruction in the region. Their leader
was an Ottawa chieftain named Pontiac, who refused to
recognize the Treaty of Paris, a self-serving pact drawn up
by diplomats unfamiliar with the territory. Fearful white
settlers created an ugly situation for the peaceful Moravian
Indians by blaming them for the attacks. In the face of
mounting antagonism, these Christian Indians surrendered
their arms, abandoned their villages once more, and suffered sixteen months' internment at Philadelphia "for their

own protection." Zeisberger stayed with his faithful Indians the whole time. He patiently endured the sneers of
the white colonists and kept the gospel alive in what
amounted to a prison camp. In 1765 pastor and people
were finally allowed to establish new homes north of the
Blue Mountains.

The Moravians had wanted their Indians to resettle near
Bethlehem, but the latter moved farther away because the
local animosities were too strong. The new settlement, on
the Susquehanna's North Branch at Machiwihilusing, was
named Friedenshütten by the German-born Moravians to
indicate the tranquillity everyone hoped it would
epitomize. The new village was a model of frugality and
order. Its success indicated how much the Delawares had
assimilated to what missionaries thought Christian civilization should embody. Friedenshütten boasted twenty-
nine log houses, each with windows and a stone chimney,
arranged facing each other along a single street. A large
chapel and schoolhouse stood in the center of the town,
immediately across from Zeisberger's house. Every home
had ample room for vegetable gardens and fruit trees. A
rail fence surrounded the village, enclosing large numbers
of cattle and hogs. Moravian Indians amazed visitors by
proving themselves to be industrious farmers who raised
plentiful crops and sold surplus corn, butter, and pork to
outsiders.[15]

But the relentless pressure of new settlers never abated.
Prosperous native towns did not convince land-hungry
whites that acculturated Indians could be trusted. The
image of churchgoing Indians simply allowed whites to
covet their fields more fervently and use harsher means to
push them westward. Zeisberger agreed with native leaders that it was better to leave their present surroundings
than to live with abusive neighbors. As early as 1767 he
began exploring the headwaters of the Allegheny River.
During the next few years he established several towns on
that stream and on the Beaver River, but Pennsylvania
afforded no real haven. So he went still farther west in

1771, preferring to stay with his Indian companions rather than enjoy physical comfort in some white settlement.

By May 1772 Zeisberger had located a favorable site in Ohio, one that promised a thriving economy and enough isolation to ensure what he hoped would be lasting peace. The Indians called the place Welhik-Tuppeek, "Beautiful Spring," and so it was translated Schönbrunn in the Moravian's missionary chronicle. Within months the first church bell summoned Indian and white parishioners to worship at a newly dedicated chapel. Mission work expanded along the Muskingum River as additional towns, such as Friedensstadt and Gnadenhütten, housed all Indians willing to live under Christian discipline. Resident Germans and trusted Delaware converts helped direct temporal and spiritual affairs, while Zeisberger supervised overall mission policy. During the next few years their efforts to spread the gospel touched many different tribes. All three divisions of Delawares had representatives in the Moravian towns, together with some Shawnee converts, Nanticoke and Conoy refugees, derivative Hurons called Wyandots or Mingoes, and a few Cherokees. Zeisberger was not satisfied with that accomplishment but wanted to travel farther afield, especially to Cherokee territory, where new missions beckoned. "Upon the whole," he wrote headquarters, "I wish I were free to leave here. There are so many other places where God's Word ought to be preached, and so many Indians who have not yet heard that their Maker is their Redeemer."[16]

Under benign Moravian care, Christian Indians wanted only freedom to pursue quiet, virtuous lives and follow their teachers' guidelines. They based community standards primarily on the Decalogue, affirming monotheistic beliefs and denouncing idolatry and the old witchcraft practices. They endorsed monogamous marriages and eschewed not only murder but lying and idleness as signs of an unregenerate life. Moreover, they vowed never to engage in warfare again, and they discouraged others from doing so by refusing to trade for goods captured in raids.

They bound themselves by written regulations to a disciplined life, where ministerial advice fostered harmony in
all daily activities.[17]

Unfortunately, international conflict again ruined whatever future that idyllic life might have had. From the beginning of the Revolution various native groups had been
advocating open warfare with whites on the frontier. In
fact, hostilities had never completely subsided since Pontiac's day, and warriors in the Northwest Territory called
for another general onslaught. Moravian Indians were
pacifists, but by 1781 it was impossible to survive between
local factions clamoring for war. So Zeisberger's mission
settlements had to move for the fourth time, but now they
were not at liberty to settle where they wanted. Pro-
English Shawnees forced the Moravians to abandon bountiful supplies at their old sites and escorted them north, to
winter on the shores of Lake Erie. Zeisberger was detained
in a Detroit prison while British troops carefully watched
his flock, which eventually settled in Ontario.

As if wartime displacement were not enough, tragedy of
another sort struck the Moravian mission in 1782. Part of
the refugee community made a quick trip south to retrieve
badly needed supplies left at their old townsites. A squad
of American militia from Fort Pitt chanced upon them
while they were packing their own possessions at Gnadenhütten. Many soldiers recognized them to be peaceful
Christian Indians, but frontiersmen argued that they harbored pro-British sympathies and should be killed. In the
past the Moravian Indians had usually dealt successfully
with native belligerents, but, as pacifists, they were not so
lucky when it came to mollifying woodsmen from Virginia
and Kentucky. Ninety of them—twenty-nine men,
twenty-seven women, and thirty-four children—were
clubbed, scalped, and burned.[18] In Canada their comrades
mourned their loss. Those who fell at Gnadenhütten were a
stark reminder of atrocities that could be committed in the
name of patriotism.

Though such events saddened him, Zeisberger con-

tinued to establish new mission settlements. He lived at
New Gnadenhütten in Ontario from 1782 to 1786, moved
to Pettquotting, or New Salem, Ohio, for four years, and
then returned to Canada, where he stayed until 1795.
After that he founded Goshen, across the Muskingum
from the old Gnadenhütten massacre site, and remained
there for a final decade. Zeisberger was seventy-four by
then, and he had to let others tend the half-dozen stations
built after the war. His last years were disappointing ones
because younger missionaries left their posts, too discouraged to continue. The Indians fell victim to the familiar pattern of drinking excessively, accepting fraudulent
land deals, and moving farther west to escape the never-
ending stream of whites who poured over the mountains
to displace them. Zeisberger died in 1808 amid the ruins
of his missionary work. He had labored on behalf of native
Americans for more than sixty years, but few white Moravians took his place, and no strong native leaders emerged
to hold the Ohio communities together. Few Christian
Indian groups survived in the United States as evidence of
Zeisberger's vocation, but faithful communities in Canada
made his teachings the foundation of strong religious testimony for succeeding generations.

Moravian missions also ended because of two larger
events that climaxed eighteenth-century Indian history:
the Battle of Fallen Timbers and the Greenville Treaty. In
August 1794, General Anthony Wayne defeated a combined force of several tribes, including Shawnees, Delawares, Miamis, and Ottawas. This military conquest
weakened native resistance to white immigration, and the
treaty, signed a year later, ceded almost two-thirds of Ohio
to federal control. In retrospect, that capitulation doomed
all tribes east of the Mississippi because it opened the door
for whites to move deeper and deeper into Indian lands.
British agents stirred up native resentment for two more
decades until the War of 1812 forced them to accept
American sovereignty in the Great Lakes region. Even
Tecumseh's eleventh-hour attempt to rally pan-Indian

resistance failed when the English no longer supported his
dream of native Americans as allies of the crown.
Greenville marked a real turning point in red-white relations, and that general situation affected missions
significantly.

As we have noted, during the eighteenth century the
European powers used native American groups for lever-
age in their imperial struggles. In doing so they usually
treated them as allies. French, British, and colonial American negotiators tacitly implied that they valued the Indian
tribes, that their power and influence made them integral
to future plans. As long as the Indians were pawns in the
larger chess game, they received a modicum of respect, but
after Fallen Timbers they lost that small advantage and
became simply obstacles in the path of American pioneers.
Once France and England withdrew from the Midwest,
American federal officials treated the Indians with a confidence bred of the knowledge that they faced no serious
rivals for territorial expansion. As the nineteenth century
began, national policy replaced foreign diplomacy as the
key factor in treating with Indians. That context greatly
affected theory and practice in subsequent Christian
missions.

6   *Missions in the Nineteenth Century (1803–90)*

Removal from the East

The possibility of British military aid to midwestern Indians ended in 1815 with the Treaty of Ghent. After that, the Indians faced a single republican government claiming sovereignty between the Great Lakes and the Gulf of Mexico. But American politicians had in fact inaugurated a new Indian policy even before the War of 1812. Instead of respecting aboriginal groups as separate nations with a right to their own distinctive cultures and to the land they inhabited, these national planners viewed them simply as impediments to expansion. Separate tribes and cultures were incompatible with homogeneous nationalism. The Indians were confronted with these alternatives: either assimilate to the body politic, with its white standards of civilization and religion, or continue their traditional practices somewhere else, without threatening the nation's prevailing ideology.

This essentially imperialistic attitude governed most red-white interaction through the nineteenth century. Missionaries worked more than ever on the assumption that one set of cultural standards—the one shared by churchmen and politicians—promoted both spiritual progress and national stability. They took it for granted that Christianity undergirded republican virtue and expressed that conviction with increased emphasis after the Con-

stitution called for the disestablishment of religion. When
most states followed federal precedent and refused to support churches with public revenues, religious leaders had
to adjust to a system of voluntary churches and to gain
wider patronage by arguing that Christianity was essential
to a properly functioning civic life. Religious principles
were supposed to pervade all facets of national experience,
including the Indians. Nineteenth-century missionaries
were citizens of the new nation who hoped to persuade the
Indians to accept civilized habits along with baptism as
integral parts of American culture. Anything that
threatened national homogeneity had either to be converted or removed.

White policymakers who wanted to assimilate the Indians into American society thought that agriculture offered the best means for changing them into civilized and
productive citizens. As early as 1793 Congress authorized
the President to furnish Indian tribes with domestic animals and farm tools, plus agents to demonstrate their use.
This assimilationist principle inspired the Intercourse Acts
of 1796, 1799, and 1802, though appropriations fluctuated.[1] Pessimists, on the other hand, arguing that Indians
would never accept white material culture and its value
system, insisted that the only lasting solution was to
quarantine them. They therefore called for treaties to provide new homelands where the Indians could follow life-
styles unacceptable among American citizens. The
Louisiana Purchase (1803) provided apparently unlimited
space for that kind of solution. So, as the nineteenth century began, President Jefferson and his successors frequently used the territory beyond the Mississippi as a
dumping ground for unassimilable eastern Indians. But
defenders of peaceful acculturation continued to promote
civilization as a desirable end too. The United States government had been vacillating between these two policies
since the Revolution.

Some agents of the advancing white population allowed
no kind thought about natives to hamper them. William

Henry Harrison, for example, did not believe that Indians had any capacity for living up to white standards, and his only policy was to remove as many of them as possible. In 1809 he negotiated the Treaty of Fort Wayne, by which much of Indiana and Illinois was acquired for white pioneer settlement. Harboring no misgivings about the Almighty's plans for this continent, he asked rhetorically, "Is one of the fairest portions of the globe to remain ... the haunt of a few wretched savages, when it seems destined by the Creator to support a large population and to be the seat of civilization?"[2] He then proceeded to back up this mandate with considerable military power. In 1811 he crippled a large force of Shawnees gathered on Tippecanoe Creek, and two years later his army crushed effective native resistance while scattering British troops at the Battle of the Thames.

To the south another forceful individual took steps to make ultramontane America safe for white settlers. Andrew Jackson did not admire native ways either, although he accepted the services of Indians who volunteered to make war against their traditional enemies. In 1813 he marched into Alabama to punish the hostile "Red Stick" Creeks for their successful attack on Fort Mims, and after five indecisive skirmishes he finally overwhelmed them in 1814, at the Battle of Horseshoe Bend. Collaborating "White Sticks" proved instrumental in that victory, but the Treaty of Fort Jackson lumped all Creeks together as if both factions had fought against Americans. Betraying his Creek allies, Jackson secured extensive new lands for white habitation by confining the bewildered natives to a small portion of their once proud domain.

Harrison and Jackson exemplified the way many whites dealt with Indians during the early national period. Perhaps few rivaled their militancy and draconian peace terms, but most of the pioneers beyond the mountains shared their opinion that different cultures required separate territories. According to these triumphant whites, America seemed chosen to rule vast stretches of the

beckoning continent, and red inhabitants would be wise to
protect themselves by moving out of the way.

Still, at the time these military conquests were reducing
Indian holdings east of the Mississippi, Congress passed a
bill (1819) that withheld the stick and offered another
carrot. It established a "civilization fund" to disburse
$10,000 annually for instructing Indians in agriculture, lit-
eracy, and other beneficial pursuits. The House Committee on Indian Affairs left no doubt about its reasons for
recommending such a bill:

> Put into the hands of their children the primer and the hoe,
> and they will naturally, in time, take hold of the plow; and as
> their minds become enlightened and expand, the Bible will be
> their book, and they will grow up in habits of morality and in-
> dustry, leave the chase to those of minds less cultured, and
> become useful members of society.[3]

Thus, measures intended to make amenable Indians
civilized and happy issued from Washington while treaties
were expelling others from the path of western farmers.
Since the government had no machinery for dispensing the
civilization fund, the churches used it to send missionaries
on a dual errand: to Christianize natives and teach them
the customs requisite to citizenship. Within that context,
schools became the most important focal point of
nineteenth-century missionary activity.

Protestants began forming missionary societies soon
after the Revolution to provide vigorous gospel witness in
the western regions. Between 1787 and 1820 they
established eleven denominational and interchurch bodies
to further missionary work. Not all evangelists enjoyed a
federal civilization-fund subsidy in the early national
period, but their efforts generally conformed to the dominant pattern it inspired.

Representative figures like the Baptist missionary Isaac
McCoy help illustrate their common objectives. Born in
Pennsylvania, McCoy, who was self-educated, moved in

his twentieth year to Indiana, where he began ministering
to white churches. His denomination's triennial conven-
tion appointed him missionary to the Indians in 1817,
seven years after his ordination. Working with natives in
Indiana and Illinois until 1829, he accompanied his
charges to Kansas when a treaty removed them from their
traditional homeland. McCoy labored there for twelve
years and in 1842 became corresponding secretary of the
American Indian Missionary Association, a post he held
until his death in 1846.

The Methodists also sponsored pioneering missionaries
in the midwestern states. Local preachers had worked occasionally with Indians in Ohio since 1806, but the first
effective evangelist was John Stewart, a freeborn mulatto
who was part Indian himself. From 1815 until his death in
1821 he lived with Wyandots in the Upper Sandusky area
and reported impressive results. James B. Finley continued Stewart's work for another seven years after the
Ohio annual conference appointed him official missionary
in 1819.

The group that sponsored the most efforts in this period
was the American Board of Commissioners for Foreign
Missions, an interdenominational agency created in 1810.
The ABCFM, which supported missions in all parts of the
country as well as overseas, expended half its funds before
1820 for evangelical work among North American Indians. Most of its workers came from Presbyterian or
Congregational churches, though missionaries of all
ecclesiastical backgrounds pursued essentially the same
goals. They included as part of their religious message a
determination to indoctrinate Indians with social and
moral qualities basic to civilized Christian behavior. One
missionary spoke for all of them when he said that the
purpose of his school was to instill in native Americans
"those habits of sobriety, cleanliness, economy, and industry, so essential to civilized life." No matter where
their stations were located, nineteenth-century mis-

sionaries agreed that proper religious influences would
Americanize the aborigines.

Mission schools everywhere tried to shape native
Americans into productive individuals whose values and
life-style would support the republic. Missionary-
sponsored farms and households served as models of piety
and industry for Indians to copy. As one supporting
agency explained its rationale in 1823,

> missionary Institutions, established to convey . . . the benefits
> of civilization and the blessings of Christianity . . . may look
> forward to the period when the savage shall be converted into
> the citizen; when the hunter shall be transformed into the
> mechanic; when the farm, the work shop, the School-House,
> and the Church shall adorn every Indian village; when the
> fruits of Industry, good order, and sound morals, shall bless
> every Indian dwelling.[4]

Evangelists in the field found it necessary to rectify
many specific details of Indian conduct. They insisted that
schoolchildren cut their hair, wear trousers and dresses,
use soap, water, and combs, adopt English names, sit in
chairs, eat with forks, and perform chores around the
house and farm. They confronted Indians with new behavior patterns based on startlingly different conceptions
of time and punctuality. Missionaries stressed industriousness as a normative work ethic; they redefined customary
sex roles in daily tasks and emphasized respect for private
property through laws that applied uniformly to everyone.
Evangelical programs amalgamated spiritual teachings with
white living standards, deliberately urging their superiority
in order to eradicate native American cultures.

The ABCFM tried to influence dozens of tribes, but the
Cherokees excelled all others in making a sophisticated
response to new religious and behavioral patterns. They
were an Iroquoian-speaking tribe, unlike most of their
neighbors, who spoke Muskhogean, but in other respects
they shared in the Southeast Woodlands culture. Located

in the mountainous sections of northern Georgia, eastern Tennessee, and western North Carolina, the Cherokees had lived there for centuries before the white explorers came. Spanish chronicles described them as established in hilltop villages by 1540, by which time they had adopted an ethos and world-view derived at least in part from ancient Mississippian motifs. By 1700 an estimated 22,000 Cherokees occupied sixty towns. There were three groups among them, speaking three separate dialects. Since they were less highly organized than the Creeks southwest of them, nothing indicated that the Cherokees would soon become nationally prominent.

Food was plentiful in the southeastern United States. Roots, berries, and nuts were the traditional Cherokee staples, and hunters supplied deer, turkey, black bear, and fish as meat supplements. The Cherokees also farmed domesticated crops in precontact times. They grew corn, beans, and squash as standard food items and cultivated sunflowers, bottle gourds, and tobacco for other purposes. They lived in small groups, using one type of building for winter, another for summer. Winter houses were built on a circular floor plan, sunk three feet below ground level, and had cylindrical walls and a conical thatched roof. Summer houses were rectangular, had gabled roofs, and sometimes reached seventy feet in length. They were often two stories high, and partially open walls provided relief from the heat. Such houses and cultivated fields denote a relatively sedentary people who seldom changed townsites. Their solid, competent material culture indicate that they had learned to deal successfully with their genial environment.

Clans, based on wide matrilineal kinship associations, were the most important Cherokee social unit. Each clan claimed a particular animal or natural phenomenon, such as Deer, Bear, or Wind, as its totem. Rather than indicating animal ancestry, their totems served as classificatory devices. Each person felt a strong sense of responsibility to other members of his fundamental identity group. Though clans did not own property collectively, some specific lineages within them did. Cherokees often practiced exogamous polygyny, a custom widely observed in the Southeast Woodlands culture area. Males usually married two or more women, often sisters. Political leadership resided in chiefs, who enjoyed no coercive power but depended on persuasive abilities to secure public cooperation. In town councils everyone, including women, could speak on whatever topics they wished. One headman was responsible for reconciling different opinions in time of war; another faced the same task in peacetime. Cherokee males were primarily warriors, but the purpose of their warfare was to retaliate upon their enemies and to gain individual honor; not to acquire land or property.

The Cherokees, like most other native American groups, achieved a symbiotic relationship with their natural surroundings by respecting supernatural forces through ritual propriety. The men performed special dances before embarking on a bear hunt and propitiated other animal spirits through raccoon-, beaver-, and buffalo-hunt dances. Human scalps were displayed to commemorate a successful foray into enemy territory. The most important religious rituals were performed during an annual eight-day ceremony, a feature of the Southeastern Ceremonial Complex, named Akawhungdin in Cherokee and generally called "Busk," or Green Corn Festival, throughout the region. At harvest time, officials rekindled the sacred fire in special houses on each town's public square. These New Year celebrations created a general atmosphere of reconciliation, in which old debts and feuds were canceled. Ceremonial leadership generally devolved on town councilors, who shared a great fund of religious lore. But there were more specialized functionaries whose training and accumulated religious wisdom definitely classifies them as priests rather than individualistic shamans.[5]

The Cherokees thought of this world as an island floating in a great body of water—imagery common to many Indian world-views. The water beetle began creation by bringing mud in typical earth-diver fashion from beneath the surface to form habitable land. By the time the Cherokees came to live in the center of their island home, a heavenly vault had been attached to it by strong cords at each of the four cardinal compass points. Great spirits—Sun, Moon, Great Thunderer (Kanati), and Corn (Selu)—lived in the upper world, but they rarely interfered with normal events. Closer to daily experience, innumerable spirits dwelt in the middle world to aid people in their daily affairs. Among these benevolent gods were the Immortals, who lived in towns inside the mountains. Another group, called the Little People, inhabited groves and caves, but their mischievous personalities did not endear them to the natives.[6]

Keepers of tribal lore told about Kanati, the first man, and Selu the first woman, in myths that sanctioned Cherokee customs. These prototypical narratives set the basic rhythms of tribal life, patterns for sex roles, and an equitable division of labor. Kanati's example showed that male responsibilities were hunting, defending the village, and making aggressive war. Selu performed the female tasks of cultivating domestic plants and maintaining the household. Sacred tales also depicted her as dying to germinate corn and other vegetables, just as seeds die to generate new plants. Both spirit beings went to the upper world and lived with the Sun, whom all Southeast Woodlands Indians revered as the most important deity. These dawn-time narratives indicate that the Cherokees regarded their universe as an orderly place, one in which causal relationships could be understood and suitable conduct could be prescribed. They thought that most spirits dealt justly with humanity and that respect for behavioral rules would yield practical advantages. As long as people enacted ritual observances properly, the gods would smile on both private ventures and communal pursuits.

The Cherokees sometimes blamed negative events—misfortune, illness, and death—on their own shortcomings, which had allowed the world to get out of

balance. But sometimes they blamed the malevolent underworld spirits, who wanted to drag things into chaos for
their own wicked reasons. Chief among these monsters
was Uktena, who possessed a huge serpentine body,
antlers, and large birdlike wings. Uktena also had a
diamond-shaped crest between its eyes that gave off
blinding flashes of light to paralyze its victims. Another
frightful being was Tlanuwa, modeled after the falcon and
said to be capable of killing unwary prey with its sharp
breast. Such demons usually lived under bodies of water or
in mountain caves, where they plotted ways to harm
people and so thwart the benevolent designs of the gods of
the upper world.

Just as there were ways to please beneficent gods, rituals
existed for diverting the evil beings who took pleasure in
ruin. Cherokee priests knew how to fend off monsters as
well as secure proper balance with supportive deities.
They helped cure diseases, predict the future, influence
weather conditions, and foster human prosperity in general. All in all, the Cherokees regarded their world as one
in which rewards and punishments confirmed their ethos
in practical terms. So they gloried in thisworldly existence
with an exuberance that presumably continued beyond
the grave. Tribesmen were uneasy about departed spirits
who stayed near their village, but they were certain that
each person's soul survived death. Most of them believed
that the souls of the dead went to live in the western sky at
a place where former social distinctions were relaxed.
There all Cherokees expected to resume the good life that
had meant so much to them in this world.

Sometime during the eighteenth century the Cherokees
decided that self-interest required them to adopt some
features of white civilization. Encouraged primarily by
mixed-bloods, they began to rely less on hunting and developed an intensive agricultural economy. Many lived in
frame dwellings and became successful businessmen. By
1817 the tribal chiefs decided to reorganize their government into a republic, patterning it after the United States

Constitution. Within a decade they had provided for a bicameral legislature, eight judicial districts, a supreme court, law-enforcement officers, and a tax system.[7] Aside from the intrinsic worth of such changes, Cherokees adopted them in a deliberate attempt to forestall removal from their beloved homeland. They reasoned that if Indians could internalize the virtues of neighboring Americans, there would be no need to move them away. Congress would not expel natives who shared the values and norms of white citizens.

Education played an important part in the Cherokee plan to appropriate American culture, and missionaries were instrumental here. As early as 1804 a Presbyterian minister named Gideon Blackburn established a school for Indian youths in eastern Tennessee. His work faltered for lack of funds, but the Cherokees, who by then considered themselves a nation, realized that schools were central to modernization and peaceful independence. They welcomed additional missionaries, who opened schools alongside model farms and chapels. In 1817 the interdenominational ABCFM sent Cyrus Kingsbury to build a network of academies along the Tennessee-Georgia boundary. He called the first mission station Brainerd in honor of the eighteenth-century pioneers, and, when he journeyed southwest to establish a mission among the Choctaws, he named that one after John Eliot.[8] In 1825 Samuel A. Worcester joined other dedicated missionaries at Brainerd, pledging himself to enhance Cherokee spiritual and material well-being through education.

Presbyterians and Congregationalists from the ABCFM were not the only missionaries to encourage rapid acculturation among the modernizing Cherokees. The Baptists sent Humphrey Posey in 1817 to establish a mission among them, but for some reason the Cherokees did not receive Posey's efforts favorably, and the mission made little progress until 1821, when Evan Jones arrived. Jones's evangelical labors produced lasting results, highlighted by the conversion and ordination, in 1829, of Kaneeds, the

first full-blooded Cherokee Baptist preacher. The
Methodists opened schools in 1825 and quickly gained
influence, counting John Ross and many other Cherokee
leaders as members. A wizened native called Turtle Fields,
veteran of the Creek War, became the first ordained
Cherokee Methodist clergyman. The Moravians also
helped teach the secular learning and moral habits the
Cherokees wanted to adopt; beginning with a mission
named Springplace, they founded another academy in
1821.

Bright native boys and girls applied themselves assidu-
ously to mission-school lessons. They quickly acquired the
rudiments of language, mathematics, and science that
placed them on a par with white children. Some became
clergymen like their mentors, and none in this category
excelled the accomplishments of Elias Boudinot, whose
Cherokee name was Galagina. After graduating from a
local academy, he studied for four more years at a mission
school in Cornwall, Connecticut, and spent another at An-
dover Theological Seminary. In 1823 he returned to help
his people identify the best aspects of white religion and
culture. Since literacy was one of the greatest boons, he
worked with Samuel Worcester to spread knowledge of
reading as far as possible. In 1819 a Cherokee silversmith
named Sequoya (Sikwayi) completed a decade's work by
producing a syllabary that reduced his native language to
written symbols. Boudinot and Worcester solicited funds
to buy a printing press and thus opened wide vistas for
people who could use the new alphabet. In 1828 the
Cherokee Phoenix became the first newspaper to publish
articles in both English and a native American language.
Worcester also translated portions of Scripture into
Cherokee, and the press at New Echota, Georgia, printed
them, plus tracts, hymnbooks, and other religious literature.

By 1828 the Cherokees had reached a pinnacle of successful acculturation. In the aggregate they owned 22,000
cattle, 46,000 swine, 7,600 horses, and 2,500 sheep. They

used innumerable plows, wagons, and spinning wheels and operated 762 looms, 31 gristmills, 61 blacksmith shops, and a powder mill. They had built many churches, 18 schools, long stretches of public road, and 18 ferries. Sequoya's alphabet made it possible for natives of all ages to master reading in a short time, and the *Cherokee Phoenix* did its part to create an enlightened citizenry. Some white plantation owners grudgingly admitted that the Cherokees were obviously civilized by southern standards, because they owned nearly 600 African slaves. Their place in American life seemed to be secure. Then two events occurred in quick succession to dispel that illusion. In 1829 Andrew Jackson became president, and whites discovered gold in northern Georgia.

Jackson had always sided with the white Americans who thought the best way to handle Indians was to push them off any land that white people wanted. He scoffed at the absurdity of respecting native Americans as independent nations, and with federal power finally at his disposal he intended to make that view the dominant one. More locally, the state of Georgia had been urging the Cherokees since 1802 to relinquish their lands and make room for a burgeoning white population. John Ross and most other native leaders had opposed making any concessions, and Jackson's election was a serious blow. The new president let it be known that Indians must acknowledge the jurisdiction of the state in which they lived or else move beyond the Mississippi. In pursuance of that principle, he pushed the Indian Removal bill through Congress in May 1830. The vote was narrow, but the victory was substantial. Most Indians in the Southeast capitulated shortly thereafter—the Choctaws in 1830, the Chickasaws, Creeks, and Seminoles in 1832.

But the Cherokees remained where they were. They sent their educated spokesmen to Washington to urge compromises and preserve cooperative independence, and Worcester and other missionaries encouraged them to maintain their own republican government where they

already were. In 1830 Georgia passed a law requiring all
whites to leave Cherokee country, but the missionaries
remained with their people. State officials subsequently
arrested eleven white clergymen and several of their assistants and sentenced them to four years in a local pen-
itentiary for violating the expulsion decree. Georgia's
governor offered to pardon the missionaries on certain conditions, but Worcester and Elizur Butler refused. To accept pardon, they said, would amount to abandoning not
only their Indian friends but their Christian duty. They
therefore languished in prison while their lawyers ap-
pealed their case to the Supreme Court of the United
States. One of the lawyers pleading on behalf of the
Cherokee nation was John Sergeant, great-nephew of the
first missionary to Indians at Stockbridge. In 1832 Chief
Justice John Marshall delivered the majority opinion in
Worcester vs. *Georgia.* He ruled that state laws did not apply
within Indian territories and that the missionaries should
be released. The state authorities of Georgia refused to
honor the decision, and Jackson declined to take any action forcing them to do so. Thus, even though the
Cherokees had won a favorable decision in the highest
American court, they still faced implacable whites who
were determined to seize their land. The ministers stayed
in jail; whites continued to encroach on Indian holdings;
and federal officials allowed the doctrine of states' rights to
harden into a mindset that contributed to civil war three
decades later.

By 1833 Worcester finally admitted that his confronta-
tion with state authorities no longer served a useful purpose. He accepted clemency and began urging his Indian
friends to accept the inevitable expulsion. Cherokee
negotiators under John Ross still held out, but a small
clique, including Elias Boudinot, signed a removal agreement at New Echota in 1835. Antitreaty factions resisted
until the bitter end, arguing that the surprise pact was
illegal because it did not represent the majority of the
Cherokees; but the officials in Washington and Atlanta had

what they wanted and proceeded with plans to expel the
Indians.[9] The federal government also cut off its appropriation ($2,500) to the ABCFM on the ground that its field-
workers had contravened national policy by resisting the
removal. Worcester left for Oklahoma in 1835 and continued missionary work there for his remaining twenty-
four years. Boudinot stayed with Indian friends in Georgia
until 1838, when most of them left their homeland at
bayonet point. Later that year several embittered
Cherokees assassinated him and two others because, in
their eyes, all of the Indian treaty-signers had betrayed
their people.

The tragic tale of human suffering in 1838–39, caused
by white greed and cruelty, has been told often enough.
The removal was traumatic, not only for the Cherokees,
but for the Indians in the west. The Plains Indians did not
welcome the refugees, and the resulting hostilities forced
the easterners to adopt warlike habits again instead of the
peaceful ways they had come to appreciate. Many found it
necessary to resume hunting rather than use their acquired
agricultural skills. After 1859 the displaced Southeast
Woodland natives became known as the Five Civilized
Tribes. At first they fell into political factions, disillusioned
and demoralized as they were by the horrors of removal.
But they refused to be broken, and they did not blame the
missionaries for their plight. Instead of rejecting Christianity as some malignancy of white culture, they continued in the faith. Cherokee support of Christian precepts
since 1838 attests to the lasting values they perceived in its
message.

Pacification in the West

Today's Indian stereotypes are usually derived from the
culture of the Great Plains Indians, who in fact constituted
a small minority within the aboriginal population and
figured only in the later years of the contact with whites.
Their impact on the white collective consciousness after

the Civil War has influenced the white imagination far out
of proportion to their numerical strength. Typical examples of these tribes were the Caddoan-speaking Pawnees,
located in Nebraska, the Algonkian-speaking Arapahoes
of Colorado, and the Cheyennes of Wyoming. Farther
north were the Crows, Siouan-speaking bands, who
flourished in Montana, and the Blackfeet, another
Algonkian derivative, who inhabited upper Montana and
Alberta. To the west of them were the Flatheads, part of a
subgroup known as Salish, who lived in Montana's Bitterroot country. Living generally north and east of them were
the Dakotas, mainstays of the Hokan-Siouan linguistic
stock, who epitomized Plains culture for most nineteenth-
century observers.

At some point the Ojibwas coined a term Nadoues-
sioux, meaning "Snakes" or "Enemies," in pointed reference to the warlike Dakotas. European chroniclers
shortened this word to Sioux, for convenience. The people
in question, however, always referred to themselves as
Dakotas (Lakotas and Nakotas in other dialects), which in
their own language meant "Friends" or "Allies." In precontact times they occupied most of the land between
Lake Superior and the two states now bearing their name.
Though Dakotas considered themselves one people with a
common baseline culture, they possessed no cohesive
political structure. Seven divisions formed three broad
alignments: the Mdewakantons, Wahpekutes, Sissetons,
and Wahpetons constituted the Santee, or eastern group;
the Yanktons and Yanktonais lived in the middle; and the
Tetons formed the great western segment. The Teton
Dakotas were by far the most numerous, counting seven
major tribes: the Oglala, the Brulé, the Hunkpapa, the
Miniconjou, the Sans Arc, the Blackfeet, and the Two-
Kettle. There are no reliable figures on the overall Dakota
population at the time of contact. Early nineteenth-century
demographers estimated that the Santee group was made
up of approximately 6,000 persons, so the overall total
probably exceeded three times that number.[10]

By the 1750s the Ojibwas in the area of the Great Lakes obtained firearms from European traders and began to use them against their Dakota enemies, many of whom consequently moved west, abandoning their marginal agricultural and woodland habits for a more nomadic life-style on the treeless plains. They pushed beyond the Minnesota River during the first half of the eighteenth century and penetrated Missouri River territory during the next fifty years. By the early decades of the nineteenth century, Dakota hunters had adapted their culture to the new conditions and formed one of the strongest native complexes to hold out against white conquest. The horse and rifle were important European culture traits, but these borrowed items were incorporated into a predominantly aboriginal ethos compatible with a precontact world-view. The Plains culture of the Dakotas shows that selective borrowing and internal cultural adjustment are not inherently destructive processes, but the white encroachment, political mismanagement, and philanthropic misunderstanding that made nineteenth-century red-white interaction a heavily one-sided exchange eventually overwhelmed this native culture too.

The Dakotas' territory offered limited food supplies, but they made the most of what they had. In the eastern sections they planted corn, but the yields were meager. The real staples were small game and wild plants, especially rice. The tribes farther west depended almost exclusively on hunting, with the buffalo (or bison) supplying most human needs. Buffalo meat was unquestionably the staff of life, the largest item in most western Dakotas' daily fare; moreover, the hides provided material for clothing, moccasins, robes, beds, and storage containers, the horns and bones were fashioned into tools and weapons, and the sinews became thread, bowstrings, and rope. Even Dakota houses were made from buffalo skins, and people used droppings from the herds for fuel. Eastern Dakotas lived in bark houses during the summer but used warmer con-

ical skin tents, called *tipis,* in the winter months. The
Western Dakotas, who had to travel with the migratory
buffalo herds, used the easily portable tipis all year long.

Like those of many hunting cultures, Dakota kinship
relations tended to emphasize patrilineal descent, but ties
with both the father's and mother's families were important. There were no strong clan affiliations to nurture personal identity. Voluntary warrior and hunting societies
partially filled those needs for men; their other ego
requirements had to be met by individual exploits. Each
Dakota band had its own chief, who sometimes inherited
his office but most often filled it by proving himself steady
and reliable. After attaining his rank through demonstrated wisdom, success as a warrior, or acquired wealth, a
chief usually managed tribal affairs by consulting majority
opinion. No single chief controlled an entire tribe, and,
when the separate bands convened for summer hunts,
spokesmen from each of them met to consider the issues
and decide on collective action.

Dakota kinship patterns and political structure both indicate that the Plains culture valued individual initiative.
Singlehanded achievements procured honor, meaning, and
status. Significant honors could be won, for example, by
stealing horses from enemy camps, by hunting or scouting
well, and by giving sound counsel for the tribe's corporate
benefit. But warfare was the supreme theater of action,
and the entire Dakota milieu encouraged young men to
increase their prestige through combat. Success consisted
primarily in touching or "counting coup" on a foe without
necessarily killing him. In exertions that achieved ritual
significance, warriors tried to break through an enemy's
sphere of spiritual protection, strike him, and live to tell
the tale. Dakota culture thus placed the greatest priority
on individual bravery, daring, and ingenuity. Whether one
acquired scalps or not was incidental to the signal
accomplishment of counting coup. This value system made
the Dakotas one of the most warlike of all native American

groups, and the emphasis on the individual meant that a Dakota faced both the human and the spiritual aspects of his universe alone.

Success in war, acceptance in men's organizations, status in the tribe, satisfactory family life, all good things came through valid contact with divine power. Dakotas expected each person to seek that contact through visions. Especially at puberty, youths participated in a religious ceremony that emphasized a solitary spiritual quest featuring isolation, fasting, sleepless vigils, and prayers for supernatural aid in subsequent endeavors. As prescribed by custom, the person left camp and found a secluded spot where he could concentrate alone. With little food, drink, or sleep, the seeker spent days imploring divine beings to touch his life through direct revelation. Sometimes, as a special sacrifice, he would gash his arms with a knife or cut off a finger joint to impress the gods with his sincerity and determination. A unique vision usually occurred, often involving natural phenomena or animals who spoke to the quester and gave him a specific orientation for his life as an adult. After returning home and recounting his experience to elders who could interpret visions, the new warrior adopted a name derived from his dream and preserved some artifact to commemorate the event. That fetish, kept in a "medicine bundle," protected its wearer in battle and helped him communicate with the divine world when he tried to reestablish contact.

Most Dakota religion consisted of private rituals in which individuals established contact with spirit power for specific ends, but one very significant ritual involved community participation. Sometime near midsummer, men volunteered for the intricate Wiwanyag Wacipi—the Sun Dance—a hallowed form of worship that redounded both to the central participants' credit and the tribe's general well-being.[11] This ceremony, which required two consecutive sets of four days to perform, included elaborate rituals that ranged from erecting a special lodge to preparing the dancers for their ordeal. The most solemn mo-

ments occurred during the final days, when volunteers
allowed supervisors to skewer their flesh (chest or back)
and connect them to a central pillar with rawhide thongs.
A buffalo skull occasionally served as a substitute dead-
weight. Then the volunteers would blow eagle-bone whistles and dance while gazing ecstatically at the sun. They
continued for hours until the thongs ripped the skewers
from the flesh and pain or exhaustion made them collapse.
The visions they experienced in this condition were especially sacred. As the paramount feature of Dakota ritual,
the Sun Dance singled out fortitude and endurance as virtues that spread general blessings to all participants in the
holy act and to the tribe as a corporate body. Together
with vision quests, they manifested the sacrificial intensity
with which Plains Indians dedicated themselves to religious propriety.[12]

There were no fixed, automatically efficacious methods
for achieving individual communion with the spirit world.
Self-denial and supplicatory prayer were always practiced,
but, apart from these, no approach to the divine realm
worked equally well for everyone. All males were expected to achieve a successful vision on their own at puberty, and Plains culture encouraged them to repeat this
experience in adult life so that the spirit beings would
continue to direct their activities. A few made the noblest
effort by undergoing the Sun Dance ordeal, but those who
did so do not appear to have formed a special class of
religious leaders. Spiritual experience thus did not produce a priesthood or even a regularly functioning class of
shamans. Some Dakotas did receive wide recognition for
outstanding spiritual accomplishments, and they were
called "holy men" or "medicine men." But there was no
office to distinguish one person's religious ability from
another in Plains culture, for the ability to communicate
with the spirit world was something everyone possessed.
Religious eminence therefore depended on the quantity of
one's attainments, not on possessing a special gift, a special
identity.

In keeping with the Dakotas' individualistic, action-oriented approach, their religious teachings formed no rigid doctrinal system; various metaphysical explanations accommodated different specific experiences. Nevertheless, they had relatively straightforward conceptions, not only of the more important divine beings, but of the origin of the created world and of the afterlife.

To begin with, they used the term Wakan Tanka as a general designation for all benevolent power. Anything that struck someone as extraordinary was said to have mana-like qualities called *wakan*. It could exist in an object, place, person, discrete event, or repeated ritual, and Wakan Tanka was the most comprehensive reference to that force.

Of all the deities who blessed mankind, the Sun was the most important. The Dakotas referred to him as Wi and considered him author of the principal virtues: bravery, fortitude, generosity, and loyalty. As the chief inhabitant of the heavens, he was the object of intense liturgical praise. His special color was red. The Sky, named Skan, also resided in the upper atmosphere and from that vantage point judged the actions of men and the other gods. His color was blue. Maka, the Earth, was thought to be mother of all material objects; green usually signified her presence as patroness of all growing things. Inyan, or Rock, symbolized by yellow, was the ancestor of all beings; he was considered to be the source of authority and vengeance. Other deities who were benevolent, like these first four, but lacked their awesome power, included Moon, Wind, and Tatanka, the buffalo god. There were also many sinister beings who threatened Dakota life. The Mini Watu, who looked and acted like maggots, sought to penetrate human bodies and cause internal disorders. The Can Oti tried to lead people astray by confusing their sense of direction. Giga and Ungala were imps and goblins who also tried to bring misfortune. Indians attributed most calamities to one or another of these wicked beings, whose central purpose was always to make trouble.

The Dakotas' fierce celebration of the life of action
valued dominance over enemies and endurance in the face
of hardships. When death came, it posed no threat to their
world-view and did not invalidate their spartan virtues.
Plains people usually placed bodies on scaffolds and left
them to deteriorate while the tribe continued to follow
roving herds of game. As they did not fear death, they did
not shun contact with those recently dead. Families often
kept mementos, such as a finger or lock of hair, to evoke
someone's memory. Sacred bundles of such articles constituted a portable graveyard, where those who had passed
beyond death could still offer consolation to the families
preserving them. Burial practices, together with ritual observances and aggressive values, show that the Dakotas
lived in a setting where spiritual powers and proper human
action complemented each other in a harmonious universe. Vigorous behavior and divine guidance coalesced to
make the Great Plains a place redolent with potential success.

Missionary activity among tribes native to the plains and
those placed there by treaty increased after 1830. Protestants and Catholics contacted almost every aboriginal
group to acquaint them with the teachings of the gospel
and with white civilization. By 1835 most tribes knew that
the missionaries wanted to alter their culture with schools,
agriculture, and Christian morals. In that year the first of
several epidemics also struck, devastating the native
population and lowering the collective resistance to white
influences. Smallpox ravaged the plains four times between 1835 and 1860. That scourge reduced many tribes
by 50 percent and in one case, the Mandans, left a bare 10
percent of its people alive. A cholera attack in 1849 produced further heavy casualties. These terrible encounters
with disease created more cultural disorientation than any
other white intrusion into Indian territory.

Many selfless Catholics conducted evangelical activities
among the Plains Indians, but none achieved more public
recognition than Pierre Jean De Smet, Jesuit missionary

and publicist. After spending two years at a struggling
Potawatomi mission near Council Bluffs, Iowa, this Bel-
gian priest visited Flathead country in the Rocky Mountains. French trappers and Iroquoian Catholics had convinced the Flatheads that the Jesuits were trustworthy, so
in 1831 they petitioned the Jesuit headquarters in Saint
Louis for a missionary. After four such requests, De Smet
went in 1840 to investigate the situation and assess the
feasibility of establishing a mission station so far away. One
year later he installed two Jesuits and three lay brothers at
Saint Mary's Mission in the Bitterroot Valley. De Smet
traveled to Europe several times, recruiting personnel and
soliciting funds to spread a mission network throughout
the Great Northwest. His peripatetic but zealous activities
greatly increased the number of gospel enterprises in Oregon.[13]

Work among the Flatheads subsided within a decade,
and Catholic overtures to the Blackfeet after 1845 also
met with little success. But the Catholic missionary
Nicholas Point initiated promising activities among the
Coeur d'Alenes in 1841, as did Adrien Hoecken among
the Kalispels in 1845, and, when these two tribes left
northern Idaho and Washington to live on a predominantly Flathead reservation, the Jesuit priests followed and
expanded their work to include all native groups residing
there. A school they started in 1864 has continued operations to the present.

Catholic missions to the Dakota tribes began in 1841,
when Augustin Ravoux went to live among the Santees in
Minnesota. No immediate successor pursued the work
after his few years' residence, but Ravoux had translated a
catechism and hymnal into native dialect, an effort that
proved useful later in the century. The Protestants also
attempted mission stations in eastern Dakota territory,
some with only temporary success; among these were the
Methodists and a contingent of Reformed clergymen from
Switzerland, who initiated evangelical programs, but
neither of these efforts lasted more than a decade. The

Protestant Episcopal church also expanded its horizon to
include the Dakotas; in 1860, inspired by the work begun
by James L. Breck among the Ojibwas and encouraged by
their new bishop, Henry B. Whipple, the Minnesota Episcopalians expanded their Indian missions. This modest beginning gave Whipple the opportunity to acquaint himself
with general conditions among native Americans, and for
four decades he was a nationally prominent advocate of
fair dealing in federal Indian policies.

It was Presbyterian and Congregational missionaries,
supported by the ABCFM, who inaugurated the first sustained missions to the eastern Dakotas. In 1835 several
individuals arrived at Fort Snelling to begin their missionary enterprise. They included Jedediah D. Stevens,
former missionary to the Stockbridge Indians in Wisconsin, and Thomas S. Williamson, a medical doctor as well as
an ordained minister. Two other activists, Samuel W. and
Gideon H. Pond, had recently arrived in the territory, but
at the moment they held no commission from the American Board. An additional clergyman and linguist, who later
contributed materially to gospel efforts, was Stephen R.
Riggs, who arrived in 1837. This group of missionaries
placed great emphasis on schools from the very beginning,
and one of the most important of these, at Lac qui Parle,
attracted approximately fifty children during each of its
first fifteen years. Mastering native idioms, Riggs helped
compile a Dakota vocabulary and saw a jointly composed
grammar and dictionary through to publication. He and
Williamson began translating the Bible into Siouan with
the help of a French trader who lived in the area. Over the
years the ABCFM missionaries published translations of
John Bunyan, Isaac Watts, elementary readers, catechisms,
and hymnals. Instead of insisting that conversion entailed
using English, they tried to build a solid understanding of
Christian principles by using the Dakotas' own linguistic
patterns.

As resident missionaries labored, white settlers
streamed into the area. Federal action protecting these

newcomers' interests led to disturbing but ultimately beneficial results for the missions. In 1851 the Santee Dakotas ceded most of their land to the United States and agreed to confine themselves to two reservations along the Minnesota River. Seven years later they accepted further restriction by giving up half of their remaining acreage. Since Lac qui Parle was the only mission left in the newly defined Dakota district, the missionaries abandoned five other stations and erected new ones in order to stay with the natives. Riggs established a new mission popularly known as Hazlewood, built near another one called Yellow Medicine. In time the Dakotas regretted losing their extensive territory; but the missionaries, noticing that many Indians hostile to Christianity chose to move away rather than accept confinement, accepted the hardships caused by the treaties because the new conditions not only screened out native opposition but curtailed the nomadic tendencies of those who stayed.

ABCFM missionaries developed a solid nucleus of native students around new boarding schools when reservation life made the Dakotas more sedentary. They taught reading and writing in Siouan and mathematics, geography, and American history, in addition to gospel lessons. The daily routine also included physical training—domestic chores for girls and manual labor for boys in the barn and woodshed. Dakota mission schools confronted the same situation that others had met in a score of different settings. White instructors tried to convince their charges that literacy and diligent habits brought their own reward by fostering Christian character. They struggled to change customary dress and general appearance, with Riggs assuring potential warriors that the "gospel of soap was indeed a necessary adjunct and outgrowth of the Gospel of Salvation."[14] Once reformed behavior had become ingrained in the students, together with a new work ethic, differentiated by sex roles, the missionaries hoped that aboriginal preferences for polygamy, subsistence hunting,

communal property, and glorification of war would dis-
appear. They also hoped the Indians would acquire such
virtues as temperance and Sabbath observance after accepting the quieter pace of settled agricultural living.

Most Indians on the Santee reservations resisted
thoroughgoing acculturation, but Riggs was quite
successful with one small group. In 1856 seventeen
Wahpeton converts, including eight mixed-bloods, formed
themselves into a separate band. They chose a new chief
and asked federal authorities to recognize them as a discrete unit having no connections with their unbaptized
tribesmen. Their constitution proclaimed the existence of
Hazlewood Republic, a community founded on explicitly
religious bases and one that attempted to reproduce a
microcosmic American culture on reservation land. The
first requirement for citizenship in Hazlewood's em-
bryonic Christian state was rejection of polytheism and
belief in the one true God. Members further pledged to
conduct their lives according to God's Word as white
ministers expounded it from the Bible. Citizens were also
urged to adopt a full range of white manners, including
their dress code. It was hoped that the constitution would
train the Hazlewood residents in responsible local government and eventually qualify them for American citizenship. Anticipating that kind of assimilation, the signers
asked federal officials to allot their agricultural land indi-
vidually and guarantee them private property rights.[15]

As often happened in missionary experiments, outside
influences disrupted the modest Christian Indian community before it had had time to become fully established. In
1862, in a time of desperate food shortage, the natives
rebelled when federal agents were unable to secure food
allotments, the only supplies that kept reservation Indians
from starving. Violence quickly escalated, and soon open
warfare spread through half of Minnesota. A minor village
chief named Little Crow reluctantly accepted leadership
because he knew that the hasty action of a few rash youths

would inevitably bring white retaliation. Most Christian
Dakotas refused to join in killing whites, and some displayed genuine heroism by rescuing missionaries from
dangerously isolated posts. Three Hazlewood citizens—
the president, Paul Mazakutemane, who was also an elder
in the church, and John Other Day and Simon
Anawangmani—were conspicuous in urging peace and
showing humanitarian concern for whites.

When the bloodshed ended, the white military forces
herded all Dakotas together with typical lack of discrimination. They had failed to capture most of the real
combatants, who moved to Canada or farther west to
blend with their Teton cousins. The prisoners, confined at
Mankato, and the noncombatants, who surrendered at
Fort Snelling, endured a winter of disease and uncertainty,
recriminations and despair. Courts-martial found hundreds of men guilty, but President Lincoln commuted
most of the death sentences. The Army hanged thirty-
eight and shipped the remainder to safer reservations.

Missionaries from several denominations visited the
prison camps and reported many conversions. Of the 400
prisoners at Mankato, all but 10 accepted some form of
Christianity. The ABCFM missioners claimed over 300;
Episcopal and Catholic priests baptized the rest. A similar
revival occurred at Fort Snelling, where the Episcopal
pastor counted 300 new Dakota converts, the Catholic
chaplain over 180, and the ABCFM missionary almost
150. Given the circumstances, the remarkable thing about
these conversions is not that they occurred but that these
new Christians remained faithful after their traumatic
prison experience had ended. In early 1863 the Mankato
prisoners were transferred to a camp near Davenport,
Iowa; at length they were reunited with their families at
Fort Thompson on the Missouri River. Finally, the whole
group settled at the mouth of the Niobrara River in Nebraska. Christian Indians still preferred to live by themselves according to gospel teachings. Many stayed at the

Niobrara, but by 1872 others gathered on small homesteads near Flandreau, South Dakota, where they maintained an inconspicuous native identity. Their community
still exists today and houses the federal government's
largest Indian boarding school.

The story of this mission, like that of so many others,
contains elements of idealistic dedication and unwarranted
suffering caused by the larger forces of intercultural conflict. Indian Christians were always a minority on the reservations. They absorbed new values and behavioral standards but did so without totally rejecting their precontact
identity. Circumstances beyond the control of either the
missionaries or their small flocks threatened to obliterate
changes in belief and ethics pursued for decades. The fact
that native churches survived uprooting and endured years
of racist discrimination attests to the fortitude with which
the converts embraced their new faith and way of life.

Government Reform, Native Revitalization

By the late decades of the nineteenth century many whites
thought a solution to the Indian problem was within their
grasp. Military forces had suppressed most of the hostile
natives, and the path to full acculturation seemed clear if
federal legislators could simply institute further reforms.
The 1875 Red River War ended major native hostilities on
the southern plains. Pockets of resistance remained, where
Indians struggled for independence, but their free days
were numbered. Most Dakota warriors reluctantly agreed
to live on reservations after their last victory on the Little
Bighorn (1876), and the surrender of Chief Joseph's Nez
Percé forces (1877) ended large-scale warfare in the
northern sector. Moreover, the buffalo herds had been
dwindling since 1820, and their virtual extinction a half-
century later destroyed the basis of Plains culture. The
new transcontinental railroad was bringing greater numbers of whites to the grasslands. The reservations seemed

to be the only place where the Indians could cling to their
traditions, but, even there, various well-intentioned reformers did not leave them alone. After generals Sherman
and Sheridan had harried the western Indians onto the
reservations, larger problems remained. Government officials and missionaries put the stick away and resorted to
the carrot again in further attempts to transform these
separate peoples into Americans.

Corrupt government officials had hampered efforts to
civilize native Americans, so in 1869 President Grant instituted reforms everyone hoped would improve the situation. Grant's Peace Policy—often called the "Quaker
policy" because influential Friends first suggested it—
covered two basic areas. It created a Board of Indian
Commissioners, on which wealthy Christian laymen
served voluntarily to monitor the government's procure-
ment system. Board members had no direct authority but
could recommend action when they pinpointed corrupt
practices. The new policy also invited churches to participate in nominating Indian agents; it was hoped that church
involvement would both weed out dishonest or in-
competent personnel and enhance the religious training of
the Indians.[16]

As a result of this policy, thirteen denominations exercised control over seventy-three agencies, with each
church monopolizing evangelical activities in designated
jurisdictions. These assignments did not acknowledge
historical missionary influences or current religious affiliations among the Indians, especially pluralistic ones. The
Methodists, for example, had not been very active in Indian missions, but, given fourteen reservations, they assumed responsibility for more tribes than any other denomination. The Catholics expected to administer a great
many native protectorates but received only seven, despite
centuries of previous contact across the continent. In 1874
they therefore formed the Bureau of Catholic Indian Missions to counteract federal prejudice and to augment their
native evangelical apostolate.

By the 1880s the interest in reforming Indian gover-
nance by nominating exemplary agents had waned. The
procedure simply did not create a more effective administration, and it produced more interdenominational rivalry
than it did native converts. Enthusiasm therefore developed for a new measure, one that promised to make natives self-supporting individuals who could live peaceably
with white neighbors.

In 1871 Congress ended its practice of treating native
groups as sovereign units, but tribal separatism persisted.
Many reformers concluded that their common ownership
of land contributed to the Indians' ethnic consciousness
and their consequent refusal to be absorbed into the
American mainstream. The Board of Indian Commissioners reflected this prevailing analysis:

> [I]t is evident that no 12,000,000 acres ... can long be kept
> simply as a park, in which wild beasts are hunted by wilder
> men. This Anglo-Saxon race will not allow the car of civiliza-
> tion to stop long at any line of latitude or longitude on our
> broad domain. If the Indian in his wildness plants himself on
> the track, he must inevitably be crushed by it.[17]

Rather than crush outright those who were unwilling to
accept Anglo-Saxon civilization, the federal authorities decided simply to erode their ability to withstand it.

In 1887 Congress passed the General Allotment Act,
sometimes named after Henry Dawes, its chief supporter.
It capped two decades of reform sentiment by authorizing
the President to carve up the Indian reservation lands and
distribute a quarter-section (160 acres) to each Indian who
headed a family and an eighth-section to each bachelor
over eighteen years of age. It also offered American
citizenship to all natives who accepted such allotments and
promised to live on their homesteads away from other
tribesmen. All surplus reservation land—that is, any that
was not apportioned to individual Indian owners—became
available for white settlement.[18] The General Allotment

Act, by pushing natives into separate ownership, threatened communal property, one of the basic foundations of Indian culture and cohesion. For all its reformist intentions, the act also opened the way for whites to acquire the "surplus" acres immediately and to gain additional holdings through leases or subsequent purchase. Between 1887 and 1934 (when the process was finally reversed), whites acquired over 60 percent of the 138 million acres held by Indians before severalty. The measure failed to make private landowners and middle-class capitalists of the Indians. It only impoverished them further and accelerated their downward psychological spiral.

The Dawes Act was not implemented in the southwestern desert regions, and that helps explain why the tribes have survived there better than in most other places. For a time the Five Civilized Tribes also escaped its application, but after a decade of negotiation they finally agreed to break up their common holdings. The Cherokees were the last to accept severalty allotments (1902), and they did so only after making sure there would be no surplus for white speculators. In 1901, when Congress passed a law making every resident of Indian Territory a citizen of the United States, the long campaign to destroy Indian exclusiveness based on communal property and tribal government came to an end. At about the same time, federal officials also cut off appropriations to the old "civilization fund," which supported mission-school activities.[19]

The Americanization process seemed to be successful in removing native obstacles to cultural homogeneity and in leaving the churches free to Christianize Indians further, according to their differing theological perspectives. But government planners failed to notice that the principal obstacle to assimilation was rooted in Indian spirituality, a wellspring of inner strength not easily affected by superficial changes. As long as independent religious vitality survived, it filled the Indians with a sense of their own identity and cultural importance, with a power that defied

alien control. An early expression of this will to survive
appeared in Tecumseh's brother Tenskwatawa, also known
as the "Shawnee Prophet." There were undoubtedly
others like him in earlier times, such as the "Delaware
Prophet" in Pontiac's day, but we have no exact record of
their message. In his youth Tenskwatawa reputedly led a
dissolute life, succumbing to whiskey and other white
vices, but sometime around 1805 he received a vision and
urged his fellow tribesmen to reform themselves as he had
done. He preached against liquor, intermarriage with
whites, and the use of white manufactures, such as clothing
and iron tools, in favor of a precontact life-style.
Tenskwatawa promised that if natives returned to their
forefathers' virtuous ways, the Master of Life would restore the happiness known in the days before the whites
had arrived. That spiritual message caught fire among several tribes and played a central role in Tecumseh's plans
for a pan-Indian state. Even when government troops destroyed the basis for separate Indian existence in the Midwest in 1811–13, the old dreams of restoration survived.

A parallel visionary, named Ganiodaio, emerged among
the Seneca of New York's once-influential Iroquois
League. By the time this young man, also known as Handsome Lake, had grown to maturity, the Senecas had fallen
from power because of their support for the British during
the Revolution. Handsome Lake, embodying the rootless
despair common to many who experienced cultural decay,
fell prey to drunkenness and other destructive habits. But
around 1800 he too began preaching moral and social reforms, grounding Indian survival on a revivified Indian
religious consciousness. He based his teachings, called
Gaiwiio or "Longhouse Religion," on a vision he had had
in which the Creator announced that his people should
preserve their precontact integrity.[20] Handsome Lake
urged his tribesmen to forsake alcohol, witchcraft,
suicides, and abortions—to reject their gloomy defeatism.
If they clung to the best parts of their ancient moral system, the Creator would sustain them in their traditional

values and strengthen their ability to endure. Many
Iroquois follow the Longhouse Religion today, and it is
one of the strongest forms in which selected precontact
traditions still flourish.

Another prophet arose to spread comfort and hope
among the tribes who were culturally disoriented after
their wars on the western plains. Sometime in the 1880s a
Paiute named Wovoka announced that he had been trans-
ported from this world to a delightful place, filled with
grass and animals, where he had seen God. After communing with those who had died (there restored to
youthful vigor), he had returned to earth with a message
urging all Indians to love one another and live in peace. If
they stopped warring and refrained from lying or stealing,
God promised to restore the world as it had been before
the whites had come. Wovoka also demonstrated a dance
he had learned in heaven, a dance that would hasten the
day when God would reward his people. This "Ghost
Dance" symbolized the new ethic of moral probity and
peace that would preserve Indian cohesion. It also anticipated the day when departed loved ones would be restored, herds of animals would return, and a world without
whites would make restitution for current afflictions.

Wovoka's gospel of hope and deliverance spread rapidly
through many western tribes. It may have influenced Chief
Joseph, who deliberately rejected his father's Christian
leanings, but a Sokulk prophet named Smohollah inspired
Nez Percé spiritual independence too. Many reservation
Indians took up the Ghost Dance ritual and yearned for
eschatological forces to restore a life-style without white
interference. Among them were some Dakotas who also
anticipated the coming new age but did not share
Wovoka's pacifism. When government troops tried to
curtail their socioreligious activities at Wounded Knee
Creek in December 1890, the Dakotas fought back. More
than 200 men, women, and children died in the ensuing
melee when what was begun as a controlled police action
deteriorated into indiscrimate slaughter.[21] That debacle

crushed Indian expectations of a speedy reversal of their sufferings, and eschatological hopes associated with the Ghost Dance faded like those of earlier prophecies.

The year 1890 thus stands as the chronological terminus for the nineteenth century as far as red-white relations are concerned. Later protagonists on both sides sought different objectives in an altered context. But subsequent native attitudes preserved the sense of revitalized spirituality and coupled it with a desire to affirm Indian identity within the ancient traditions. Missionaries and politicians had tried unsuccessfully for a hundred years to eradicate an elemental component of cultural survival. The persistence of the Indians' spirituality shows that the reservoir of their self-consciousness did not dry up, and, in the twentieth century, powerful new spiritual expressions stemming from traditional ceremonialism have demonstrated anew the vitality of the Indians' religious consciousness.

7

Missions in the Twentieth Century

In recent times the managers of red-white interaction have followed different directions with regard to Indian cultural separatism and religious diversity. As the century began, federal policymakers for the most part pursued assimilationist objectives, using nineteenth-century rationalizations as they did so, and the Christian missionaries usually followed suit. In the 1920s, however, some new voices began to defend cultural pluralism as an alternative to destroying minority life-styles. The twentieth century has thus witnessed a protracted struggle between the two sides: between those who would repress and those who would encourage the Indians' vitality as Indians. Neither side has won to date, and only grudgingly does either acknowledge that the other view contains a partial truth. Policy reversals and continuing debates in this century have allowed the Indian religions to assert themselves more fully. These new forms have not only recovered vital precontact rituals but have also increased the number of valid Christian liturgical practices.

White Policies

Twentieth-century missionary work has expanded its scope while losing its earlier narrow focus. In 1908 most Protestant agencies joined the Home Missions Council, a newly created subsidiary of the Federal Council of

Churches. That coalition of fourteen denominations formed a Committee on Indian Affairs, with leaders drawn from the YMCA and YWCA, the American Bible Society, and the Indian Rights Association, to correlate the work of evangelism among native Americans. In 1950 the Federal Council of Churches became the National Council of Churches, and the Home Missions Council merged with twelve other departments to form the Division of Home Missions. Not long after these structural revisions had been made, the special office for Indian affairs went out of existence.

Modern statistical surveys have tended to be sketchy and sporadic, but they provide some record of missionary efforts on reservations and other communities with heavy Indian population. A 1921 survey reported twenty-six Protestant denominations engaged in Indian missions, totaling 32,164 communicants with more than 80,000 additional constituents. Their work touched 161 reservations, where 428 pastors and evangelists serviced 597 churches and mission stations. The same charts indicate that a Roman Catholic staff of 705 people worked on programs at 149 missions, maintaining 336 churches, chapels, and schools; secular priests and religious orders combined their efforts to reach a total of 61,456 native American Catholics.[1] But there were still forty reservations where no resident missionary of any sort represented Christianity on a continuing basis.

In 1950 another partial survey showed that ten more Protestant denominations had inaugurated missionary work and that 833 of their resident and visiting workers were in attendance at 437 mission stations. Despite that expansion, the Protestant denominations, now thirty-six in number, had increased native communicants to only 39,200, while claiming influence among another 140,000 persons. Staff members were still predominantly white, but at least 213 native Americans had entered the field.[2] Another report on Protestant churches appeared in 1974, covering denominations that cooperate with the Cook

Christian Training School in Tempe, Arizona. At that time, the United Presbyterian, Protestant Episcopal, United Methodist, American Baptist, United Church of Christ, Reformed, and Christian Reformed participants listed 452 Indian parishes with staffs numbering 177 missionaries. Statistics on recent Catholic missions are difficult to obtain, primarily because a great deal of Indian work now falls within standard diocesan categories. Fortunately, we now have another general survey that reports both the location and present strength of Indian churches of all denominations.[3]

Twentieth-century missionaries to the Indians have usually perpetuated assimilationist tactics, but some are modifying that approach. In 1958 the National Council of Churches conducted a study that substantiates this generalization in several important ways. Only 22 percent of the Protestants who responded to the questionnaire said that they utilized native leadership in any capacity; half of the Catholic missionaries did so. Regarding the use of native languages, 14 percent of the Protestants claimed to know the local dialect well, but only 6 percent of the Catholics reported that they did. On the Dakota and Navajo reservations, where the use of native tongues is still quite vigorous, the number of Protestants who used no Indian language at all was 48 percent, that of Catholics, 40 percent. Only a small fraction in each confessional division expressed strong sympathy for Indian customs. No more than 9 percent of all Protestant missionaries favored preserving native American values and life-styles; 11 percent of the Catholics indicated a similar openness to cultural diversity.[4]

Protestants supporting the old assimilationist ideal numbered 35 percent of the total, and Catholic missionaries who favored complete Indian acceptance of white standards reached 44 percent. Still, 51 percent of the Protestants took a middle ground and said that they found some native values worth preserving; 31 percent of the Catholics supported a compromise that blended cul-

tural patterns. Missionary attitudes about native religions
were more varied. Among those who considered Indian
faith and ritual "almost entirely unreconcilable" with
Christianity were Southern Baptists (100 percent), Reformed (89 percent), Presbyterians (70 percent), and
American Baptists (55 percent). But several denominations thought elements in native American religions were complementary to Christian teachings; these
included the Episcopalians (81 percent), the Congregationalists (75 percent), the Catholics (74 percent), and the
Methodists (53 percent).[5] Many of these contemporary
missionaries reported that they view their task largely in a
pastoral context rather than an evangelical one. Few regarded saving souls as their primary goal because educational programs, medical care, and social welfare have
eclipsed preaching activities. This 1958 study shows that
some missionaries have become less antagonistic toward
Indian cultures and indigenous religious values but that,
on the whole, missionaries continue to denounce religious
toleration. Evangelical publicists have also condemned
both new native rituals and the resurgence of ancient
ones.[6]

As early as the 1920s some liberal government
administrators took the lead in creating a more tolerant
atmosphere, and perhaps their efforts contributed to more
positive attitudes about native culture and religion among
missionaries. These liberal innovators were in a minority,
and the legislation they sponsored always faced objections
from many quarters. But reforms initiated under Roosevelt's New Deal revived hope for Indian renewal. Before
that time the Bureau of Indian Affairs had routinely
pressed the Indians to become peaceful, self-sufficient
farmers, sharing their white neighbors' morality and mate-
rialism. In 1921, for example, the Bureau of Indian Affairs
commissioner urged reservation superintendents to prepare Indians for citizenship by encouraging missionaries to
teach them "higher" conceptions of family life. In the same
directive he also condemned the Sun Dance and other

religious ceremonies involving elements of self-torture as well as those in which substances like peyote were used to procure visions. Most whites thought that such rituals endangered health and promoted idleness or superstition. Nevertheless, these native practices survived and grew as the mainstays of a resurgent Indian spirituality.

In 1924 Congress passed the Citizenship Act, which made all Indians citizens of the United States. Several hundred thousand had already become citizens through prior agreements that specified education and probationary periods before granting voting privileges. After 1924 all of them became technically enfranchised. During the first three decades of this century the BIA continued to break up communally held land and allot it in parcels to individuals. White businessmen then leased or bought most of it from inexperienced natives. An average of two million acres passed annually from Indian ownership to white control under the severalty program. By 1928 more than 100,000 red citizens were landless and poverty-stricken. In that year Lewis Meriam conducted a monumental study, released through the Institute for Government Research, which demonstrated that the vast majority of native Americans suffered from inadequate health and educational facilities. They had not benefited from or assimilated to white economic and social standards. The Great Depression created more hardships for Indians than for other Americans. Reformers had all the facts they needed to revise policies that had rarely accommodated tribesmen to mainstream American culture in the first place.

In 1933 President Roosevelt appointed John Collier to be Commissioner of Indian Affairs. Collier had been an officer of the American Indian Defense Association for ten years, and, as commissioner, he was to chart a new official policy, based on self-government and religious freedom for tribal groups. A romantic visionary who idealized the pre-Columbian Indian communities, Collier believed that their example could help rootless whites, overdependent

on technology. He was also a political administrator who
made giant strides in helping Indian groups protect their
spiritual values and perpetuate their existence as distinct
peoples. Despite his utopian ideology, his practical contributions to Indian improvement reversed many earlier
policies and inaugurated significant changes in land ownership, conservation, and tribal government. He fostered a
rebirth of the artistic and ceremonial expressions that were
the heart of precontact cultures.

Collier had spent years criticizing the assimilationists for
what he considered their bigotry and their predatory tactics. He saw government service as an opportunity to rev-
olutionize administrative procedures from the top. As a
humanitarian he wished to ease the plight of natives who
suffered the twin evils of sickness and extreme poverty. As
a social scientist he wanted to restore tribal cultures that
had been eroded by missionaries and government agents
bent on making Indians conform to white civilization.
With BIA authority behind his new approach, he hoped to
improve Indian life by offering material advantages without forcing the tribes to accept alien values.[7] He therefore
tried to recover reservation lands for original owners, restore political cohesion to tribal units, and protect distinctive Indian customs and values in the name of cultural and
religious freedom. If government placed modern education and scientific knowledge in the hands of independent
Indians, he was confident they would incorporate useful
change into their different systems without destroying the
cooperative institutions, rituals, and traditional values that
had originally given them proud identities.

A few months after assuming office, Collier persuaded
President Roosevelt to abolish the Board of Indian Commissioners. He opposed that group not because it cost too
much, as some claimed, but because it consistently favored
the assimilationist policies associated with the 1887 General Allotment Act. Many board members had worked
closely with missionaries to make BIA schools provide
both salvation and citizenship for those who attended.

Collier removed the board because it encumbered his plan
to preserve Indian cultures and restore tribal lands. Within
a year he attacked the monopoly many missionaries enjoyed on various reservations. Declaring that Indians had
constitutional rights in spiritual matters, he urged Indian
Service personnel to respect native liberties. He also
ended compulsory attendance at religious services in BIA
schools. Then he invited all religious leaders, native
traditionalists as well as Christian ministers, to use government facilities for instruction and worship. Every
church was free to conduct services as it wished. Indians
could support any group, or none, as they saw fit.

Collier's administrative directives provided some improvement on the reservations, but the real basis for reform lay in the new legislation that he and BIA staff members drafted. After asking many tribes what changes they
wanted, bureau lawyers wrote an omnibus bill that placed
Indian destinies substantially in Indian hands again. Native
reactions to this draft caused further revisions, and the
1934 Indian Reorganization Act represented a notable departure from former government policy. Sometimes
known as the Wheeler-Howard Act because of its chief
supporters—Senator Burton K. Wheeler and Representative Edgar Howard—the IRA allowed Indians to regain
self-esteem and self-determination in their own affairs. In-
dicative of Collier's respect for native response, he submitted the bill to each tribe for possible adoption after
Congress passed it. If any tribe chose not to accept the
help proffered (some large tribes, such as the Navajos,
rejected certain central features of the Act), the federal
authorities were not to force it upon them. But when
tribes accepted the IRA (192 of them eventually approved
its provisions), federal machinery and native peoples were
to cooperate in implementing practical steps toward Indian
recovery.

Perhaps the IRA's most beneficial feature was its pro-
scription of all future land allotments. It also provided for
consolidating checkerboard reservations, and it restored

unallotted land to tribal ownership. Further, it authorized
the Interior Department to begin conservation measures
on Indian sites, and it secured an appropriation of two million dollars annually to expand reservation holdings. The
IRA called for new civil-service criteria to increase the
number of native Americans in the Indian Service. It provided $250,000 each year in scholarships for Indian stu-
dents, to benefit their tribes through advanced education.
The act also invited, but did not require, each tribe to organize its political and social life under a charter of limited
home rule. Its financial provisions empowered tribes as cor-
porations to borrow money from a federal credit fund, to
utilize legal services, and to improve communal economic
development with modern management techniques.[8] At
first the IRA did not apply to Indians in Oklahoma or
Alaska, but before Collier's resignation in 1945 they too
could adopt its guidelines.

Many conflicts arose when Collier tried to apply a new
set of political and economic ideas to groups with different
cultural orientations. The Dakotas, for instance, had never
experienced much political solidarity, and it was difficult
for them to participate in a single self-governing structure.
The deeply conservative Pueblos were also wary of accepting notions of majority rule. Indians who had already
adjusted to democracy, private property, and other
middle-class cultural norms opposed the IRA as a back-
ward step. Missionaries criticized the new measures because they thought that, in reviving tribalism, it subsidized
segregation and perpetuated racial prejudice. Undeterred
by such opposition, Collier influenced native groups to
adopt his strategy wherever possible. Most found that
their communal life flourished in the new tolerant atmosphere. On balance, they developed stronger local institutions, capable of withstanding the traumas of marginal
sociological status. Those who resisted the Indian New
Deal had little to recommend in its place but the old assimilationist program, which eroded tribal assets and ensured further cultural deterioration.[9]

It was impossible for Collier fully to reinstate Chief Justice John Marshall's early dictum that the Indian tribes were sovereign entities. Many acculturated Indians declined to be classified into separate groups again. Others could not see how restoring cooperative institutions would solve modern problems better than yeoman individualism did. But Collier's determination to sustain group consciousness produced two beneficial results: it paved the way for more selective acculturation, and it avoided the worst features of the personality disintegration that had accompanied earlier programs. By mid-century over 100 tribes had adopted constitutions for local self-government; twice that number had formed economic cooperatives. There was less overuse of grazing lands, and yields increased; agricultural production on reservations multiplied by 400 percent; soil and wildlife conservation reclaimed vast tracts that had been slipping into wasteland. A streamlined system of federal claims courts improved the legal process through which various tribes were compensated for fraudulent land deals. Agents reorganized Indian schools with an eye toward making them more useful to the local communities. Health-care facilities were still inadequate, but encouraging advances were made against such major diseases as tuberculosis and trachoma.

Aside from the practical aspects of Collier's legacy, he raised central issues about Indian cultures. He questioned whether future progress should come at the expense of repudiating traditional patterns formed before contact with white civilization. Perhaps his most far-reaching action in this context was to lift the ban on native ceremonies. His invoking the doctrine of religious freedom to protect native rituals may prove to be the key to our country's continual dilemma over separate cultures.

After Collier resigned in 1945, the BIA pendulum swung back to conservative policies again. Government agents under Dillon S. Myer, commissioner from 1950 to 1953, began once more to promote assimilation by withdrawing Bureau services and restricting credit funds. Myer developed several vocational training programs for urban workers and urged Indians to relocate in industrial cities. In 1954 his successors tried to repudiate IRA practices altogether. Public Law 280 and House Concurrent Resolution 108 declared Indians subject to the same laws and privileges as other citizens, thus terminating Indian wardship. True to their intention of getting government "out of the business of Indian affairs," BIA agents also broke up several large reservation holdings. These included the Menominees' rich forests in Wisconsin and the Klamaths' timber range in Oregon. President Eisenhower commented that many of the Indian bills Congress rushed through for his approval were "most un-Christian." But he signed every one of them into law.

By 1958, however, a new Secretary of the Interior acknowledged that federal measures could not obliterate tribal consciousness. He promised that government agencies would revise their dealings with a tribe only with that group's consent. The Kennedy and Johnson administrations restricted unilateral decisions even further, and more recent government-Indian negotiations have made native voices an essential component in resolving specific problems. In the last quarter of the twentieth century many whites and some Indians still support the old assimilationist goals, but most Indians and some whites now favor a cultural pluralism based on cooperative diversity. Neither view dominates government action, and the best that can be said is that Indians are increasingly defining their own roles in American society.

Native Tenacity

One of the generalizations about Indian life made in chapter 1 was that native American cultures have been changing for quite some time. Hunters and warriors modified their tactics when craftsmen invented more efficient weapons. Farmers modified theirs when new techniques yielded a better and more varied food supply.

Central values, involving divine power and human relationships, changed at a less rapid pace, but ceremonies
and belief systems gradually replaced earlier ones in the
slow dynamics of cultural adjustment. It is a mistake to
assume that aboriginal groups thought in static terms or
could not meet challenges with refined innovations. It is
equally wrong to conclude that more recent experiences
have destroyed core Indian qualities. Cultural transformation has become much more rapid and extensive
since whites arrived in the New World, but forced acculturation has not eradicated native values, especially religious
ones.

How have the Indians adapted to change? When, in the
twentieth century, they abandoned their customary warfare, subsistence farming, and nonliterate tribal records,
they did not readily adopt white substitutes. Most sought
to redefine themselves by borrowing rituals and communal
processes from other Indians. This pan-Indian response
has emerged primarily in the shape of fraternal and religious organizations that help to preserve alternative, more
meaningful, life-styles. Pan-Indianism is old in that it continues the familiar struggle against social and psychological
deterioration, invoking ethnic solidarity to combat cultural
aggression. It is new in that the Indians have moved beyond intratribal action and are now willing to accept intertribal leadership as well as outside resources.

Pan-Indian sympathies often found outlet in religious
alignments that blended aboriginal traits and Christian
ideology. An early example is the Shaker Religion, begun
around 1881 among Coast Salish natives in the southern
Puget Sound area. Its name and origins had nothing to do
with the earlier communitarian sect known as Shakers; the
fact that they also were given to physical tremors during
worship was quite coincidental. The new church's native
leadership developed a wide following. They used simple
liturgical aids, such as bells and candles, to conduct unpretentious services, featuring songs, prayers, and dancing,

during which members often reached psychic levels where spirits made them tremble with power. Such contact often cured disease and gave general purpose to their lives.[10] Their syncretistic rituals recapitulated many shamanistic practices and made it possible for everyone to share the power once controlled by specialists. Pentecostal missionaries have since noticed many parallels between Indian Shakers and their own spiritual emphasis, but the Indians still resist collaborating with white religionists and try to preserve indigenous qualities in their independent church. Today's Shaker churches fuse shamanistic influences with distinctively Christian beliefs to invigorate life as many Pacific Northwest native Americans experience it.

Indian rituals connected with peyote illustrate in a larger geographical area how aboriginal forms persist alongside Christian theology and ethics. Spanish chroniclers observed peyote worship in the sixteenth century; how much earlier these practices existed we do not know. Despite Hispanic efforts to eradicate it, Indians in northern Mexico still utilized the substance religiously in the 1800s. Peyote (*Lophophora williamsii*) is a small turnip-shaped cactus that grows in the arid Rio Grande Valley. The plant contains nine isoquinoline alkaloids, not to be confused with the addictive narcotics found in both mescal and the hallucinatory mushroom *teonanacatl*. Though it has a bitter taste, people eat the dried top, or peyote "button," to induce temporary physiological derangements, including heightened perceptions of sound and color. Those who consume it during religious activities claim that it enhances concentration and highlights central truths with vivid imagery. Far from producing irreverence or promiscuity, peyote users say that it induces a solemn respect for spiritual power and serious moral behavior.

Sometime around 1870–80 the Mescalero Apaches and Kiowas began to use peyote in conjunction with their ritual dances. By 1885 the Comanches had joined them in making the plant a central feature of tribal rites. When enthusiasm for the popular Ghost Dance subsided after the massacre at Wounded Knee (1890), peyote cults diffused rapidly through the Plains cultures. Other new religions, such as the Hand Game and the Grass Dance and its midwestern variant, the Dream Dance, also attracted followers despondent over military defeat and reservation confinement, but peyote gained more support than all the others. Centered primarily in Oklahoma by 1910, peyote users emerged on reservations from Iowa to Arizona and from Wisconsin to Wyoming. There were regional variations—many, for instance, combined strong Christian influences with flexible local preferences—but all peyote religionists adhered to a common core of belief and ritual.

The first peyotist group to gain specific legal recognition was the First Born Church of Christ in Redrock, Oklahoma, whose state charter dates from 1914. When white officials harassed them and tried to prohibit peyote use, several tribes formed a larger organization in 1918 and invoked their constitutional right to freedom of religion to protect themselves. In that year delegates representing 12,000 adherents organized the Native American Church and elected trustees from the Apache, Comanche, Kiowa, Oto, Ponca, Cheyenne, and Arapaho tribes. Their declared intention was

to foster and promote the religious belief of the several tribes of Indians in the State of Oklahoma, in the Christian religion with the practices of the Peyote sacrament as commonly understood and used among the adherents of this religion . . . and to teach the Christian religion with morality, sobriety, industry, kindly charity and right living, and [to] cultivate the spirit of self respect, [and] brotherly union among the members of the native race of Indians.[11]

In 1934 the nuclear ecclesiastical unit expanded to a national federation of peyote churches covering a dozen states. By 1945 they had spread to eighteen states, and a

decade later they changed their name to the Native
American Church of North America to acknowledge
Canadian membership as well. According to a recent
estimate 250,000 adherents participate in this strong expression of contemporary Indian religious vitality.

The Native American Church has no officially authorized body of doctrine and no single system of ideas
and symbols, but some broad generalizations still apply to
most church members. They usually equate God with the
Great Spirit, a power widely reverenced as the ultimate
source of being. Jesus often replaces native culture heroes
or guardian spirits to intercede between God and humanity, and He is sometimes identified with Peyote Woman in
the cultus. The members also refer to the Holy Spirit, but
they assign it a vague role, as do most Christian theologies;
occasionally they link the Holy Spirit with peyote as a
latter-day incarnation conveying special sympathy and
compassion for Indians. They refer to angels, too, as mes-
senger spirits and associate them with the traditional compass points or with the winds from those directions.
Thunderbird imagery has also blended readily with the
biblical dove symbol, and crosses, present in many settings, may stem from either aboriginal or white origins.
Crucifixes and rosaries among peyotists are more obviously due to Catholic influence. Peyote buttons replace
bread and wine in the central ritual, but Native American
churchmen remain within the classical concept of sacrament.[12] Because of such compatibilities, many participants
do not consider peyote religion and membership in
another Christian church to be exclusive or antagonistic.

Just as peyotists have blended native religious forms
with trinitarian theology, cruciform symbolism, and sacramental liturgy, they have also synthesized diverse ethical
emphases. White customs such as those based on the Ten
Commandments dominate their syncretistic morality, but
few rules directly contravene Indian cultural traditions.
Native American Church leaders urge brotherly love

among those who strive to "follow the peyote road." They exhort their followers to deal honestly with other members of the group and to offer as much mutual encouragement as possible. Peyotists stress the value of kinship solidarity and self-reliance in the secular world, where members work to support their families. Perhaps most significantly, Native American churchmen avoid all forms of alcohol. Those who conform to this ethic have adopted the white man's eschatology somewhat by saying that good moral behavior will be rewarded in a pleasant future life. Though they say little about punishment for those who violate the code, they appear to have abandoned the pre-contact notion that all Indians will share indiscriminately in future rewards.[13]

Peyotist groups usually hold services on Saturday nights in a special tipi, hogan, or other indigenous structure. Officials prepare a crescent-shaped earthen mound inside the ceremonial chamber and place a large peyote button on the top, together with crosses as additional sacred symbols. Between the points of the crescent they lay a V-shaped fire for later use. Other liturgical aids include an eagle-bone whistle, a gourd rattle, a water drum, a staff, cedar and sage incense, and a feather fan. The Roadman, as chief officer, is essential to conducting worship services, but he does not mediate between divine power and those who attend. The way to spiritual communication is open to all who participate. When the Roadman opens worship with singing, his assistant, the Drummer, accompanies him. Lesser officials include the Cedar Chief, who occasionally puts incense on the fire, and the Fireman, who keeps the blaze alive all night. These four ceremonial leaders are commonly present, but services without this traditional number are still valid.

The ceremonies begin at nightfull, when worshipers gather in the special chamber around the sacred fire. The Roadman stands and sings four songs, holding the staff, fan, and sage in his left hand and rattling the gourd with his right. Then he prays aloud, expressing spontaneous thoughts in his native tongue. Each person seated in a circle around the crescent follows suit, singing and praying in Indian languages and passing the ceremonial aids in turn to his neighbor. After this congregational litany, the members distribute peyote buttons for everyone to eat. Worshipers normally consume four buttons during a night's service or drink "tea" brewed from peyote. As the substance takes hold, participants quietly turn inward to contemplate the colorful visions that result from eating peyote. The material causes remarkable psychological effects, and this temporary state of mind highlights all peyote ceremonies.[14] During the night the worshipers also speak of personal problems or confess breaking their moral code. Group members always express sympathy to sustain them in meeting future difficulties. Consoled with private visions and communal support, the congregation departs, after sharing a morning meal of corn, meat, and fruit.

Peyotists cling to their church because most of them have suffered social and physical disabilities; their visions provide welcome release from present ills by allowing them to approach God directly. But many people oppose the Native American Church. Leaders in the traditional Indian religions frequently object to its Christian references and mixed symbols. The Navajos have been particularly adamant against peyote use among their people, and their reservations are still beset with thorny legal disputes over religious freedom. Government agents have frequently viewed peyote rituals with alarm too. The BIA favored cultural uniformity during this century's early decades, and its agents criticized peyotism because it reinforced native cultures and competed with Christianity; they also denounced peyote as an intoxicant or narcotic, to be prohibited from the reservations, and they charged that peyotists endangered their own health by relying on the plant as medicine instead of consulting trained physicians.

In 1918 Representative Carl M. Hayden of Arizona introduced a bill in Congress to outlaw peyote. Public hearings on the proposed legislation attracted many who condemned the substance as another item in the sad train of personal and social deterioration among Indians. Others defended the plant, however, and proved that most allegations regarding it came from unscientific hearsay based on prejudice against native American cultures. Hayden's bill passed the House amid conflicting opinions, but it never became federal law.[15] Local enforcement was another matter. Thirteen western states had passed laws against peyote by 1937, and Native American churchmen became more secretive than ever before. It is still difficult to obtain full information about their religious practices. Opposing attitudes regarding peyote abound in great confusion, but in 1961 the Arizona Supreme Court made a ruling that helps resolve some central issues. It determined that peyote is not a narcotic or habit-forming in any way; there are no harmful aftereffects associated with its use. No significant number of people use the substance outside religious ceremonies, and in churches it poses no threat to public health, morals, or welfare.[16] In 1964 the California Supreme Court also exonerated peyotists, and since 1972 the Navajos have won the right to practice their religion more openly on Arizona reservations. Some local sheriffs still attack peyote as a "cheap drunk," and many people have groundless fears about what the "drug" really does; but there are no federal laws prohibiting it, and many states have repealed their earlier strictures. In an era of greater understanding it may yet be possible for Native American churchmen to display their distinctive liturgy alongside other Christian expressions.

This modern form of Indian Christianity has survived and expanded for several reasons. It retains native themes that preserve the Indians' pride in their own traditional ways while utilizing Christian symbols and doctrines in harmony with most white churches. The church's ethical code emphasizes peace and hard work, domestic virtues that white missionaries have been urging on native Americans for centuries. Its members support the slogan "Peyote and alcohol don't mix" to prevent liquor from debilitating their lives, and the evidence suggests that they have been successful in that campaign. The emotional impact of religious services helps peyotists regain their self-esteem and accept rather stoically the subordinate sociological status that is usually their lot. From a white perspective, this religion makes Indians industrious and cooperative with mainstream culture. From the natives' viewpoint, peyote gives them solace from an oppressive world and replenishes their ability to endure injustices that have become a social inheritance.

The Native American Church is also a rallying point for ethnic pride and cultural survival. Its religious leaders do not exclude whites from participating, but they consider its emphases especially suited to Indians. Though churches employ a syncretistic theology and ethics, they respect a traditionally individualistic approach to religious power. Peyote ceremonies succeed primarily because they have perpetuated the aboriginal custom of private vision quests. They provide individuals with the means of working in collective isolation to achieve personal spiritual goals. Vision quests have always been difficult, and peyotists say it is hard to follow their road. In precontact times questers prayed for spirits to reward their zeal by granting a theophany; within a similar context, peyotists do the same. Adherents have found enough supernatural power there to make their secular lives tolerable. Within the church they have also found a supportive community for resisting cultural deterioration. Other institutions perform this social function too, but syncretism and ethnic self-consciousness help explain the contemporary strength of the peyote religion.

Revived interest in the Sun Dance is another example of native tenacity in the face of white domination. Algonkian tribes in the Great Plains culture area began that ritual in precontact times. Enough tribes had added Sun Dance ceremonies and ideology to their worship patterns so that by the early nineteenth century it constituted the most widespread sacred ritual in the Plains region. Supporters ranged from Comanches in central Texas to Blackfeet and Crees in southern Alberta. Different tribes varied the practices slightly, but recurrent patterns formed a "web of essential features" that characterized every version of the shared ritual.[17] Many incorporated self-torture and mutilation in this sacred ceremony, but few besides the Dakotas considered this essential to proper performance. More pervasive features involved the taboos the dancers observed: choosing and erecting a center pole correctly, using sacred bundles properly, and seeing to it that hunting or warrior societies supervised the ceremonial events. The common liturgical core enabled tribal participants to experience the beauty and dignity inherent in this special medium.

In precontact times Sun Dance participants undertook ritual ordeals for many reasons. They danced to fulfill vows made in distress, to secure protection in warfare, or to make the buffalo plentiful. Others wanted to demonstrate bravery, receive new visions, or acquire spirit power to cure ailing tribesmen. But white encroachment destroyed the buffalo-centered economy and the native life-styles that had nurtured the traditional religions. As white officials gained increasing control over the western Indians, they tried to suppress the Sun Dance. Missionaries and reservation agents objected to its "pagan" symbolism and physical abuses; the dance contravened the American values and customs the white imperialists wanted the natives to adopt, and by 1890 they had virtually extinguished it. The defeated Indians responded with new religious expressions, hoping thus to compensate for physical deterioration or psychological depression. In that setting individualistic emphases gave way to community survival. The modern rituals concentrated on social cohesion and corporate welfare instead of isolated personal gains.

The Wind River Shoshones were particularly effective in

reviving the Sun Dance rituals. They had adopted it
around 1800 and assimilated the new religious form in the
following decades. During enforced acculturation the
Wind River Shoshones supported their traditional religions, especially after the Ghost Dance had failed to rectify the loss of their territory, their declining population,
and their subjugation to federal authority. Between 1890
and 1905 they reshaped the Sun Dance in ways that adjusted it to the white Christian standards imposed on their
culture. After modifying some practices, they urged new
reasons for worshiping in the old manner and proselytized
their neighbors. By 1933 they had extended the revised
ceremonial complex to Bannocks, Utes, and other
Shoshones in Idaho, Utah, and Nevada. In 1941 the Sun
Dance began spreading eastward, back to its former
heartland, and contemporary evidence suggests a positive
future for this distinctive means of spiritual communication.

Some observers say that modern Indians have grafted
Christian symbols onto Sun Dance activities to perpetuate
their traditional format. For example, they point out that
the dancers endure much less personal torture than before. When participants experience physical pain, syn-
cretists correlate their acts with the suffering that Jesus
experienced for others, and because many dance corrals
now feature twelve posts instead of ten, as before, they
suggest that the center pole is Jesus or the crucifix surrounded by twelve disciples. Warriors no longer display
weapons in the dance area or pray for successful raids;
moreover, there are no ceremonial buffalo hunts to follow
the annual dance. Many attribute such modifications to
peaceable Christian influence plus direct missionary efforts to have natives abandon their glory in killing. But
these attempts to legitimate the Sun Dance by drawing
parallels with Christian symbols are not ultimately convincing. They fail to see that the fundamental attitudes do
not rely on any important Christian feature.[18]

There is no strong correspondence between today's Sun

Dance practitioners and the white religious or educational programs on their reservations. Few Shoshones or Utes have converted to Christianity, and those who have maintain only nominal affiliation. Wind River natives have long resisted the missionaries' claims to exclusive truth and denominational superiority. The twentieth-century Indians who keep the Sun Dance alive are more skeptical and egalitarian than their white neighbors. From a less normative perspective, their ritual celebration of traditional power reinforces native religious patterns without drawing on or contributing to Christian symbolism in any meaningful way.

Plans for contemporary Sun Dances begin during the winter months, when individuals announce their intention of dancing later that year. Other community members, such as singers and drummers, start practicing their ancillary roles to make sure that they will perform correctly at the appointed time. No one joins the annual ceremonies because of social pressure, but those who dream about it feel a special obligation to participate the following summer. The Sun Dance leader inaugurates the solemn proceedings by selecting a spot for erecting the center pole. Elaborate ceremonies are involved in this and then in choosing and marking the tree that will serve as the pillar of the microcosmic universe, cutting the tree, and hauling it to the chosen location. Men cut additional poles to form a circular wall with posts, and they fashion rafters into a conical roof, taking special care to make the final beam run in a direct east-west line from the center pole to a post in the rear so as to form a "backbone," aligning the temporary structure with the spiritual forces that animate the great universe. The officials prepare a buffalo skull, using ritual paint, clay, and sage, and place this atop the central pillar as another focal point of the sacred drama that is about to begin.

Modern Sun Dances last for three days and two nights, during which time the dancers neither eat nor drink.

Shoshone references to it as *taguwënër,* "thirsting dance"
or "standing in thirst," confirm the ordeal's austerities. The
participants arrange themselves around the center pole
and blow on eagle-bone whistles. Their rhythmic movements keep pace with the accompanying songs and drum-
beats that punctuate each day's agenda. The dancers con-
serve their energy so that they will not collapse too early in
the grueling pageant. They rest at intervals in special huts,
but from dawn to late evening they dance at specified
periods and entreat spirit beings to show their presence at
the ceremony. This marvelously intricate ritual includes
important paraphernalia, such as special clothing, feathers,
and paint, together with unique prayers, songs, and dance
steps that achieve a solemn liturgical beauty.

The dancers expect visions to occur on the third day, if
they come at all; two days and nights of dancing plus the
cumulative effect of hunger, fatigue, and thirst bring the
participants to a climactic threshold. If any young men
seem reluctant to continue, they are reminded that they
are about to acquire special strength for leading an Indian
way of life. Fellow tribesmen encourage the dancers to
persevere, urging them to bolster family solidarity and
preserve the integrity of traditional culture patterns. In
these harangues they also warn dancers not to abuse themselves with alcohol or other white vices, which they denounce in scathing terms. The dancing continues, and
some dancers now reach the ceremony's anticipated high
point. Witnesses know that a dancer is receiving a vision
when he collapses and his body turns cold. The others
continue to pursue their own visions while officials cover
their fallen companion and leave him to commune un-
molested with the spirits who have chosen to contact him.
When those favored with visions revive, they drink a special mixture of water and clay, which they afterward share
with the general community. The participants exchange
gifts and payments with dance officials; then all join in the
communal feast that terminates the proceedings.[19]

Traditional Sun Dance emphasis on individual achievement persists, but in the contemporary rites this is secondary to the need to preserve the cultural integrity of the
group. Successful dancers have significant dreams later in
life, and these important communications help them use
new truths to cope with daily affairs. Some of them keep
the office of shaman alive with heightened spiritual perceptions; others rely on a strengthened sense of personal
worth to protect themselves from the despair resulting
from poverty, slum conditions, and white domination.
Those who receive visions also contribute their religious
experience to the larger community. Using insights gained
through traditional means, dancers comfort tribesmen
suffering from undiagnosed maladies and those who fear
that ghosts are causing their misfortunes. Sun Dance
participants try to raise the general well-being of communities oppressed by outside influences. They help re-
build collective self-esteem and make folkways more
resilient. But whatever the uses of Sun Dance power, positive good comes from its revival. The ceremony conveys a
protective blend of individual and community activities
relevant to both spiritual and temporal spheres, and all
these values derive from a religion that is proudly Indian
rather than white.

At the end of a historical survey such as this, one wonders
what these resurgent religions tell us about the future. Is
there any hope for beneficial cultural interaction? Diseases
and wars crippled many sophisticated cultures in the past,
but native Americans survived those physical calamities.
Religious consciousness lay at the core of their cultural
resistance, and it is clear by now that Indian spiritual vitality will persist despite all white attempts to suppress it.
Some expressions of it flourish in the accommodation-
oriented Native American Church, others in the deliberately autonomous Sun Dance. Each of these examples
points to the dynamism inherent in native cultures that has
enabled them to survive the missionaries and government

agents who—often with good intentions—sought to submerge native Americans in mainstream white culture. Private property, citizenship, and modern technology have not eradicated the fundamental integrity of Indian self-consciousness. Recent claims-court decisions, religious autonomy, and pan-Indian solidarity suggest that this persistence will grow rather than diminish in the years to come.

Historical understanding can help whites deal knowledgeably with Indian affirmations in this century's penultimate decade. People who support mainstream patterns can respond favorably to revitalized minority cultures by envisioning a pluralistic American society, or they can reject diversification again in favor of the old myth of homogeneity. Either way, religion will be a significant factor in future exchanges. Religions lay deeply embedded in precontact syntheses of world-view and ethos, and they have sustained Indian survival through almost five centuries of red-white interaction. The religious consciousness of American Indians is now experiencing a renaissance, and this new growth provides an opportunity to move toward a healthy cultural diversification instead of repeating earlier aggressive policies. Native American cultures, if left to flower on their own, will enrich world religions with fresh expressions of profound spiritual significance, whether these take form in powerful new symbols, liturgies, or ethical priorities. For American society, Indian life points the way to greater diversity and expanded tolerance. Ethnic persistence is already a fact, whether today's demographers recognize the importance of Indians or not. If the nation as a whole restricts the Indians' freedom to act and worship along indigenous lines, it will perpetuate a shortsighted parochialism and deny what is best for itself as an amalgam of many peoples.

Notes

Chapter One

1. Robert F. Spencer, Jesse D. Jennings, et al., *The Native Americans: Prehistory and Ethnology of the North American Indians* (New York: Harper & Row, 1965), p. 97.
2. Charles M. Hudson, *The Southeastern Indians* (Knoxville: University of Tennessee Press, 1976), p. 55.
3. James B. Griffin, "The Northeast Woodlands Area," in Jesse D. Jennings and Edward Norbeck, eds., *Prehistoric Man in the New World* (Chicago: University of Chicago Press, 1964), pp. 236–38.
4. Olaf H. Prufer, "The Hopewell Complex of Ohio," in Joseph R. Caldwell and Robert L. Hall, eds., *Hopewellian Studies,* Scientific Papers, vol. 12 (Springfield: Illinois State Museum, 1964), pp. 71–72.
5. William H. Sears, "The Southeastern United States," in Jennings and Norbeck, *Prehistoric Man in the New World,* pp. 277–78.
6. Antonio J. Waring, Jr., "The Southern Cult and Muskhogean Ceremonial," in Stephen Williams, ed., *The Waring Papers,* Papers of the Peabody Museum of Archaeology and Ethnology, vol. 58 (Cambridge, Mass.: Peabody Museum, 1968), p. 66.
7. James H. Howard, *The Southeastern Ceremonial Complex and Its Interpretation,* Missouri Archaeological Society Memoir no. 6 (Columbia, Mo.: Missouri Archaeological Society, 1968), pp. 11–12.
8. James O. Brown, "Spiro Art and Its Mortuary Contexts," in Elizabeth P. Benson, ed., *Death and the Afterlife in Pre-Columbian America* (Washington, D.C.: Dumbarton Oaks Research Library, 1975), p. 8.

9. Howard, *Southeastern Ceremonial Complex,* p. 19.
10. Waring, "Southern Cult and Muskhogean Ceremonial," p. 64.

Chapter Two

1. Edward H. Spicer, *Cycles of Conquest: The Impact of Spain, Mexico, and the United States on the Indians of the Southwest, 1533–1960* (Tucson: University of Arizona Press, 1962), pp. 153–55. See also Albert H. Schroeder, "Rio Grande Ethnohistory," in Alfonso Ortiz, ed., *New Perspectives on the Pueblos* (Albuquerque: University of New Mexico Press, 1972), p. 48.
2. Edward P. Dozier, "Rio Grande Pueblos," in Edward H. Spicer, ed., *Perspectives in American Indian Culture Change* (Chicago: University of Chicago Press, 1961), pp. 106–7. See also Paul Kirchhoff, "Gatherers and Farmers in the Greater Southwest," in Roger C. Owen, James J. F. Deetz, and Anthony D. Fisher, eds., *The North American Indians: A Sourcebook* (New York: Macmillan, 1967), p. 427.
3. Alfonso Ortiz, "Ritual Drama and the Pueblo World View," in A. Ortiz, ed., *New Perspectives on the Pueblos,* pp. 153–54.
4. Leslie A. White, "The Pueblo of Santa Ana, New Mexico," *American Anthropologist* n.s. 44, no. 4, pt. 2 (October–December 1942): 321–22. See also Elsie C. Parsons, *Pueblo Indian Religion* (Chicago: University of Chicago Press, 1939), vol. 1, pp. 63–64, 107–8.
5. Alfonso Ortiz, *The Tewa World: Space, Time, and Becoming in a Pueblo Society* (Chicago: University of Chicago Press, 1969), pp. 98, 104, 116.
6. Clifford Geertz, *Islam Observed: Religious Development in Morocco and Indonesia* (New Haven: Yale University Press, 1968), p. 97. See also Clifford Geertz, "Ethos, World-View, and the Analysis of Sacred Symbols," *Antioch Review* 17 (1957): 424–25, and Ortiz, "Ritual Drama," p. 136.
7. Edward P. Dozier, *The Pueblo Indians of North America* (New York: Holt, Rinehart & Winston, 1970), pp. 203–4. See also Leslie A. White, *The Pueblo of Sia, New Mexico* (Washington, D.C.: U.S. Government Printing Office, 1962), pp. 115–21, and White, "Santa Ana," p. 87.
8. Parsons, *Pueblo Religion,* 1:182.

9. Ortiz, *Tewa World,* p. 50. See also Parsons, *Pueblo Religion,* 1:216.

10. George P. Hammond, *Don Juan de Oñate and the Founding of New Mexico* (Sante Fe: El Palacio Press, 1927), pp. 98–99.

11. F. W. Hodge, G. P. Hammond, and A. Rey, eds., *Fray Alonso de Benavides' Revised Memorial of 1634* (Albuquerque: University of New Mexico Press, 1945), pp. 35, 99. See also Ralph E. Twitchell, *The Leading Facts of New Mexican History* (Cedar Rapids, Ia.: Torch Press, 1911), vol. 1, p. 337; and Frank D. Reeve, *History of New Mexico* (New York: Lewis Historical Publishing Co., 1961), vol. 1, p. 154.

12. Lansing B. Bloom, "Fray Estevan de Perea's *Relacion,*" *New Mexico Historical Review* 8 (1933): 233. See also *Benavides' Revised Memorial of 1634,* pp. 53, 58.

13. Dozier, *Pueblo Indians,* p. 50. See also Spicer, *Cycles of Conquest,* pp. 167–68, and Parsons, *Pueblo Religion,* 2:1102.

14. Edward H. Spicer, "Spanish-Indian Acculturation in the Southwest," *American Anthropologist* 56 (1954): 669–70. One quotable attitude summarizes the prevailing impasse: "To this day no external influence has damaged this bastion of faith; the Pueblo Indians have unhesitatingly fitted alien realities into their own view of the cosmos . . . . The rain-makers behind the mesas, the animal gods on the rim of the world, the mask gods beneath the sacred lake, are still the only realities. Even the mushroom clouds from the atomic explosions which take place in their deserts have not caused them to waver; they still know where the middle of the world is." See Walter Krickeberg et al., *Pre-Columbian American Religions* (London: Weidenfeld & Nicholson, 1968), pp. 208–9.

Chapter Three

1. Conrad Heidenreich, *Huronia: A History and Geography of the Huron Indians, 1600–1650* (Toronto: McClelland & Stewart, 1971), pp. 15, 103. See also Bruce G. Trigger, *The Huron: Farmers of the North* (New York: Holt, Rinehart & Winston, 1969), pp. 12–13, for a slightly higher estimate.

2. Bruce G. Trigger, *The Children of Aataentsic: A History of the Huron People to 1660* (Montreal: McGill-Queen's University Press, 1976), vol. 1, p. 102.

3. Trigger, *Huron,* pp. 36–39.

4. Heidenreich, *Huronia*, pp. 226–27, 293; see also Trigger, *Children*, 1:50.

5. Elisabeth Tooker, *An Ethnography of the Huron Indians, 1615–1649*, Bureau of American Ethnology Bulletin no. 190 (Washington, D.C.: U.S. Government Printing Office, 1964), pp. 52–55; see also Mary W. Herman, "The Social Aspects of Huron Property," in R. C. Owen, J. J. F. Deetz, and A. D. Fisher, eds., *The North American Indians: A Sourcebook* (New York: Macmillan, 1967), p. 589.

6. Trigger, *Children*, 1:79–80; see also Trigger, *Huron*, p. 87.

7. Tooker, *Ethnography*, pp. 86–88; see also Anthony F. C. Wallace, "Dreams and the Wishes of the Soul: A Type of Psychoanalytic Theory among the Seventeenth-Century Iroquois," *American Anthropologist* 60 (1958): 237–38.

8. Trigger, *Children*, 1:73; see also Trigger, *Huron*, p. 51.

9. Trigger, *Huron*, pp. 108–12.

10. Trigger, *Children*, 1:77–78.

11. Ibid., p. 76; see also Tooker, *Ethnography*, pp. 80–81.

12. Trigger, *Children*, 1:87; see also Tooker, *Ethnography*, p. 140.

13. Bruce G. Trigger, "The Jesuits and the Fur Trade," *Ethnohistory* 12 (1956): 38; see also Bruce G. Trigger, "The French Presence in Huronia: The Structure of Franco-Huron Relations in the First Half of the Seventeenth Century," *Canadian Historical Review* 49 (1968): 140–41.

14. Trigger, *Children*, 2:510; see also Cornelius J. Jaenen, *Friend and Foe: Aspects of French-Amerindian Cultural Contact in the Sixteenth and Seventeenth Centuries* (New York: Columbia University Press, 1976), p. 61.

15. Jaenen, *Friend and Foe*, pp. 52–53.

16. Peter Duignan, "Early Jesuit Missionaries: A Suggestion for Further Study," *American Anthropologist* 60 (1958): 726–29; see also Jaenen, *Friend and Foe*, p. 50.

17. Brébeuf's shrewd counsel to other Jesuits on how not to offend their hosts can be found in two of his reports. See R. G. Thwaites, ed., *The Jesuit "Relations" and Allied Documents* (Cleveland: Burrows, 1896–1901), vol. 10, pp. 87–115; vol. 12, pp. 117–23.

18. Trigger, *Children*, 2:699–700.

19. Tooker, *Ethnography*, p. 88.

20. Trigger, *Children*, 2:711; see also Jaenen, *Friend and Foe*, p. 157.

Chapter Four

1. Early population estimates can be found in James Mooney, "The Aboriginal Population of America North of Mexico," *Smithsonian Miscellaneous Collections* 80 (1928): 4; Sherburne F. Cook, "Interracial Warfare and Population Decline among the New England Indians," *Ethnohistory* 20 (1973): 12–13, 22; Francis Jennings, *The Invasion of America: Indians, Colonialism, and the Cant of Conquest* (Chapel Hill: University of North Carolina Press, 1975), p. 29. These works have now been superseded by Neal Salisbury, *Manitou and Providence: Indians, Europeans, and the Making of New England, 1500–1643* (New York: Oxford University Press, 1982).

2. Wilcomb E. Washburn, *Red Man's Land/White Man's Law: A Study of the Past and Present Status of the American Indian* (New York: Scribner's, 1971), pp. 38–39.

3. T. J. C. Brasser, "The Coastal Algonkians: People of the First Frontiers," in Eleanor B. Leacock and Nancy O. Lurie, eds., *North American Indians in Historical Perspective* (New York: Random House, 1971), p. 72; see also Wilbur R. Jacobs, *Dispossessing the American Indian: Indians and Whites on the Colonial Frontier* (New York: Scribner's, 1972), pp. 11–12.

4. Ruth Underhill, *Red Man's Religion: Beliefs and Practices of the Indians North of Mexico* (Chicago: University of Chicago Press, 1965), pp. 84–94.

5. Ruth F. Benedict, "The Concept of the Guardian Spirit in North America," *Memoirs of the American Anthropological Association* 29 (1923): 43, 84.

6. Joan M. Vastokas and Romas K. Vastokas, *Sacred Art of the Algonkians* (Peterborough, Canada: Mansard Press, 1973), pp. 38–39.

7. Alfred G. Bailey, *The Conflict of European and Eastern Algonkian Cultures, 1504–1700: A Study in Canadian Civilization* (Toronto: University of Toronto Press, 1969), p. 142. Thomas Mayhew, Jr., reported that a local sachem once listed for him a total of thirty-seven principal gods that he acknowledged in his serious religious responsibilities. See *Collections of the Massachusetts Historical Society* 3d ser., 4, p. 111.

8. Wording of the Massachusetts charter along these lines is cited in Jennings, *Invasion*, p. 230.

9. Lloyd C. M. Hare, *Thomas Mayhew: Patriarch to the Indians, 1593–1682* (New York: D. Appleton, 1932), p. 86.

10. Nicholas P. Canny, "The Ideology of English Colonization: From Ireland to America," *William and Mary Quarterly* 3d ser., 30 (1973); see also Jennings, *Invasion,* pp. 45–46.

11. By way of qualification we should note that some eschatological thinkers, such as John Cotton, argued that conversion of the Jews had priority over concern for Indians. Seventeenth-century missionaries did not share that ordering of events, however, for they held either that Indians were descended from the ten lost tribes of Israel or that conversion of "gentiles" could eventually include Jews and thus hasten the millennium with universal acceptance of Christian principles. See J. A. De Jong, *As the Waters Cover the Sea: Millennial Expectations in the Rise of Anglo-American Missions, 1640–1810* (Kampen, Netherlands: J. H. Kok, 1970), pp. 55–57, 69, 76.

12. William Kellaway, *The New England Company, 1649–1776, Missionary Society to the American Indians* (London: Longmans, Green, 1961), pp. 103–5.

13. Nancy O. Lurie, "Indian Cultural Adjustment to European Civilization," in James M. Smith, ed., *Seventeenth-Century America: Essays in Colonial History* (Chapel Hill: University of North Carolina Press, 1959), p. 45; see also Jennings, *Invasion,* p. 48.

14. Kellaway, *New England Company,* pp. 6–7.

15. Douglas E. Leach, *The Northern Colonial Frontier, 1607–1763* (New York: Holt, Rinehart & Winston, 1966), p. 184.

16. Daniel Gookin, "Of the Language, Customs, Manners, and Religion of the Indians," *Collections of the Massachusetts Historical Society* 1 (1792), as cited in Roy H. Pearce, "The 'Ruines of Mankind': The Indian and the Puritan Mind," *Journal of the History of Ideas* 13 (1952): 208–9; see also Washburn, *Red Land/White Law,* pp. 22–23.

17. Neal Salisbury, "Red Puritans: The 'Praying Indians' of Massachusetts Bay and John Eliot," *William and Mary Quarterly* 3d ser., 31 (1974): 50–51.

18. Ibid., pp. 28–29; see also Kellaway, *New England Company,* p. 8.

19. Frederick Weis, "The New England Company of 1649 and Its Missionary Enterprises," *Publications of the Colonial Society of Massachusetts* 38 (1947–51): 140; see also Jennings, *Invasion,* pp. 250–51.

20. Douglas E. Leach, *Flintlock and Tomahawk: New England in King Philip's War* (New York: Norton, 1958), pp. 150–54;

see also Ola E. Winslow, *John Eliot: "Apostle to the Indians"* (Boston: Houghton Mifflin, 1968), pp. 167, 178.

Chapter Five

1. Verner W. Crane, *The Southern Frontier, 1670–1732* (Ann Arbor: University of Michigan Press, 1956), pp. 145, 308.

2. John Calam, *Parsons and Pedagogues: The S.P.G. Adventure in American Education* (New York: Columbia University Press, 1971), pp. 47–49; see also Frank J. Klingberg, *American Humanitarianism in Colonial New York* (Philadelphia: Church Historical Society, 1940), pp. 103–4.

3. Mather, as cited in *Massachusetts Historical Society Collections* ser. 6, 1 (1886): 401–2.

4. William Kellaway, *The New England Company, 1649–1776: Missionary Society to the American Indians* (London: Longmans, Green, 1961), pp. 238–39.

5. As cited in Harold Blodgett, *Samson Occom* (Hanover, N.H.: Dartmouth College, 1935), p. 73.

6. James D. McCallum, *Eleazar Wheelock: Founder of Dartmouth College* (Hanover, N.H.: Dartmouth College, 1939), pp. 109–10; a complete list of native missionaries and their subsequent careers can be found on pages 134–38.

7. Blodgett, *Occom*, p. 57.

8. Samuel K. Lothrop, *Life of Samuel Kirkland: Missionary to the Indians* (Boston: Little, Brown, 1848), p. 207; the letter is dated 13 August 1768.

9. Clinton A. Weslager, *The Delaware Indians: A History* (New Brunswick: Rutgers University Press, 1972), p. 42.

10. William W. Newcomb, Jr., *The Culture and Acculturation of the Delaware Indian,* University of Michigan Museum Anthropological Papers no. 10 (Ann Arbor: University of Michigan Museum, 1956), pp. 59–78; see also Frank G. Speck, *A Study of the Delaware Indian Big House Ceremony* (Harrisburg: Pennsylvania Historical Commission, 1931), pp. 26 ff.

11. Isaac Sharpless, "The Quakers in Pennsylvania," in Rufus M. Jones, *The Quakers in the American Colonies* (London, 1911; reprinted, New York: Norton, 1966), p. 435.

12. As cited in David Wynbeek, *David Brainerd: Beloved Yankee* (Grand Rapids, Mich.: Eerdmans, 1961), p. 205. Another instance epitomized that attitude for Brainerd: "I told him that I had a desire (for his benefit and happiness) to instruct them in

Christianity.... [H]e inquired why I desired the Indians to become Christians, seeing the Christians were so much worse than
the Indians are in their present state. The Christians, he said,
would lie, steal, and drink, worse than the Indians. It was they
first taught the Indians to be drunk; and they stole from one
another, to that degree, that their rulers were obliged to hang
them for it, and that was not sufficient to deter others from the
like action.... [I]f the Indians should become Christians, they
would then be as bad as these. And hereupon he said, they
would live as their fathers lived, and go where their fathers were
when they died" (ibid., p. 86).

 13. Thomas Brainerd, *The Life of John Brainerd: The Brother of
David Brainerd, and His Successor as Missionary to the Indians of
New Jersey* (Philadelphia: Presbyterian Publication Committee,
1865), pp. 258–59.

 14. Ibid., p. 281; italics in the original.

 15. Edmund A. de Schweinitz, *The Life and Times of David
Zeisberger: The Western Pioneer and Apostle of the Indians*
(Philadelphia: Lippincott, 1870; reprinted, New York, 1971),
pp. 316–17.

 16. Ibid., p. 394.

 17. See ibid., pp. 378–79, for a list of the statutes drawn up
and agreed upon by natives at Schönbrunn and Friedensstadt.
See also Weslager, *The Delaware Indians,* pp. 283–84.

 18. A list of the martyrs appears in de Schweinitz, *Zeisberger,*
pp. 551–52.

Chapter Six

 1. Francis Paul Prucha, *American Indian Policy in the Formative
Years: The Indian Trade and Intercourse Acts, 1790–1834* (Cambridge, Mass.: Harvard University Press, 1962), pp. 213–15.

 2. As cited in William T. Hagan, *American Indians* (Chicago:
University of Chicago Press, 1961), p. 69; see also Prucha, *Formative Years,* pp. 240–41, for a compilation of similar statements
from John Winthrop to Thomas Hart Benton.

 3. The House of Representatives Committee on Indian Affairs report of 1818 can be found in *American State Papers: Indian Affairs,* vol. 2, p. 185; see also R. Pierce Beaver, *Church,
State, and the American Indians* (St. Louis: Concordia, 1966), p.
68, and Prucha, *Formative Years,* pp. 220–21.

4. Robert F. Berkhofer, Jr., *Salvation and the Savage: An Analysis of Protestant Missions and American Indian Response, 1787–1862* (Lexington: University of Kentucky Press, 1965; reprinted, New York, 1972), pp. 35–42.

5. Charles Hudson, *The Southeastern Indians* (Knoxville: University of Tennessee Press, 1976), pp. 337–40; see also John R. Swanton, *The Indians of the Southeastern United States,* Bureau of American Ethnology bull. 137 (Washington, D.C.: U.S. Government Printing Office, 1946).

6. Hudson, *Southeastern Indians,* pp. 126–32, 169–71; see also James Mooney, "Myths of the Cherokee," *Bureau of American Ethnology Annual Report* no. 19 (Washington, D.C., 1900).

7. Grace Steele Woodward, *The Cherokees* (Norman: University of Oklahoma Press, 1963), pp. 139–40, 145–46.

8. William E. Strong, *The Story of the American Board: An Account of the First Hundred Years of the American Board of Commissioners for Foreign Missions* (Boston: Pilgrim Press, 1910; reprinted, New York, 1969), pp. 36, 38–39.

9. Grant Foreman, *Indian Removal: The Emigration of the Five Civilized Tribes of Indians* (Norman: University of Oklahoma Press, 1932), pp. 267 ff.; see also Walter G. Cooper, *The Story of Georgia* (New York: American Historical Society, 1938), vol. 2, pp. 305–13.

10. James H. Howard, "The Cultural Position of the Dakota: A Reassessment," in Gertrude E. Dole and Robert L. Carneiro, eds., *Essays in the Science of Culture in Honor of Leslie A. White* (New York: Crowell, 1960), pp. 250–57.

11. J. R. Walker, "The Sun Dance and Other Ceremonies of the Oglala Division of the Teton Dakota," *Anthropological Papers of the American Museum of Natural History* 16 (New York, 1917): 60–62, 116–19; see also Royal B. Hassrick, *The Sioux: Life and Customs of a Warrior Race* (Norman: University of Oklahoma Press, 1964), p. 246.

12. Much of this description has to do with the western Dakota, because we are better informed about them. The Sun Dance was not of much importance to the Santee until after the Dakota War of 1862, when they came under more western influence. Much of the Santee Dakotas' early culture bore strong Woodland traits, similar to the Ojibwas and others in the Great Lakes region.

13. Hiram M. Chittenden and Alfred T. Richardson, *Life, Letters, and Travels of Father Pierre-Jean De Smet, S.J., 1801-1873* (New York: Francis P. Harper, 1905; reprinted, New York: Arno Press, 1969), vol. 1, pp. 31–58, 315–92; vol. 2, pp. 403–7, 553–69.

14. Stephen R. Riggs, *Mary and I: Forty Years with the Sioux* (Chicago, 1880; reprinted, Williamstown, Mass.: Corner House, 1971), p. 42.

15. Stephen R. Riggs, *Tah-koo Wah-kan, or The Gospel among the Dakotas* (Boston: Congregational Publishing Society, 1869; reprinted, New York, 1972), pp. 393–99.

16. Francis Paul Prucha, *American Indian Policy in Crisis: Christian Reformers and the Indian, 1865–1900* (Norman: University of Oklahoma Press, 1976), pp. 40–53; see also Beaver, *Church, State, and American Indians*, pp. 138–40.

17. As cited in Loring B. Priest, *Uncle Sam's Stepchildren: The Reformation of the Indian Policy, 1865–1887* (New Brunswick: Rutgers University Press, 1942), pp. 219–20.

18. Prucha, *American Indian Policy in Crisis*, pp. 252–55.

19. Beaver, *Church, State, and American Indians*, pp. 167–68.

20. Anthony F. C. Wallace, *The Death and Rebirth of the Seneca* (New York: Knopf, 1970), pp. 239–53, 272–84.

21. James Mooney, "The Ghost-Dance Religion and the Sioux Outbreak of 1890," *Bureau of American Ethnology Annual Report* no. 14, pt. 2 (Washington, D.C., 1896; reprinted, Chicago, 1965), pp. 2–35, 115–20.

Chapter Seven

1. Gustavus E. E. Lindquist, *The Red Man in the United States: An Intimate Study of the Social, Economic, and Religious Life of the American Indian* (New York: Doran, 1923), pp. xii–xiii, 428–30.

2. Gustavus E. E. Lindquist, *Indians in Transition: A Study of Protestant Missions to Indians in the United States* (New York: National Council of Churches of Christ in the U.S.A., 1951), pp. 32–33.

3. R. Pierce Beaver, ed., *The Native American Christian Community: A Directory of Indian, Aleut, and Eskimo Churches* (Monrovia, Calif.: Missions Advanced Research and Communication

Center, 1979); see also Beaver, "The Churches and the Indians: Consequences of 350 Years of Missions," in R. P. Beaver, ed., *American Missions in Bicentennial Perspective* (South Pasadena, Calif.: William Carey Library, 1977), p. 305.

4. Anne O. Lively, *A Survey of Mission Workers in the Indian Field* (New York: National Council of Churches in the U.S.A., 1958), pp. 15, 19.

5. Ibid., pp. 17–18 and appendix, p. 5.

6. Lindquist, *Indians in Transition*, pp. 19, 28–29.

7. Kenneth R. Philp, *John Collier's Crusade for Indian Reform, 1920–1954* (Tucson: University of Arizona Press, 1977), pp. 97, 118; see also John Collier, *From Every Zenith: A Memoir and Some Essays on Life and Thought* (Denver: Sage Books, 1963), pp. 173, 203.

8. Philp, *John Collier's Crusade,* p. 159; see also John Collier, "The United States Indian," in Joseph B. Gittler, ed., *Understanding Minority Groups* (New York: Wiley, 1964), pp. 46–47.

9. Philp, *John Collier's Crusade,* pp. 185–86.

10. Erna Gunther, "The Shaker Religion of the Northwest," in Marian W. Smith, ed., *Indians of the Urban Northwest* (New York: Columbia University Press, 1949), pp. 48–59, 70–71.

11. As cited in Omer C. Stewart, "The Native American Church and the Law," in Deward E. Walker, Jr., ed., *The Emergent Native Americans* (Boston: Little, Brown, 1972), p. 385.

12. James S. Slotkin, *The Peyote Religion: A Study in Indian-White Relations* (Glencoe, Ill.: Free Press, 1956), pp. 44–45, 65, 68–71.

13. Ibid., pp. 41–42, 71.

14. Ibid., pp. 72–76.

15. Hazel W. Hertzberg, *The Search for an American Indian Identity: Modern Pan-Indian Movements* (Syracuse, N.Y.: Syracuse University Press, 1971), pp. 259–64, for opinions favoring the bill against peyote; see pp. 264–71 for opinions against the restrictive bill.

16. Stewart, "The Native American Church and the Law," pp. 391–92.

17. Leslie Spier, "The Sun Dance of the Plains Indians: Its Development and Diffusion," *Anthropological Papers of the American Museum of Natural History* 16 (New York, 1921): 473–75, 491–94.

18. Joseph G. Jorgensen, *The Sun Dance Religion: Power for the*

Powerless (Chicago: University of Chicago Press, 1972), pp. 142, 173, 211; see also Demitri B. Shimkin, "The Wind River Shoshone Sun Dance," Anthropological Paper 41 in *Bureau of American Ethnology Bulletin* no. 151 (Washington, D.C.: U.S. Government Printing Office, 1953), pp. 429–30, 435–37.

19. Jorgensen, *The Sun Dance Religion,* pp. 179–93, contains the best overall description of modern Sun Dance activities. For an elaborate description of the ritual among the Cheyennes, see Peter J. Powell, *Sweet Medicine* (Norman: University of Oklahoma Press, 1969), vol. 2, chaps. 43–51.

Suggestions for
Further Reading

Readers seeking a general introduction to American Indian studies can find it in several basic texts. One such volume, edited by Roger C. Owen, James J. F. Deetz, and Anthony D. Fisher, is *The North American Indians: A Sourcebook* (New York: Macmillan, 1967); additional perspective can be gained from Paul S. Martin, George I. Quimby, and Donald Collier, *Indians before Columbus: Twenty Thousand Years of North American History Revealed by Archeology* (Chicago: University of Chicago Press, 1947), and from Robert F. Spencer, Jesse D. Jennings, et al., *The Native Americans: Prehistory and Ethnology of the North American Indians* (New York: Harper & Row, 1965). Somewhat more specialized but crucial to summarizing this important area are Jesse D. Jennings and Edward Norbeck, eds., *Prehistoric Man in the New World* (Chicago: University of Chicago Press, 1964), together with Joseph R. Caldwell and Robert L. Hall, eds., *Hopewellian Studies,* Illinois State Museum Scientific Papers, vol. 12 (Springfield: Illinois State Museum, 1964). Pioneering scholarship in the most elaborate of the precontact cultures is found in the works of the gifted amateur, Antonio J. Waring, Jr., edited by Stephen Williams, *The Waring Papers,* Papers of the Peabody Museum of Archaeology and Ethnology, vol. 58 (Cambridge, Mass., 1968); see also James H. Howard, *The Southeastern Ceremonial Complex and Its Interpretation,* Missouri Archaeo-

logical Society memoir 6 (Columbia, Mo., 1968), for solid
treatment of fascinating materials. For an overall view see
Dean R. Snow, *Native American Prehistory: A Critical
Bibliography* (Bloomington: Indiana University Press,
1979).

Systematic investigation of any Indian culture begins
also with periodical literature, which, over the years, has
provided data for varied purposes. Most important in this
genre are writings sponsored by the Bureau of American
Ethnology, whose *Annual Reports* (published since 1881)
and *Bulletins* (since 1887) contain a wealth of information
on a wide range of topics. The same can be said for entries
in the *American Anthropologist* (since 1899) and *Memoirs of
the American Anthropological Association* (since 1905). New
students and specialists alike profit from many works by
the foremost author in general Indian studies today, Wilcomb E. Washburn. The value of his recent major effort,
*The American Indian and the United States: A Documentary
History* (New York: Random House, 1973), increases as
readers learn to appreciate the solidity of his four-volume
work during the course of their own investigations.

Those who wish to learn about a specific tribe or culture
area should begin by consulting George P. Murdock and
Timothy J. O'Leary, *Ethnographic Bibliography of North
America,* 5 vols., 4th ed. (New Haven: Human Relations
Area Files Press, 1975). For perspective on general trends
in Indian studies, a good beginning is William N. Fenton,
*American Indian and White Relations to 1830: Needs and
Opportunities for Study* (Chapel Hill: University of North
Carolina Press, 1957; reprinted, New York, 1971). A
similar review of literature that helps readers get their
bearings in the field of religion is Åke Hultkrantz, "North
American Indian Religion in the History of Research, A
General Survey," *History of Religions* 6, 7 (1966–67). For
an understanding of contributions by anthropologists in
fields of general theory and more specific application see
Michael Banton, ed., *Anthropological Approaches to the
Study of Religion* (London: Tavistock, 1966); Ralph Linton,

ed., *Acculturation in Seven American Indian Tribes* (New York: Appleton-Century, 1940); Fred Eggan, *The American Indian: Perspectives for the Study of Social Change* (Chicago: Aldine, 1966); Edward H. Spicer, ed., *Perspectives in American Indian Culture Change* (Chicago: University of Chicago Press, 1961); and Eleanor B. Leacock and Nancy O. Lurie, eds., *North American Indians in Historical Perspective* (New York: Random House, 1971).

Those working with Indians in the American Southwest should begin with a useful overview: Alfonso Ortiz, ed., *Southwest,* vol. 9 of William C. Sturtevant, genl. ed., *Handbook of North American Indians* (Washington, D.C., 1979). For another interpretive survey they might consult Edward H. Spicer, *Cycles of Conquest: The Impact of Spain, Mexico, and the United States on the Indians of the Southwest, 1533–1960* (Tucson: University of Arizona Press, 1962). After digesting that extremely valuable survey, students concentrating on local cultural expressions are fortunate to have the exemplary Alfonso Ortiz, *The Tewa World: Space, Time, and Becoming in a Pueblo Society* (Chicago: University of Chicago Press, 1969). Besides that indispensable study, there are also the durable work of Edward P. Dozier, *The Pueblo Indians of North America* (New York: Holt, Rinehart & Winston, 1970), the volume edited by Alfonso Ortiz, *New Perspectives on the Pueblos* (Albuquerque: University of New Mexico Press, 1972), and the old but still useful work by Elsie C. Parsons, *Pueblo Indian Religion,* 2 vols. (Chicago: University of Chicago Press, 1939). Anthropological reports on separate pueblos can be found in the periodical literature, but sample independent publications include Leslie A. White, *The Pueblo of Sia, New Mexico* (Washington, D.C.: U.S. Government Printing Office, 1962), and Elsie C. Parsons, *The Pueblo of Jemez* (New Haven: Yale University Press, 1925). For those interested in early Spanish activities, no better cache of materials can be found than that presented by France V. Scholes and Lansing B. Bloom in *New Mexico Historical Review* articles published from 1928 to 1945.

Sources on the Iroquoian-speaking peoples of the
Northeast are few in number but of remarkably high qual-
ity. Early works were those by Elisabeth Tooker, *An
Ethnography of the Huron Indians, 1615–1649* (Washing-
ton, D.C.: U.S. Government Printing Office, 1964), and
Bruce G. Trigger, *The Huron: Farmers of the North* (New
York: Holt, Rinehart & Winston, 1969). These two hand-
books are now superseded by Trigger's two-volume work
*The Children of Aataentsic: A History of the Huron People to
1660* (Montreal: McGill-Queen's University Press, 1976).
One can find additional information, presented with great
care, in Cornelius J. Jaenen, *Friend and Foe: Aspects of
French-Amerindian Cultural Contact in the Sixteenth and
Seventeenth Centuries* (New York: Columbia University
Press, 1976), and Conrad Heidenreich, *Huronia: A History
and Geography of the Huron Indians, 1600–1650* (Toronto:
McClelland & Stewart, 1971). More specialized studies are
available in limited quantity; two examples are William N.
Fenton, "'This Island, The World on the Turtle's Back,'"
Journal of American Folklore 75 (1962), and Elisabeth
Tooker, *The Iroquois Ceremonial of Midwinter* (Syracuse:
Syracuse University Press, 1970). Tooker has recently
edited an impressive anthology as well: *Native North
American Spirituality of the Eastern Woodlands: Sacred
Myths, Dreams, Visions, Speeches, Healing Formulas, Rituals
and Ceremonies* (New York: Paulist Press, 1979).

Students can find documentary evidence of early French
missionary activity in Reuben G. Thwaites, ed., *The Jesuit
"Relations" and Allied Documents,* 73 vols. (Cleveland: Burrows, 1896–1901)—a large amount of material, but necessary reading for serious inquirers into the topic. A solid
interpretive volume that treats of three types of European
Catholicism in the New World comes from John Tracy
Ellis, and general students might well begin with his *Catholics in Colonial America* (Baltimore: Helicon Press, 1965).
More specialized studies on Jesuit activities tend to be less
objective, but there is some merit to be found in Joseph P.
Donnelly, *Jean de Brébeuf, 1593–1649* (Chicago: Loyola

University Press, 1975); John H. Kennedy, *Jesuit and Savage in New France* (New Haven: Yale University Press, 1950); Francis X. Talbot, *Saint among the Hurons: The Life of Jean de Brébeuf* (New York: Harper, 1949); and Talbot's earlier volume, *Saint among Savages: The Life of Isaac Jogues* (New York: Harper, 1935).

Anthropological materials on Algonkians in the Northeast are fairly meager and are too often dependent on early white chronicles. The latest and best overview is contained in Bruce G. Trigger, ed., *Northeast,* vol. 15 of William C. Sturtevant, genl. ed., *Handbook of North American Indians* (Washington, D.C., 1978). Those interested in precontact civilizations should also consult Regina Flannery, *An Analysis of Coastal Algonquian Culture* (Washington, D.C.: Catholic University of America Press, 1939), and Alfred G. Bailey, *The Conflict of European and Eastern Algonkian Cultures, 1504–1700: A Study in Canadian Civilization* (Toronto: University of Toronto Press, 1969), though these two studies mix sources from different time periods, and Bailey concentrates on hunters in Maine and eastern Canada. Another valuable study of a related group in southern New England is William S. Simmons, *Cantautowwit's House: An Indian Burial Ground on the Island of Conanicut in Narragansett Bay* (Providence, R.I.: Brown University Press, 1970).

Two recent publications dominate the field at the moment, though neither sustains the balance and fair-minded judgment required for definitive historical analysis. Still, readers cannot afford to ignore either Francis Jennings, *The Invasion of America: Indians, Colonialism, and the Cant of Conquest* (Chapel Hill: University of North Carolina Press, 1975), or Alden T. Vaughan, *New England Frontier: Puritans and Indians, 1620–1675* (Boston: Little, Brown, 1965). As outstanding as their work is, these authors have not settled many important questions about white settlement in New England. A more promising work on this crucial early period will soon appear, Neal Salisbury's

*Manitou and Providence: Indians, Europeans, and the Mak-
ing of New England, 1500–1643* (New York: Oxford University Press, 1982).

Other valuable contributions in this area include James
M. Smith, ed., *Seventeenth-Century America: Essays in Colo-
nial History* (Chapel Hill: University of North Carolina
Press, 1959); Howard Peckham and Charles Gibson, eds.,
Attitudes of Colonial Powers toward the American Indian
(Salt Lake City: University of Utah Press, 1969); Wilbur
R. Jacobs, *Dispossessing the American Indian: Indians and
Whites on the Colonial Frontier* (New York: Scribner's,
1972); and Douglas E. Leach, *The Northern Colonial Fron-
tier, 1607–1763* (New York: Holt, Rinehart & Winston,
1966). For early missionary efforts in Puritan territory see
William Kellaway, *The New England Company, 1649–
1776, Missionary Society to the American Indians* (London:
Longmans, Green, 1961); Ola E. Winslow, *John Eliot,
"Apostle to the Indians"* (Boston: Houghton Mifflin, 1968);
Lloyd C. M. Hare, *Thomas Mayhew: Patriarch to the Indians, 1593–1682* (New York: D. Appleton, 1932).

Works on eighteenth-century missions are limited
mostly to biographical studies of those who pioneered in
various fields. John Calam's *Parsons and Pedagogues: The
S.P.G. Adventure in American Education* (New York: Columbia University Press, 1971) is the central source of
information on Anglicans. James D. McCallum, *Eleazar
Wheelock: Founder of Dartmouth College* (Hanover, N.H.:
Dartmouth College, 1939), and Harold Blodgett, *Samson
Occom* (Hanover, N.H.: Dartmouth College, 1935), give
some idea of Congregationalist work in New England. The
dated family portrait by Samuel K. Lothrop, *Life of Samuel
Kirkland: Missionary to the Indians* (Boston: Little, Brown,
1848), is useful for New York. Early versions of Jonathan
Edwards' biography of David Brainerd are hardly im-
proved on by the more accessible David Wynbeek, *David
Brainerd: Beloved Yankee* (Grand Rapids, Mich.: Eerdmans,
1961). A far more useful volume is Thomas Brainerd's *The*

*Life of John Brainerd: The Brother of David Brainerd, and
His Successor as Missionary to the Indians of New Jersey*
(Philadelphia: Presbyterian Publication Committee,
1865), which covers some of the same ground as the
adulatory ones about John's unjustly famous brother. The
classic volume by Edmund A. de Schweinitz, *The Life and
Times of David Zeisberger: The Western Pioneer and Apostle of
the Indians* (Philadelphia: Lippincott, 1870), is once again
available in reprint (New York: Arno Press, 1971), and
Elma E. Gray's *Wilderness Christians: The Moravian Mission to the Delaware Indians* (Ithaca: Cornell University
Press, 1956) continues the story of Moravian missionary
work in the Middle Colonies into the nineteenth century.

There are some early dubious works about native
Americans in the Middle Colonies, but a recent publica-
tion, Clifton A. Weslager, *The Delaware Indians: A History*
(New Brunswick, N.J.: Rutgers University Press, 1972),
presents the best collation of reliable data and sound
judgment. He has also compiled *The Delawares: A Critical
Bibliography* (Bloomington: Indiana University Press,
1978). Other useful information can be found in William
W. Newcomb, Jr., *The Culture and Acculturation of the
Delaware Indians* (Ann Arbor: University of Michigan
Press, 1956), and Frank G. Speck, *A Study of the Delaware
Indian Big House Ceremony* (Harrisburg: Pennsylvania
Historical Commission, 1931).

Anthony F. C. Wallace, *King of the Delawares: Teedy-
uscung, 1700–1763* (Philadelphia: University of Pennsylvania Press, 1949), is apologetic in tone and occasionally goes beyond steady interpretive balance, but it must
be consulted as one of the few full-length biographies of an
important Indian figure. For additional insight, drawn from
a related Algonkian tribe, see Ruth Landes, *Ojibwa Religion and the Midewiwin* (Madison: University of Wisconsin
Press, 1968), and A. Irving Hallowell, "Ojibwa Ontology,
Behavior, and World View," in Dennis and Barbara Ted-
lock, eds., *Teachings from the American Earth* (New York:
Liveright, 1975).

Those approaching nineteenth-century materials for the
first time should consult Robert F. Berkhofer, Jr., *Salvation and the Savage: An Analysis of Protestant Missions and
American Indian Response, 1787–1862* (Lexington: University of Kentucky Press, 1965; reprinted, New York:
Atheneum, 1972); it is indispensable in its coverage of
materials and perception of issues. Charles Hudson has
produced, in *The Southeastern Indians* (Knoxville: University of Tennessee Press, 1976), the best book on the
Cherokees and other native Americans in that culture
area, and a survey of the literature is now available in
Raymond D. Fogelson, *The Cherokees: A Critical Bibliography* (Bloomington: Indiana University Press, 1978).

For information on the Dakotas as representatives of
Plains culture, readers should consult Roy W. Meyer,
*History of the Santee Sioux: United States Indian Policy on
Trial* (Lincoln: University of Nebraska Press, 1967), Royal
B. Hassrick, *The Sioux: Life and Customs of a Warrior Race*
(Norman: University of Oklahoma Press, 1964), and
Robert M. Utley, *The Last Days of the Sioux Nation* (New
Haven: Yale University Press, 1963). Modern reports on
how Plains Indians express themselves can be found in
John G. Neihardt, *Black Elk Speaks: Being the Life of a Holy
Man of the Oglala Sioux* (New York: Morrow, 1932; re-
printed, Lincoln: University of Nebraska Press, 1961), and
in Joseph E. Brown, *The Sacred Pipe: Black Elk's Account of
the Seven Rites of the Oglala Sioux* (Norman: University of
Oklahoma Press, 1953). A general survey of literature is
also available in Herbert T. Hoover, *The Sioux: A Critical
Bibliography* (Bloomington: Indiana University Press,
1979).

Material on nineteenth-century federal policy regarding
American Indians is quite extensive. The most notable
author in this area is Francis P. Prucha, whose many works
include *American Indian Policy in the Formative Years: The
Indian Trade and Intercourse Acts, 1790–1834* (Cambridge,
Mass.: Harvard University Press, 1962), and *American Indian Policy in Crisis: Christian Reformers and the Indian,*

1865–1900 (Norman: University of Oklahoma Press, 1976), which set standards of accuracy and interpretive scholarship for others to follow. The early years receive attention in a good study by Ronald N. Satz, *American Indian Policy in the Jacksonian Era* (Lincoln: University of Nebraska Press, 1975), while Robert W. Mardock, *The Reformers and the American Indian* (Columbia: University of Missouri Press, 1971), and Henry E. Fritz, *The Movement for Indian Assimilation, 1860–1890* (Philadelphia: University of Pennsylvania Press, 1963), provide the general context undergirding government debates. Loring B. Priest's *Uncle Sam's Stepchildren: The Reformation of United States Indian Policy, 1865–1887* (New Brunswick, N.J.: Rutgers University Press, 1942) is dated but still useful. A shorter but better-balanced account is Wilcomb E. Washburn's *The Assault on Indian Tribalism: The General Allotment Law (Dawes Act) of 1887* (Philadelphia: Lippincott, 1975). On the question of establishing Oklahoma as Indian Territory see Grant Foreman, *Indian Removal: The Emigration of the Five Civilized Tribes of Indians* (Norman: University of Oklahoma Press, 1932), Arthur H. DeRosier, Jr., *The Removal of the Choctaw Indians* (Knoxville: University of Tennessee Press, 1970), and Angie Debo, *The Road to Disappearance* (Norman: University of Oklahoma Press, 1941), for representative studies of specific tribes in that general process.

Works on nineteenth-century missionary activity rarely measure up to the quality exhibited by Berkhofer. One exception is R. Pierce Beaver's *Church, State, and the American Indians: Two and a Half Centuries of Partnership in Missions between Protestant Churches and Government* (Saint Louis: Concordia, 1966), but most studies are parochial and tend to follow denominational lines with somewhat hagiographical emphases. Some firsthand reports of Minnesota missions are Stephen R. Riggs, *Mary and I: Forty Years with the Sioux* (Chicago: Privately published, 1880; reprinted, Williamstown, Mass.: Corner House, 1971), and Samuel W. Pond, *Two Volunteer Mis-*

sionaries among the Dakotas (Boston: Congregational
Sunday-School and Publishing Society, 1893). A valuable
work on Catholic activities in later years of the century is
Peter J. Rahill, *The Catholic Indian Missions and Grant's
Peace Policy, 1870–1884* (Washington, D.C.: Catholic Uni-
versity of America Press, 1953).

Data on more contemporary evangelical work are dis-
tressingly meager. The two volumes by Gustavus E. E.
Lindquist, *The Red Man in the United States: An Intimate
Study of the Social, Economic, and Religious Life of the American Indian* (New York: Doran, 1923), and *Indians in
Transition: A Study of Protestant Missions to Indians in the
United States* (New York: National Council of Churches in
the U.S.A., 1951), convey some pertinent material along
with the typical missionary conviction that Indian cultures
must be eradicated.

A recent outstanding book on the Indian New Deal is
by Kenneth R. Philp, *John Collier's Crusade for Indian Re-
form, 1920–1954* (Tucson: University of Arizona Press,
1977); it provides essential reading in this important area.
A later valuable study is Graham D. Taylor's *The New Deal
and American Indian Tribalism: The Administration of the
Indian Reorganization Act, 1935–45* (Lincoln: University of
Nebraska Press, 1980). John Collier's own book, *From
Every Zenith: A Memoir and Some Essays on Life and Thought*
(Denver: Sage Books, 1963), supplements Philp's and
Taylor's more objective studies with personal views.

For new Indian religious expressions see Homer G.
Barnett, *Indian Shakers: A Messianic Cult of the Pacific
Northwest* (Carbondale, Ill.: Southern Illinois University
Press, 1957). A durable study of peyotism by James S.
Slotkin, *The Peyote Religion: A Study in Indian-White Re-
lations* (Glencoe, Ill.: Free Press, 1956), is still the best
survey for general readers, but specialists may also wish to
consult David F. Aberle, *The Peyote Religion among the
Navaho* (Chicago: Aldine, 1966), and Omer C. Stewart,
Washo-Northern Paiute Peyotism (Berkeley: University of
California Press, 1944). Those investigating modern forms

of the Sun Dance should begin by reading Joseph G.
Jorgensen, *The Sun Dance Religion: Power for the Powerless*
(Chicago: University of Chicago Press, 1972), because it is
the best summary of recent data and the gateway to earlier
studies. For those interested in pursuing Christian theo-
logical reflection and positive dialogues with traditional
native religions, see Carl F. Starkloff, *The People of the
Center: American Indian Religion and Christianity* (New
York: Seabury Press, 1974). Good sources for getting ac-
quainted with some of the larger contemporary bodies for
Indian action are Hazel W. Hertzberg, *The Search for an
American Indian Identity: Modern Pan-Indian Movements*
(Syracuse: Syracuse University Press, 1971), and Stan
Steiner, *The New Indians* (New York: Harper & Row,
1968).

Index